Implementing Data Mesh

*Design, Build, and Implement Data
Contracts, Data Products, and Data Mesh*

Jean-Georges Perrin and Eric Broda
Foreword by Scott Hirleman

Beijing · Boston · Farnham · Sebastopol · Tokyo

Implementing Data Mesh

by Jean-Georges Perrin and Eric Broda

Published by O'Reilly Media, Inc., 1005 Gravenstein Highway North, Sebastopol, CA 95472.

O'Reilly books may be purchased for educational, business, or sales promotional use. Online editions are also available for most titles (*http://oreilly.com*). For more information, contact our corporate/institutional sales department: 800-998-9938 or *corporate@oreilly.com*.

Acquisitions Editor: Aaron Black	**Indexer:** nSight, Inc.
Development Editor: Shira Evans	**Interior Designer:** David Futato
Production Editor: Beth Kelly	**Cover Designer:** Karen Montgomery
Copyeditor: Shannon Turlington	**Illustrator:** Kate Dullea
Proofreader: Krsta Technology Solutions	

September 2024:   First Edition

Revision History for the First Edition

2024-09-04:   First Release

See *http://oreilly.com/catalog/errata.csp?isbn=9781098156220* for release details.

978-1-098-15622-0

[LSI]

Liz,

*Thank you for supporting my crazy ideas, like this book
(and the next ones we have not yet talked about).
Je t'aime.*

—Jean-Georges

Susan, Davis, and Graeham,

*Thanks for your support, ideas, and help!
You guys are the best!*

—Eric

Table of Contents

Part II.   Designing, Building, and Deploying Data Mesh

Part III.   GenAI, Teams, Operating Model, and Roadmap for Data Mesh

Foreword

When I first encountered the Data Mesh concept in late 2020, I was much more steeped in the best practices of the operational world, especially site reliability engineering (SRE) and distributed systems. Zhamak Dehghani, the creator of the Data Mesh concept, proposed a number of ways of doing analytics, machine learning, and data work that felt very familiar and a bit obvious because of how long they had been adopted in the software world, like shifting ownership left, product thinking, continuous integration and continuous delivery (CI/CD), etc.

However, after I spent a few weeks digging deeper, including into what people were actually saying about Data Mesh in posts on LinkedIn and Twitter—so not just the articles, presentations, and podcasts—there was a resounding question underlying everything: OK, but *how*? The data world in general hadn't done work in any way close to what Data Mesh calls for, and trying to simply jump into entirely new ways is 1) disruptive in general and 2) abhorrent to most data people....

Because of all the questions around Data Mesh, I created a community that is now over 10,000 people strong (Data Mesh Learning) and a podcast as well to explore this with more than 300 episodes (Data Mesh Radio). Because that question is still the most pertinent and pernicious one about Data Mesh today: OK, but *how*?

From the very early days of the community, both Jean-Georges and Eric have been helping people to explore this question. Not just what is Data Mesh—I do not miss the days when there were 15 new articles with that title each week—but how do we go about actually implementing Data Mesh as a concept in our organizations?

There aren't exact answers because it's like asking how someone can live a good life—everyone's sense of what matters and what is of value is different, as is everyone's starting point. If you think reasonably, there can't be an exact answer to how we do Data Mesh because every organization is different: the aims of the organization, maturity levels, what data can do to help the organization compete, the org structure, and so on. If you are already very distributed, but your data work is very siloed and sharing between lines of business (aka domains) is not the status quo, the steps you have to take to move forward are vastly different from a highly centralized, command-and-control-type organization's steps.

But there is hope. There have been a number of organizations driving significant value through a Data Mesh approach. Jean-Georges and Eric have been exploring since the beginning of the Data Mesh community what patterns actually *matter* to getting from where you are today toward better. And of course, how to keep getting better and better. Because it's always about not getting things perfect but getting to good enough for now. There are potentially thousands of decisions someone leading a Data Mesh journey might have to make, but the question becomes which decisions matter when and why.

I will emphasize this point because it is actually probably the second most important one to make: in a Data Mesh implementation, there are *thousands* of decisions to make. Most don't matter too much in the greater scheme. Still go for good answers, but this book will help you focus on what decisions provide the best path to success as well as the ones that provide the most leverage to success.

Much like choosing what you wear to do yard work probably isn't going to impact your life much (do wear safety gear, though!) but it might impact the outcome of a date or an interview, there will be many questions in a Data Mesh journey where you aren't sure of the right answer. But this book will help you better assess which ones really matter *and* how to measure the success of your approach so that you can improve it as you continue to drive to better.

There are multiple paths to success with Data Mesh—we've seen that across the hundreds of companies that have talked publicly about their journeys. So we need to decontextualize what is working and why from those organizations and learn from them. And that's what Jean-Georges and Eric are doing in this book for you. It is a very difficult task, so they've made your life far easier with this book!

I have probably spoken with close to 500 people across a 1,000-plus conversations about Data Mesh, and there are few I would put at the same level as Eric and Jean-Georges on their ability to figure out what matters when and why, and then especially be able to succinctly communicate that. Because that communication part is crucial, and they do it extremely well.

It's also crucial to pay attention to one word used over and over in Data Mesh literature: *journey*. You do *not* have to get this perfect up-front. You will learn, and the most important thing is to realize that you can try, test, and iterate. It's about getting to better, not getting to perfect. And the journey of a thousand miles starts with but one first step. We're all still learning how to do Data Mesh well, and this book crystallizes much of what the broader community and industry have learned to date. It can help you immensely with doing Data Mesh better *and* lowering your stress by focusing on what matters instead of getting bogged down in those thousands of less impactful decisions.

I also want to emphasize again that there is no exact playbook. Take what you read here, and understand the reasoning behind the decisions and adapt them to your organization. If you want an easy approach, just throw all your data into a data swamp and be done with it. This is going to take some work on your end, but I promise you, Data Mesh can bring incredible value to the organization and incredible personal value and fulfillment to those leading the implementation.

In wrapping up so that you can get to the good stuff, I will give you, dear reader, my more succinct warning and encouragement I give to everyone exploring Data Mesh in an attempt to try to make their organization better in oh so many ways: you can't copy someone else's blueprint, but you absolutely should dig into what decisions were the key leverage points. And don't get so bogged down in the exact technical details—Data Mesh is a crucial driver in making your organization better able to leverage data, but it's about so much more than the platform. Have patience and give yourself the grace of making not-so-great decisions with an eye on constantly making better ones. And good luck, it's gonna be a heck of a ride. :)

— Scott Hirleman
Founder, Data Mesh Learning
Host, Data Mesh Radio

Preface

In 2019, Zhamak Dehghani came up with the concept of Data Mesh (*https://oreil.ly/NxrtY*). It took her 18 months to refine her ideas into the four principles of Data Mesh: domain ownership, data as a product, self-serve data platform, and (my favorite) federated computational governance (*https://oreil.ly/u6iSU*). The movement was launched. It has the strength of the tide—nothing is stopping it. Her foundational book, *Data Mesh* (O'Reilly), was published in 2022 and confirmed the strength and desire of an entire industry to change to a better model.

But…

To implement Dehghani's vision, practitioners needed a guide—a hands-on, practical way to build Data Mesh. We took on this task in early 2023 and are delivering it to you now. We hope you will enjoy it.

If this book is not enough for you, remember that both of us are available to help you make your Data Mesh a reality!

Who Is This Book For?

This book is for all those who are interested in Data Mesh concepts and implementation, regardless of their level of expertise. We value your interest and are excited to share our insights with you.

If you are a data engineer, you will learn how your job and tasks will evolve with Data Mesh. Don't worry—it will make your day-to-day a lot more interesting.

If you are an architect, you will discover how this software architecture will benefit data architecture and will allow you to build better data platforms.

If you are a technology leader, this book will give all the help you need to build and implement Data Mesh. Most importantly, Part III imparts a lot of knowledge about change management and the social aspects of Data Mesh.

If you are a nontechnical C-level, this book may not be the best investment for you, but it is for all the technology staff in your organization. Think about end-of-year gifts, birthdays, anniversaries... You will make people happy.

Overview of the Parts and Chapters

This book is divided into 3 parts and 16 fast-paced chapters.

Part I, "The Basics", sets up the basics and gives a quick reminder of Dehghani's work:

- Chapter 1, "Understanding Data Mesh: The Essentials", outlines the fundamental principles of Data Mesh, a modern data architecture paradigm that promotes decentralized data ownership, treats data as a product, and implements self-serve infrastructure for domain teams. Building on Dehghani's foundational work, this chapter emphasizes how Data Mesh introduces agility into data management by enabling local autonomy and faster response times as well as by fostering a culture of innovation and collaboration.

- Chapter 2, "Applying Data Mesh Principles", summarizes the key principles of Data Mesh and focuses on how they apply to data products, including the FAIR (findable, accessible, interoperable, and reusable) product, as well as what constitutes a good data product and the lifecycles of data products. The goals of this chapter are to create a practical Data Mesh roadmap, translate your strategy and vision into an achievable plan, secure executive sponsorship and funding, empower a skilled data product owner with decision-making authority, and engage customers while maintaining flexibility and alignment with business objectives.

- Chapter 3, "Our Case Study: Climate Quantum Inc.", introduces Climate Quantum Inc., a fictional company leveraging Data Mesh capabilities to address the complexities of managing climate data, making it more accessible, usable, and trustworthy. By decentralizing data ownership and using a domain-oriented architecture, Climate Quantum Inc. aims to streamline the discovery, consumption, sharing, and verification of vast and varied climate data, thus providing a scalable solution to the multifaceted challenges posed by climate change.

Part II, "Designing, Building, and Deploying Data Mesh", focuses on the technology aspect of Data Mesh:

- Chapter 4, "Defining the Data Mesh Architecture", explores the core components of Data Mesh, focusing on the architecture of data products as well as the broader Data Mesh architecture and highlighting how various artifacts and development, runtime, and operational capabilities come together to create discoverable, observable, and operable data products. This chapter also delves into how these components are integrated through Data Mesh backbone services, marketplaces, and registries, using Climate Quantum Inc. as a case study to illustrate the practical application of these principles for managing complex climate data.

- Chapter 5, "Driving Data Products with Data Contracts", discusses the implementation of data products, emphasizing the role of data contracts in establishing trust by ensuring data quality and service levels and using examples from Climate Quantum Inc. to illustrate these concepts. The chapter explores the principles of product thinking, details the elements of data contracts, and introduces the data quality of service (data QoS) framework for combining dimensions of data quality with service-level agreements, which promotes a standardized, reliable approach to data management.

- Chapter 6, "Building Your First Data Product", guides you through the steps of creating your initial data product by understanding its components, leveraging data contracts, connecting data sources, and building endpoints while ensuring that observability, discovery, and control services are integrated. The chapter emphasizes the standardization and modularity of data products, facilitated by using sidecars and open standards like the ones promoted by the Bitol project to streamline development and operations.

- Chapter 7, "Aligning with the Experience Planes", explains how to separate responsibilities across three functional areas in a Data Mesh: the infrastructure experience plane for data infrastructure, the data product experience plane for independent data products, and the mesh experience plane for interconnecting data products and managing enterprise-level tools. Each of these areas has specific capabilities to streamline organization and reduce cognitive load. The chapter also delves into how these planes communicate, particularly focusing on feedback loops, both user and system, which travel across planes to enhance data reliability and inform continuous improvement.

- Chapter 8, "Meshing Your Data Products", explains how to register, assemble, and utilize multiple data products within a Data Mesh to enhance their value and ensure data quality and governance. This chapter also focuses on the key concepts of producer-aligned and consumer-aligned data products. Finally, you will learn how Data Mesh can simplify data lineage.

Part III, "GenAI, Teams, Operating Model, and Roadmap for Data Mesh", focuses mainly on the operating and social aspects of Data Mesh:

- Chapter 9, "Running and Operating Your Data Mesh", explores how to make data products discoverable, observable, and secure, highlighting the dynamic nature of data within Data Mesh, the crucial interfaces and processes involved in ensuring seamless operation, and the opportunities for enhanced data management through standardization and self-serve capabilities, all of which ultimately foster a more agile and efficient data ecosystem.

- Chapter 10, "Creating a Data Mesh Marketplace", addresses the challenge of finding data products in a growing Data Mesh ecosystem by proposing a Data Mesh Marketplace, which, unlike traditional data catalogs, provides a dynamic, user-friendly platform for data discovery, consumption, and sharing that leverages self-serve capabilities and minimizes metadata duplication.

- Chapter 11, "Establishing Data Mesh Governance", explains how the self-serve capability and embedded agents within dynamic data products facilitate a more agile, federated approach to data governance, emphasizing certification for compliance, which decentralizes policy enforcement to data product owners while maintaining centralized policy definition.

- Chapter 12, "Understanding Data Product Supply Chains", explains how the embedded services and self-serve capabilities of data products enable the creation of consistent, efficient, and repeatable "data product factories" and establish a dynamic data supply chain ecosystem analogous to modern manufacturing supply chains.

- Chapter 13, "Integrating Data Mesh and Generative AI", reveals that by combining the decentralized wonders of Data Mesh with the mind-blowing capabilities of generative AI, organizations can turbocharge their data-driven decision-making processes, creating a future where even your data products have the brains to make your business smarter!

- Chapter 14, "Establishing Data Mesh Teams", emphasizes that successful Data Mesh implementation relies 20% on technology and 80% on winning over people, with data product teams acting like autonomous "data product factories" within a sociotechnical ecosystem while interacting with platform and enabling teams to create a flourishing data-driven environment.

- Chapter 15, "Defining a Data Mesh Operating Model", explains how Data Mesh requires a shift from traditional centralized data management to a decentralized, domain-centric approach, involving the creation of an operating model that aligns people, processes, and technology to manage, share, and utilize data products efficiently across an organization.

- Chapter 16, "Establishing a Practical Data Mesh Roadmap", outlines a pragmatic roadmap for Data Mesh implementation, emphasizing the need to balance technology, organizational culture, data product creation, and governance, structured into parallel work streams (technology, factory, operating model, socialization) to build a scalable and efficient Data Mesh ecosystem.

What This Book Isn't

This book is not the only recipe for building Data Mesh (although we think it is the best, the most righteous, and the leading one). At times when we were writing this book, we didn't always agree, and you may disagree with us too when reading some chapters. We all have different ideas and perspectives, so it's only natural that the tone and spirit will sometimes differ a bit.

Conventions Used in This Book

The following typographical conventions are used in this book:

Italic
:   Indicates new terms, URLs, email addresses, filenames, and file extensions.

`Constant width`
:   Used for program listings, as well as within paragraphs to refer to program elements such as variable or function names, databases, data types, environment variables, statements, and keywords.

`Constant width bold`
:   Shows commands or other text that should be typed literally by the user.

`Constant width italic`
:   Shows text that should be replaced with user-supplied values or by values determined by context.

> This element signifies a general note.

O'Reilly Online Learning

 For more than 40 years, *O'Reilly Media* has provided technology and business training, knowledge, and insight to help companies succeed.

Our unique network of experts and innovators share their knowledge and expertise through books, articles, and our online learning platform. O'Reilly's online learning platform gives you on-demand access to live training courses, in-depth learning paths, interactive coding environments, and a vast collection of text and video from O'Reilly and 200+ other publishers. For more information, visit *https://oreilly.com*.

How to Contact Us

Please address comments and questions concerning this book to the publisher:

O'Reilly Media, Inc.
1005 Gravenstein Highway North
Sebastopol, CA 95472
800-889-8969 (in the United States or Canada)
707-827-7019 (international or local)
707-829-0104 (fax)
support@oreilly.com
https://oreilly.com/about/contact.html

We have a web page for this book, where we list errata, examples, and any additional information. You can access this page at *https://oreil.ly/implementing-data-mesh*.

For news and information about our books and courses, visit *https://oreilly.com*.

Find us on LinkedIn: *https://linkedin.com/company/oreilly-media*

Watch us on YouTube: *https://youtube.com/oreillymedia*

Acknowledgments

Of all people, I want to express my deepest gratitude to Eric. It is true what they say: Canadians are kind. But Eric, you have been more than kind. You have been patient, understanding, and not a pushover when it came to this project. Thank you, my friend, for your invaluable help.

Without the support of Kimberly Thies and Todd Nemanich, my dear partners at AbeaData, I would not have been able to finish this book. Thanks, gang!

I would like to deeply thank the team at O'Reilly. Shira Evans was instrumental in making this book a success and coordinating Eric's work with mine while keeping us (mostly me) on track.

I have a special place in my heart for Colleen Tartow, John Y. Miller, Karin Håkansson, Ole Olesen-Bagneux, and Max Schultze. They took the time to review the book without fear of our wrath. They changed this book for the better.

The volunteers for the Bitol project at the Linux Foundation kept giving me the energy I needed to move forward and keep innovating. I am grateful to Andrew Jones, Andy Petrella, Atanas Iliev, Dirk Van de Poel, Gene Stakhov, Georges Kopp, Jochen Christ, Manuel Destouesse, Martin Meermeyer, Peter Flook, Sandro Pugliese, Simon Harrer, Todd Nemanich (again!), and Tom Baeyens.

Finally, this book has been the fruit of a community. The Data Mesh Learning Community, created by Scott Hirleman, has been our source of inspiration and friendship for the last few years. Both Eric and I are there often, and this is a great way to get in touch with us. Special thanks to Scott Hirleman, Paul Au, Melissa Logan, Yuliia Tkachova, Tom De Wolf, Wannes Rosiers, Olivier Wulveryck, Paul Cavacas, Amy Raygada, Charlotte Ledoux, and many others for your kindness and friendship.

I am dedicating this book to my parents, a tribute to their unwavering support and love. My first book, in the mid-90s, was dedicated to my sisters. My first published book was dedicated to my wife and children who stood by me throughout a three-year-long process. It is about time I express my gratitude to my parents for shaping me into the person I am today. Merci Maman, merci Papa. Je vous aime.

— Jean-Georges

When we agreed to write this book, Jean-Georges told me it would be a very long journey—after all, Jean-Georges was a veteran author, and this was my first book. Now, having completed the book, I can honestly say it was a challenge—lots of late nights writing chapters and lots of debates. So yes, Jean-Georges was absolutely right—it was a long journey.

But the journey was made much easier by having such an experienced, smart, and wise coauthor. So first, I wish to offer a huge THANK YOU to Jean-Georges, who invited me to coauthor this book and then offered the guidance and healthy debates that followed to allow us to address such a wide-ranging and complex topic.

Ralph Waldo Emerson wrote, "Life is a journey, not a destination." And similarly, writing this book was not just about reaching a destination for me, but the realization that the journey itself has been immensely rewarding. I have learned a lot, and I have been able to apply the concepts in this book to real situations with my clients. But perhaps most importantly, I met a lot of interesting people (I never would have thought that the Data Mesh community was so large), and I made some new friends along the way.

Like Jean-Georges, I would like to deeply thank the team at O'Reilly, and in particular, Shira Evans, who kept us on track and ever so gently pointed out many errors or inconsistencies in our early drafts.

I would also like to thank our technical reviewers Colleen Tartow, John Y. Miller, Karin Håkansson, Ole Olesen-Bagneux, and Max Schultze. Having been a technical reviewer in the past, I know this is a tough job, and all too often you don't get the thanks you deserve. So thank you!

While John Miller is one of our tech reviewers, I also would like to acknowledge his help, encouragement, and guidance along the way. I have had the pleasure of working with John for more than 15 years, and recently, we have been able to test-drive many of the concepts laid out in this book. This has gone a long way toward refining the concepts in this book. So, a huge thank you goes out to you, my friend!

I am dedicating this book to my wife, Susan, and my sons, Davis and Graeham. Each of you has heard me talking about writing this book, and you have heard my frustrations while writing this book. But you have always been encouraging. And for me, the coolest part is that Davis, Graeham, and I are actually working on client engagements together implementing the concepts in this book. It does not get much better than this!

— Eric

The Basics

The first part of this book sets the stage for the rest of the book: by the end of this part, you will be familiar with our terminology and our use case.

Chapter 1, "Understanding Data Mesh: The Essentials", outlines the fundamental principles of Data Mesh, a modern data architecture paradigm that promotes decentralized data ownership, treats data as a product, and implements self-serve infrastructure for domain teams. Building on Dehghani's foundational work, this chapter emphasizes how Data Mesh introduces agility into data management by enabling local autonomy and faster response times as well as by fostering a culture of innovation and collaboration.

Chapter 2, "Applying Data Mesh Principles", summarizes the key principles of Data Mesh and focuses on how they apply to data products, including the FAIR (findable, accessible, interoperable, and reusable) product, as well as what constitutes a good data product and the lifecycles of data products. The goals of this chapter are to create a practical Data Mesh roadmap, translate your strategy and vision into an achievable plan, secure executive sponsorship and funding, empower a skilled data product owner with decision-making authority, and engage customers while maintaining flexibility and alignment with business objectives.

Chapter 3, "Our Case Study: Climate Quantum Inc.", introduces Climate Quantum Inc., a fictional company leveraging Data Mesh capabilities to address the complexities of managing climate data, making it more accessible, usable, and trustworthy. By decentralizing data ownership and using a domain-oriented architecture, Climate Quantum Inc. aims to streamline the discovery, consumption, sharing, and verification of vast and varied climate data, thus providing a scalable solution to the multifaceted challenges posed by climate change. We have included references to Climate Quantum Inc. throughout the book.

CHAPTER 1

Understanding Data Mesh: The Essentials

In the rapidly changing landscape of enterprise data management, Data Mesh has evolved from an emerging concept into a cornerstone of modern data architecture. Its ascent marks a significant shift in how organizations handle the ever-increasing complexity and scale of their data ecosystems. The foundational principles of Data Mesh, articulated in Zhamak Dehghani's seminal work, *Data Mesh* (O'Reilly), have set the stage for a new era in data handling and utilization.

Building on Dehghani's principles, this book aims to bridge the gap between theoretical understanding and practical application, turning the principles of Data Mesh into practice for data professionals. Recognizing that many of our readers are likely familiar with Dehghani's principles, we delve deeper, not just reiterating these concepts but also expanding on them to demonstrate their implementation in real-world scenarios.

For those new to Data Mesh, we provide an accessible introduction, ensuring that all readers are on the same footing. Our book is anchored in the core principles of Data Mesh but extends well beyond this solid foundation to illustrate how these principles can be effectively implemented and operationalized within your organization.

Let's start by reiterating Dehghani's transformative vision, which rests on several key principles:

Data as a product
> Data is treated as a valuable product, with domain teams responsible for developing and delivering data solutions tailored to their specific needs.

Decentralized domain ownership
> Responsibility for data is distributed among domain-specific teams, each accountable for the quality, accessibility, and governance of their data.

Self-serve
> This is a framework that empowers domain teams to manage their data independently, reducing dependence on centralized data teams.

Federated computational governance
> In this model, domain teams enforce data governance within their purview, in alignment with overarching organizational policies.

Making Data Agile

These principles echo the spirit of the Agile methodology in software development. The Manifesto for Agile Software Development (*https://oreil.ly/a3xr5*), published in 2001, is still a pivotal document in the software industry that, at its core, emphasizes individuals and interactions, working software, customer collaboration, and response to change. These principles were translated into practices through frameworks like scrum and kanban, which promote iterative development, regular feedback loops, and close collaboration among cross-functional teams.

More than 20 years of turning core Agile principles into practice have passed since the Agile manifesto was published. We now deliver software faster, better, and cheaper: McKinsey & Company, a consulting firm, has shown (*https://oreil.ly/Zqr0X*) that "agile organizations have a 70 percent chance of being in the top quartile of organizational health, the best indicator of long-term performance." Simply put, the software engineering world has never been the same.

Similarly, Data Mesh introduces agility into the data landscape, emphasizing decentralized ownership, responsive data management, and collaborative cross-functional teams. Just as Agile promotes self-organizing teams, Data Mesh advocates for domain-oriented decentralized ownership, putting the power of data in the hands of individual domain teams. In an Agile context, customer collaboration involves continuous engagement with stakeholders to understand their evolving needs. Likewise, Data Mesh encourages domain teams to engage with data consumers within their organization, gathering feedback and iterating on their data products to meet their specific requirements.

Just as Agile values working software, Data Mesh places a premium on delivering high-quality data products. Agile-based user stories define the desired functionality; data products outline the features, quality requirements, and accessibility of data, enabling domain teams to build and deliver data products that provide real value to their stakeholders.

Simply put, Data Mesh brings Agile practices to data and, by doing so, makes data agile!

Local Autonomy + Speed = Agility

Data Mesh offers several benefits that address the challenges organizations face in data management, particularly in relation to adopting local autonomy and speed, which, in turn, drives agility.

First, Data Mesh advocates for local autonomy. Traditional centralized approaches often result in overloaded data teams and bottlenecks in decision making. In contrast, Data Mesh empowers individual domain teams with the ownership of and responsibility for their data. This decentralization allows teams to have a deeper understanding of their specific data needs and requirements, leading to more effective decision making and faster response times. By fostering local autonomy, Data Mesh enables teams to adapt quickly to changing data demands and make data-driven decisions in a timely manner. With local autonomy, Data Mesh enables speed and, with increased speed, faster time to market.

With its focus on a self-serve data infrastructure, Data Mesh enables domain teams to access and manage their data independently. This eliminates the need for at-times bureaucratic processes and time-consuming requests to centralized data teams, reducing wait times and accelerating the data development lifecycle. By putting the necessary tools and resources into the hands of data practitioners, Data Mesh enables rapid iteration, experimentation, and delivery of data products. This increased speed allows organizations to capitalize on data insights more efficiently, gaining a competitive advantage in today's fast-paced business landscape.

And with local autonomy comes speed and agility: by distributing data ownership and fostering collaboration, Data Mesh enables teams to respond swiftly to changing business needs and data requirements. Domain teams have the flexibility to adapt their data products—and even infrastructure in some cases—to meet evolving demands, avoiding the constraints of rigid, centralized systems. This agility empowers organizations to seize emerging opportunities, make data-driven decisions in real time, and stay ahead of the competition.

Perhaps the most interesting by-product of agility is the establishment of a culture of innovation and experimentation. With local autonomy, teams are encouraged to explore new ideas, test hypotheses, and iterate on their data products. This fosters a sense of ownership and accountability that can spur creativity and drive continuous improvement.

By embracing Data Mesh principles, organizations can unlock the potential of their data assets, enabling teams to discover valuable insights, develop innovative solutions, and drive business growth.

Solving Today's Data Challenges

What problems will Data Mesh and its promise of "agile data" address? Can data silos be bridged? Can data quality—always a challenge—be improved? Can gaps in data governance be transformed into a recognized driver of business value?

Bridging Data Silos

Let's start with data silos. Data silos hinder accessibility and collaboration, making it difficult to gain a holistic view and leverage the full potential of the available data. They present a real, immediate, and formidable challenge that almost all data practitioners experience in modern enterprises.

Data silos, much like isolated islands in an immense ocean, are repositories of data that are confined within specific departments or systems and thus disconnected from the broader organizational data landscape. This segregation results in a fragmented data ecosystem, where valuable insights remain untapped and the collective intelligence of the enterprise is underutilized.

The existence of these silos often stems from historical organizational structures, disparate technology platforms, and departmental boundaries that have solidified over time. As a result, critical business decisions are frequently made based on incomplete or outdated information, leading to inefficiencies, missed opportunities, and a weakened competitive edge.

The ramifications of data silos extend beyond mere inefficiencies; they actively hinder collaboration and innovation within an organization. When data is trapped in silos, it becomes difficult for teams to access the information they need to collaborate effectively. This lack of accessibility and visibility leads to duplicated efforts, inconsistent data practices, and a general sense of organizational disjointedness.

In today's data-driven business environment, the inability to integrate data from different parts of the organization can impair a company's ability to respond to market changes, understand customer needs, and optimize operations. The challenge is compounded in organizations with a global footprint, where the diversity of data sources, regulations, and business practices adds layers of complexity to the already intricate task of data integration and harmonization.

Overcoming the challenge of data silos requires a strategic, concerted effort to foster a culture of data sharing and collaboration. This involves not just the adoption of new technologies but also a fundamental shift in organizational mindset and practices.

In this light, Data Mesh becomes highly relevant, offering a decentralized yet cohesive framework for data management. Data Mesh advocates for domain-driven ownership of data, enabling individual teams to manage and share their data effectively while aligning with the overall organizational objectives. By embracing this paradigm, enterprises can gradually dismantle the barriers of data silos, paving the way for a more integrated, agile, and data-centric organizational culture.

Shifting Toward Higher Quality Data

As data volume and variety grow, ensuring data quality and integrity becomes an increasingly difficult task. Poor data quality can lead to incorrect or bad business decisions, misguided strategies, and ultimately, a detrimental impact on business outcomes. Making matters worse, the sheer complexity of data can obstruct compliance efforts, as understanding the nuances of data privacy regulations becomes more difficult when data is scattered and convoluted. For global organizations, this challenge is amplified by the need to navigate a patchwork of regional and international data laws.

Mastering this complexity requires a multifaceted approach, blending technology, strategy, and organizational culture. Advanced technologies such as machine learning (ML) and artificial intelligence offer powerful tools for analyzing complex datasets, uncovering patterns, and generating insights that would be impossible for humans to discern unaided. However, technology alone is not a cure-all; it must be coupled with a robust data strategy that prioritizes data governance, quality, and integration. Organizations need to foster a data-literate culture where employees across departments understand the importance of data and are equipped with the skills and tools to leverage it effectively.

A shift toward more agile, flexible data architectures, such as those advocated by Data Mesh, can also play a crucial role. By decentralizing data ownership and management, Data Mesh allows domain-specific teams to handle their data more effectively, reducing bottlenecks and enhancing responsiveness to change. This approach not only helps manage complexity but also empowers teams to extract maximum value from their data, turning a potential obstacle into a strategic asset.

Transforming Data Governance

Last but not least comes every data practitioner's favorite topic: data governance.

Data governance is an indispensable component in the architecture of modern enterprise data management, primarily because of the need to adhere to regulatory, privacy, and enterprise security policies. Effective governance ensures that data is managed and utilized in a way that meets these external and internal requirements.

However, the ever-increasing regulatory requirements add another layer of complexity, with stringent requirements like the European Union's General Data Protection Regulation (GDPR), the Health Insurance Portability and Accountability Act (HIPAA) in the United States, and other regulations imposing strict guidelines and constraints on data handling, privacy, and protection. Navigating this intricate web of regulations demands not only robust security infrastructure but also a vigilant, proactive approach to data management and governance.

Given the penalties for noncompliance and the risks associated with data breaches, governance is not just a compliance issue but a critical business necessity. In this evolving landscape, data governance must be agile, responsive, and deeply integrated into the day-to-day handling of data.

Traditionally, data governance has often been managed through centralized models. While such models offer uniformity and central control, they frequently lead to slow and bureaucratic practices, creating bottlenecks that hinder the dynamic use of data. In centralized governance systems, decisions about data access, quality, and security are often made by a detached central authority, far removed from the context in which the data is used.

This distance can lead to inefficiencies and misalignments between governance policies and the actual needs and realities of different business units. The result is often a governance model that is seen more as a hindrance than an enabler, slowing innovation and responsiveness to changing business and market demands.

Far too often today, data governance is viewed as a task that must be done, a command from on high, rather than a task that drives inherent value. Data Mesh offers an alternative.

Data Mesh addresses challenges in data governance by advocating for a federated governance model, which positions accountability for governance with the data owners who are most knowledgeable about the data. In this model, governance is decentralized, with each domain team responsible for the governance of its data products. This approach ensures that governance decisions are made by those who have the deepest understanding of the data's context, use, and risks. It leads to more relevant, efficient, and effective governance practices that are closely aligned with the specific needs of each domain.

To better understand the federated governance model of Data Mesh, consider an analogy with the American National Standards Institution (ANSI) or the Canadian Standards Association (CSA)—almost every country or region has an equivalent organization. In this context, the ANSI or CSA sets rules and policies and offers a certification process that enables vendors to ensure that their products meet established standards. This certification process acts as a "brand" or "logo" of trust. Vendors can then publish their certification status, signaling to consumers that their products meet high standards.

In the Data Mesh governance model, general or broadly scoped policies are established centrally—akin to the ANSI/CSA establishing product standards and policies—and data product owners (DPOs) are responsible for implementing and reporting on adherence to policies. DPOs ensure that their data products comply with the established governance standards and, once compliant, can be certified as meeting the enterprise's governance criteria.

This certification not only serves as a mark of trust and quality within the organization but also streamlines the process of governance by empowering those closest to the data. It ensures that governance is not a top-down, bureaucratic process but rather a collaborative, integrated practice that enhances the value and security of data across the enterprise.

Furthermore, DPOs—who are closest to the data and its use cases—are in a unique position to understand and manage the compliance requirements effectively. They can publish and update their certification statuses, making this information transparent and accessible within the Data Mesh ecosystem.

This method contrasts starkly with the conventional centralized governance model, where compliance is often managed by a central group that oversees and polices all data activities. While this model has its strengths in maintaining control and uniformity, it can also lead to bottlenecks, delays, and a disconnect between the governance process and the real-world application of data.

In a federated model, the responsibility for compliance is distributed, fostering a culture of accountability and agility among DPOs. They can respond more swiftly to changes in regulations or business needs, updating certification status and ensuring that their data products remain compliant. This not only streamlines the governance process but also embeds compliance into the fabric of the Data Mesh, making it an integral part of the data product lifecycle rather than an external, enforced process.

Data Volume, Variety, and Variability

What about the characteristics of the data itself?

Today, the velocity of data creation and consumption has become a defining challenge for organizations. This rapid generation and consumption of data, akin to a high-speed train, necessitates a continuous and agile approach to data management.

Traditional data infrastructures often struggle to keep pace, leading to bottlenecks and delays in data processing and analysis. The challenge is not just in storing this vast amount of data but also in processing and extracting value from it in real time. Organizations need to adapt their infrastructure, tools, and processes to manage this deluge of data as well as to leverage it effectively for timely decision making and insights.

Data Mesh offers a compelling solution to the challenge of data velocity. First, local autonomy, as discussed earlier, delegates decision making—how data is handled, how it is transformed, and how it is consumed most effectively and efficiently—to those closest to the data and who best understand the data. If data velocity increases, decision making must commensurately increase, and local autonomy offered by Data Mesh is one part of the solution to this problem.

By its very design, Data Mesh is oriented toward handling large volumes and high velocities of data efficiently. It does so by decentralizing data ownership and management. In a Data Mesh framework, data is no longer a centralized asset to be managed from a single point. Instead, it is distributed across multiple domain-specific teams, each equipped with the tools and autonomy to manage its slice of the data ecosystem.

This decentralized approach allows for distributed teams to process data independently, thereby significantly reducing the time it takes to ingest, process, and analyze data. By empowering domain teams, Data Mesh ensures that data handling is more responsive and aligned with the specific needs and dynamics of each domain, enabling faster and more effective decision making.

Now combine local autonomy with Data Mesh's "self-serve" capability. Consumers can access data at any time, using standard, well-known, published interfaces. Data providers can create data products with minimal involvement from central groups. And platform capability required to scale data products is available on demand.

By adopting Data Mesh, organizations can transform the challenge of data velocity into an opportunity, leveraging the rapid flow of data to drive innovation, enhance customer experiences, and make more informed, agile business decisions. Simply put, Data Mesh lets enterprises keep up with the velocity, variety, and variability in their data.

Turning Principles into Practice

By now, we hope that you will see that Data Mesh offers clear benefits. But realizing these benefits means turning the revolutionary Data Mesh principles into practice. That is what we think the core purpose of this book is. This book is driven by three foundational goals, each carefully crafted to guide professionals on their journey to mastering Data Mesh.

Our first goal is to demystify the transition from Data Mesh theory to practice. We don't just discuss the principles abstractly; we illustrate them through real-world examples, detailed case studies, and practical strategies that can be directly applied in your organizational context.

Second, we aim to accelerate your journey through the Data Mesh landscape. Understanding the intricacies of Data Mesh is one thing; applying them efficiently and effectively is another. This book offers a suite of techniques and best practices, distilled from leading industry experts and pioneering organizations, to fast-track your Data Mesh implementation. We delve into advanced topics such as automating governance, optimizing data-product design, and leveraging cutting-edge technologies to amplify the benefits of Data Mesh in your enterprise.

Third, our intention is to chart a clear, actionable roadmap to Data Mesh success. This roadmap is more than a theoretical guide—it is a practical toolkit that addresses the common challenges and pitfalls encountered in implementing Data Mesh. From establishing a robust self-serve data infrastructure to nurturing a data-oriented culture, we provide a step-by-step guide to navigating the complexities of Data Mesh, ensuring a smooth, successful journey from inception to execution.

In embracing these principles and translating them into actionable practices, we envision a future where organizations can fully harness the transformative power of Data Mesh. We believe that the adoption of Data Mesh principles can propel data initiatives to unprecedented heights, enabling businesses to become more agile, data-driven, and competitive.

Our aspiration in writing this book is rooted in a humble yet bold vision: two decades from now, we hope to look back and see Data Mesh as a pivotal force in bringing Agile methodologies to the realm of data management. Our contribution, though a modest part of this larger movement, aims to empower organizations to derive better, faster, and more cost-effective insights and business value from their data. In the pages of this book, we seek to inspire a new generation of data professionals, equipping them with the knowledge and tools to revolutionize data management practices and drive their organizations toward a future where data is not just an asset but also a catalyst for innovation and growth.

In today's data-driven landscape, organizations face a myriad of challenges when it comes to managing and harnessing the power of data. The sheer volume and variety of data sources can be overwhelming, resembling an overflowing river that organizations struggle to navigate. Making sense of this deluge of data, ensuring its quality, and extracting valuable insights pose significant hurdles.

Zhamak Dehghani's Data Mesh principles offer a revolutionary vision for data management. They advocate for decentralized ownership, self-serve data platforms, federated computational governance, and cross-functional collaboration. By applying Agile principles to data, Data Mesh promotes local autonomy, speed, and agility. Organizations that translate these principles into practice can overcome data challenges and unlock the benefits of Data Mesh, improving accessibility, quality, and responsiveness to changing data demands.

The remainder of this book aims to provide practical guidance on implementing Data Mesh, establishing self-serve data infrastructure, fostering a data-product mindset, implementing federated computational data governance, creating decentralized ownership, promoting cross-functional collaboration, and facilitating knowledge sharing within organizations. We will touch on several topics:

Defining the essentials

We will define data products (Chapter 2), and how they are members of the Data Mesh ecosystem. We will introduce our case study (Chapter 3)—applying Data Mesh to make climate data easy to find, consume, share, and trust—that will be used throughout the book to demonstrate how to implement Data Mesh practices. And of course we will offer a perspective on Data Mesh architecture (Chapter 4).

Embracing a data-product mindset

We will describe how data contracts (Chapter 5) enable all members of the Data Mesh ecosystem to find one another and interact. We will explain how to encourage domain teams to think of data as a product, define clear boundaries for data products, and establish the APIs, documentation, and support mechanisms required for your first data product (Chapters 6–8). Finally, we will describe a "test and learn" mindset that encourages teams to iterate and improve their data products based on feedback and evolving business needs as well as to promote a culture of continuous improvement and innovation within each data product team.

Making data agile

We will then describe the core interfaces for data products in your Data Mesh ecosystem (Chapter 9) that make data products discoverable, observable, and operable. We will introduce the key "superpower" of data products that become available through discovery and observability: the Data Mesh Marketplace (Chapter 10). We will also describe a transformational approach that replaces traditional data governance with a delegated "certification" approach modeled on modern, real-world examples (Chapter 11) and a "factory" method of building data ecosystems and their data "supply chains" that allows your Data Mesh to grow and evolve (Chapter 12). Finally, generative AI—OpenAI, ChatGPT, and their open source counterparts—promises to shake the foundations of the modern enterprise. Data Mesh obviously is no different. In fact, we see material and widespread uses for generative AI that we will explain (Chapter 13).

Creating a domain-oriented decentralized ownership

We will describe the "team topology" required to implement your Data Mesh (Chapter 14). We will define and then describe the intricacies of an operating model for Data Mesh (Chapter 15). Then we will discuss the incentives and organizational structure that allow a Data Mesh to evolve and grow gracefully.

Creating your Data Mesh roadmap

We will provide a tried and tested "roadmap" (Chapter 16) that starts with a strategy and then shows how to implement the core data product and Data Mesh foundational elements as well as establish data product teams and the broader Data Mesh operating model. We will also show how to establish channels for collaboration and knowledge sharing among domain teams through communities of practice, regular cross-functional meetings, or data councils. We will demonstrate how to socialize Data Mesh within your organization to encourage teams to share best practices, lessons learned, and data assets to leverage the organization's collective knowledge and expertise.

Summary

By putting these principles into practice, organizations can overcome data management challenges and realize the benefits of Data Mesh. They can achieve the local autonomy that they crave and need, giving data product teams ownership and control over their data, allowing them to operate at a faster pace, leveraging self-serve infrastructure, and enabling rapid iteration and experimentation. Finally, they can embrace agility by fostering collaboration, adopting a data-product mindset, and implementing federated computational data governance. Following these practical steps, organizations can transform their approach to data management and unlock the full potential of their data assets.

Enjoy!

CHAPTER 2

Applying Data Mesh Principles

At its simplest, a *Data Mesh* is just an ecosystem of interacting data products, as shown in Figure 2-1. As in any ecosystem, there are many moving parts, each operating somewhat independently, that are connected through common standards and a communications backbone. And data products in a Data Mesh ideally have a common technical implementation with a consistent set of interfaces.

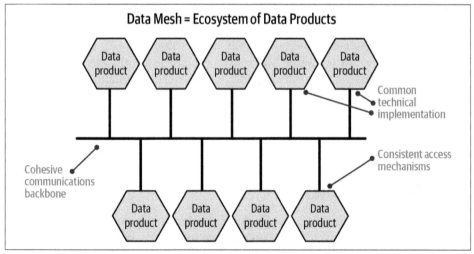

Figure 2-1. Data Mesh: an ecosystem of interacting data products

Data Mesh is, at its foundation, a conceptual framework in the realm of data architecture, which emphasizes decentralized data ownership and architecture. It recognizes that in large organizations, data is vast and varied, where each business domain has a significant degree of autonomy over (as well as local knowledge and mastery of) its own data. By decentralizing control, Data Mesh empowers individual domains to manage and make decisions about their data while maintaining a cohesive overall structure. With this autonomy presumably comes better, more localized, and faster decisions, which in turn lead to more speed and agility.

In the context of a Data Mesh, a *data product* is a package of data that is self-contained, self-descriptive, and oriented toward a specific business purpose or function. Data products are packages of data crafted to address specific business objectives within an organization. These are not mere collections of data; rather, they are comprehensive units that encapsulate the data itself along with essential tools, documentation, and metadata. This ensures that the data is not only present but also understandable and usable. Each data product is purpose oriented, tailored to serve a particular business need or solve a specific problem, making them much more than just repositories of information.

The structure of a data product is self-contained, meaning that it includes everything necessary for its effective utilization. It adheres to strict standards of quality and governance, thereby ensuring reliability, security, and compliance with relevant regulations. This comprehensive approach makes data products a trusted and dependable resource within the organization. They are designed with user accessibility in mind, offering interfaces and documentation that are easily navigable by a wide range of users, from data experts to those with minimal technical expertise.

Furthermore, the lifecycle of each data product is meticulously managed. Every data product has an assigned owner who is responsible for its maintenance, updates, and overall management. This stewardship ensures that the data product remains relevant and continues to deliver value over time. The continuous oversight and improvement of these data products underpin their evolving nature, ensuring that they stay aligned with the dynamic needs and objectives of the organization. This lifecycle management is a critical aspect of data products, distinguishing them as not just static datasets but rather evolving assets within the Data Mesh ecosystem.

We will have much more to say about the Data Mesh ecosystem in Chapter 4.

Data Mesh Principles

As we mentioned in Chapter 1, a set of guiding principles stands at the core of Data Mesh, and each of these principles plays a crucial role in the framework's efficacy and sustainability. Let's go through them in more detail here.

Data as a Product

The first of these principles is to treat data as a product. In traditional product management, a product fulfills a need, has an owner (more on that later), and has a long-term roadmap (in contrast to projects, which have a start and an end time). All of these characteristics also apply to data products.

These characteristics establish a clear boundary for each data product. This boundary demarcation, which describes a domain, is essential in defining what the data product represents, its scope, and its limitations. A clear boundary in a Data Mesh ensures that every data product is a well-defined entity within the larger ecosystem. This clarity establishes a clear understanding of the data product's purpose, and it helps manage expectations and direct efforts and resources appropriately, ensuring that each data product can effectively fulfill its intended role.

But there is more. In Zhamak Dehghani's book *Data Mesh*, she describes data products as being discoverable, addressable, understandable, trustworthy and truthful, natively accessible, interoperable and composable, valuable on their own, and secure. We will discuss these specific attributes more in later chapters.

Decentralized Domain Ownership

Another fundamental principle in the Data Mesh framework is the concept of decentralized domain ownership, which effectively establishes an empowered owner (and team) for each data product. This aspect of the framework borrows from the idea of having a dedicated manager for each city block, someone who is deeply invested and responsible for its well-being. In a similar vein, each data product within a Data Mesh has an owner who bears the responsibility for its performance, quality, and compliance with governance standards.

The role of an empowered DPO is multifaceted. The DPO is tasked with ensuring that the data product aligns with both specific business requirements and the overarching governance framework. This alignment is crucial for maintaining the integrity and usefulness of the data product, ensuring that it remains a valuable asset within the organization's data landscape.

Self-Serve Data Platform

A third principle central to the Data Mesh concept is the provision of self-serve capability—for both consumers and producers.

For a data consumer, "self-serve" means being able to easily find, consume, and trust data, all without assistance from a third party (or central team, or engineering group). This is typically implemented as a "marketplace" that offers a portal (web/mobile site) with groupings of data products that consumers can use.

Now, a quick word about the term *marketplace*: the unique characteristic of a marketplace in comparison to a data catalog is that the marketplace offers both consumer and producer functionality. The common term for this is a *two-sided marketplace*, which lets consumers find data but also makes it easy for data producers to publish data. In this sense, the producer capability of the marketplace is also self-serve. A

Data Mesh should make it easy for anyone (subject to normal security provisions) to publish data products.

Self-serve capability in a Data Mesh not only empowers users but also fosters a culture of innovation and agility. It enables individuals to leverage data for their specific needs, encouraging experimentation and personalized analysis. This capability reduces bottlenecks typically associated with centralized data systems, where requests for data access and analysis can slow decision-making processes.

Federated Computational Governance

The final principle guiding the Data Mesh framework is federated computational governance, which refers to a decentralized approach to managing and enforcing data policies, standards, and quality across different domains or teams within an organization.

Instead of having a centralized data governance team that imposes rules and standards, federated governance distributes these responsibilities to domain-specific teams. Each team governs its own data while adhering to overarching principles set at the organizational level. Federated computational governance ensures that despite the decentralized nature of data ownership, there is a unified framework governing how data is managed, used, and shared.

At this point, it is probably safe to say that the opportunities that Data Mesh provides to improve data governance are in their infancy. Hence, implementing federated computational governance requires a delicate balance. It involves creating governance structures that are robust enough to ensure consistency and compliance yet flexible enough to accommodate the unique needs and contexts of different data products. This balance is key to fostering an environment where innovation can thrive without compromising the standards and protocols essential for a cohesive data ecosystem.

Defining a "Good" Data Product

As stated earlier, a Data Mesh is an ecosystem of data products. Practically speaking, a data product is the foundational building block and, in fact, the smallest indivisible unit, a "data quantum" of sorts, for any Data Mesh. Clearly, data products are crucial, but what is the definition of a "good" data product? There are many attributes that span technical, business, ease of use, and other characteristics that constitute a "good" data product, as shown in Figure 2-2.

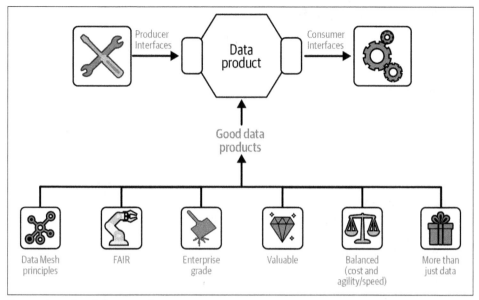

Figure 2-2. Good data products

Defining a Principled Data Product

So, where to start? Let's start with a simple and perhaps obvious statement: good data products adhere to Data Mesh principles. Let's look at these principles and apply them to data products.

First, good data products align to decentralized domain ownership: they should align to a domain (large or small) with a clear boundary and have an empowered owner. Second, good data products are treated as their name implies—as a product and not a project. Good data products, like other products, have a lifecycle, clear consumers, and a clear value proposition. Good data products are self-serve, meaning that users can get what they need from a data product without undue participation from third parties. Good data products have a federated governance mechanism that provides for local autonomy and decision making at the data-product level by the DPO and their team. This also means that DPOs and their teams are responsible and accountable for ensuring that their data products adhere to enterprise guidelines and standards as needed.

Defining a FAIR Data Product

Good data products should also adhere to FAIR principles (*https://oreil.ly/4Mp_d*). Data should be:

- Findable
- Accessible
- Interoperable
- Reusable

According to FAIR (*https://oreil.ly/4Mp_d*), the "principles emphasize machine-actionability (i.e., the capacity of computational systems to find, access, interoperate, and reuse data with none or minimal human intervention) because humans increasingly rely on computational support to deal with data as a result of the increase in volume, complexity, and creation speed of data."

Let's elaborate on these principles and apply them to data products. *Findability* is the first of the FAIR principles. For a data product to be valuable, it must be easily discoverable within the organization's broader data landscape.

Accessibility is another key principle (note that we use *accessibility* in the general sense—being easily consumable—and not in the specific context of addressing specific user-accessibility needs). It's not enough for data to be findable: once found, a data product must also be easily accessible. Accessibility includes providing comprehensive documentation that explains how to use the data as well as ensuring that the data can be easily integrated into various applications and workflows. A good data product should be as straightforward to use as a well-designed software application, with clear instructions and support.

Interoperability is a critical aspect of the FAIR principles. This refers to the ability of data products to work together and integrate effectively. In practical terms, this means that data products should be created using standard data formats and protocols. For example, if one data product uses XML format and another uses JSON, there should be tools or services in place to allow these different formats to be used together seamlessly. Similarly, interoperability may also mean using common standards (for example, SQL or RESTful APIs) or common identifiers. This interoperability is essential for combining and leveraging data from various sources.

The fourth principle, *reuse*, focuses on the ability to apply data in multiple contexts. This principle is particularly important in maximizing the value of data. Data products designed to be modular and reusable can be used across different projects and applications. For instance, a data product that contains customer demographic information can be used by marketing teams for campaign planning, by sales teams for development of sales strategies, and by product development teams for market analysis.

In addition to these technical aspects, adhering to FAIR principles involves fostering a culture of collaboration and data sharing. This cultural shift is crucial for breaking down silos and encouraging the reuse of data products. It means promoting an organizational mindset where data is seen as a shared resource that can be leveraged for multiple purposes.

In conclusion, "good" data products in a Data Mesh are those that are FAIR: findable, accessible, interoperable, and reusable. These principles ensure that data is not just stored but also actively managed and used in a way that adds value to the organization. Data products that adhere to FAIR principles become more than just repositories of information; they transform into dynamic assets that drive innovation and decision making across the enterprise.

Defining an Enterprise-Grade Data Product

FAIR principles provide one lens for understanding a "good" data product. But what makes a data product "good" in an enterprise? Or more specifically, what is the definition of a "good" enterprise-grade data product? In the realm of enterprise-grade data products, several key attributes come together to define their quality and effectiveness. These attributes—encompassing security, reliability, observability, operability, deployability, and comprehensive documentation—form a cohesive structure that ensures the data product's value within an organization.

Practically, the strength of an enterprise-grade data product lies in the seamless integration of its key attributes. Security, reliability, observability, operability, deployability, and comprehensive documentation are not isolated aspects; they are interconnected, each playing a vital role in the product's overall functionality and value. A product that meets these requirements is not just a repository of data but a dynamic asset that drives business efficiency, innovation, and decision making. Understanding how these attributes interplay and support one another is crucial in creating a data product that meets the stringent demands of enterprise environments.

Security probably stands at the forefront of these enterprise-grade attributes. An enterprise-grade data product must be fortified against unauthorized access and breaches, ensuring the confidentiality and integrity of the data it holds. This security is not only about safeguarding information but also about maintaining user trust and adhering to regulatory standards, such as GDPR or HIPAA. Implementing robust encryption, access controls, and regular security audits is integral to this process, creating a fortified barrier against potential cyber threats.

Yet security alone is not sufficient. The *reliability* of the data product is equally important. Users need to trust that the data product will provide accurate, consistent information at all times. Ensuring reliability involves implementing validation checks and error-detection algorithms as well as maintaining high data availability. This is where the concept of reliability intersects with security: a secure data product is inherently more reliable as it protects against data tampering and loss.

Observability extends the concept of reliability. It's about having the ability to monitor the health and performance of the data product. By using tools to track various metrics like response times and error rates, organizations can proactively manage the data product's health, or data quality. This proactive management plays a crucial role in maintaining the product's reliability, as it allows for the early identification and resolution of potential issues before they escalate.

Closely linked to observability is the aspect of *operability*. A data product with high operability is easier to manage and operate. This involves capabilities that streamline the data product's lifecycle management, including deploying, scaling, updating, and troubleshooting. High operability supports the product's reliability by ensuring that it remains functional and effective throughout its lifecycle, adapting to changing requirements with minimal disruption.

Deployability is another critical attribute, especially in dynamic business environments. A highly deployable data product can be easily implemented and integrated into various business processes and technological environments. This flexibility is crucial for keeping pace with the evolving needs of a business, whether it's scaling to accommodate growth or integrating with new systems and applications.

Underpinning all these attributes is the role of *comprehensive documentation*. Documentation serves as the backbone of a data product, providing clarity on its use, management, and integration. It includes everything from user guides and API documentation to operational procedures and architectural diagrams. Good documentation not only aids in the effective utilization of the data product but also ensures compliance with regulatory standards, facilitating audits and compliance checks.

The interplay among these attributes creates a holistic enterprise-grade data product. For instance, robust documentation enhances security by outlining precise data-handling procedures, while observability informs reliability strategies by identifying predictive maintenance needs. Similarly, the ease of operability is often facilitated by well-structured documentation, which provides clear guidelines for managing and updating the data product.

Defining a Valuable Data Product

Beauty is in the eye of the beholder, as they say. Nevertheless, there are a few objective characteristics of a data product that we can use to clearly and unambiguously attribute value. First, a valuable data product is fundamentally defined by its relevance and utility. The primary purpose of such a product is to address specific business needs or questions, making it a crucial tool for informed decision making and insight generation. The value is directly tied to its practical application in solving real-world business problems or enhancing operational efficiency. Therefore, a data product's utility is gauged by its ability to facilitate actions, support decisions, or provide insights that are directly applicable to the users' needs.

Quality and reliability are indispensable attributes of a valuable data product. These attributes encompass not only the accuracy, consistency, and completeness of the data but also its timeliness and relevance to current business scenarios. Furthermore, reliability extends to the technical aspects of the data product, including its performance capabilities, such as processing speed and availability. Ensuring high quality and reliability is crucial as these factors directly affect the trustworthiness and dependability of the data product in operational and decision-making processes.

Usability is a key determinant of a data product's value: if it is complex or unintuitive, its potential utility diminishes irrespective of the underlying data quality. Therefore, the design and interface of a data product should facilitate ease of use to ensure that it can be effectively employed by its target users. Somewhat related to this is interoperability—in other words, the data product is also usable from an operations perspective. A valuable data product should not only function in isolation but also integrate seamlessly with other data products. This interoperability is vital for comprehensive analytics and insight generation, as it allows for the combination and analysis of data across various domains. Additionally, compliance with regulatory requirements and security standards is nonnegotiable. Ensuring data privacy, adhering to regulations like GDPR or HIPAA, and maintaining robust security protocols are fundamental to the integrity and value of a data product.

Finally, scalability and maintainability are key aspects of a valuable data product. It should be capable of handling increasing volumes of data or user demands without necessitating significant redesign or rework. Alongside scalability, maintainability—the ease with which a data product can be updated, modified, or repaired—is critical for its long-term utility. This includes the product's ability to evolve based on user feedback and changing business needs, ensuring that it remains relevant and valuable over time. Aligning with the organization's strategic objectives and contributing to business goals—whether through cost reduction, revenue generation, or risk management—solidify a data product's value within the organization's ecosystem.

Defining a Balanced Data Product

Traditionally, IT organizations—especially those that are highly centralized—have leaned heavily toward optimizing for cost control. Cost control—a focus on efficiency—is common when IT is not closely linked or only indirectly linked to business outcomes. This focus, while financially prudent, often comes into conflict with the business's growing need for speed and agility—attributes that are increasingly crucial in today's fast-paced market environment. A key attribute of a valuable data product is achieving this balance between cost and efficiency on the one side and speed and agility on the other.

However, a shift in perspective reveals an interesting dynamic. In fact, experience has shown that prioritizing speed and agility doesn't necessarily compromise cost-effectiveness, and by focusing on these aspects, businesses can achieve more efficient product delivery, which can lead to cost savings in the long run. This efficiency is born out of the ability to adapt quickly to market changes, customer needs, and new technological advancements, thereby reducing the time and resources spent on lengthy project cycles.

This does, however, suggest an approach that involves incremental development, where data products, or their constituent capabilities, are broken down into smaller, manageable delivery units. This allows for rapid iteration and adaptation based on feedback and changing requirements. The use of prototypes and minimum viable products (MVPs) is central to this approach, enabling teams to test ideas and concepts without committing extensive resources to full-scale development. Obviously, organizations that are new to Data Mesh should consider this approach.

The incremental approach has several benefits. First, it allows for quicker response times to market demands and customer feedback, as changes can be implemented and tested in shorter cycles. Second, it reduces the risk associated with larger data products since adjustments can be made along the way, avoiding the costly pitfalls of fully committing to a single, rigid delivery plan.

Defining a Modern Data Product—More than Just "Regular" Data

Data products in a Data Mesh are often perceived as revolving exclusively around "traditional" data: databases, tables, and the like. This view is somewhat limited, though, and maybe even dated. While this type of data is indeed the foundational element, a data product encompasses a much more expansive set of artifacts.

In this context, *artifacts* are any objects, entities, or items that the DPO decides to make available to the data product's users or a broader audience, as shown in Figure 2-3.

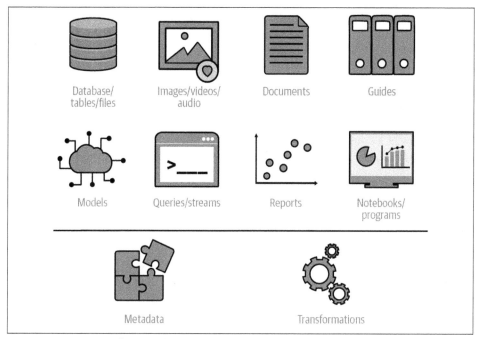

Figure 2-3. Data product artifacts

These artifacts are the "internals" of the data product and may include:

- "Regular" data, such as databases, tables, or files. We call this "regular" data as it is the most common type of artifact within data products today. Data products will likely continue to prioritize the integration and management of traditional data forms, such as databases, tables, and files, as these structured data types are foundational for most analytical and operational processes.

- Images, videos, and audio, which are becoming commonplace in our modern multimodal data environment. These data forms provide rich, contextual information that can significantly enhance analytics, ML models, and decision-making processes. As organizations aim to derive more comprehensive insights, the ability to seamlessly handle and analyze both structured and unstructured data, such as visual content, becomes increasingly critical.

- Documents, such as PDFs or other text-oriented unstructured data.

- Guides, which may help consumers understand or consume a data product. It goes without saying that clear and comprehensive documentation aids users in understanding how to leverage each artifact effectively. Of course, this documentation should be easily accessible and understandable, catering to users with varying levels of expertise.

- Models, including older AI/ML models as well as newer generative AI large language models. In many modern data products, the data is used to train or fine-tune ML or AI models. These models, when included as artifacts and offered for consumption, can offer unique insights about data in the data product.

- Queries that have been vetted (safe, performant, etc.), which simplify consumption of the data product. These can include prewritten SQL queries or other access methods that provide users with ready-to-use insights. These queries are particularly valuable for users who may not have deep technical expertise but need to derive meaningful information from the data product. Streams represent a dynamic aspect of data products where users can subscribe to specific topics within the data product and receive notifications when there are changes or updates to the data.

- Reports, which provide a preformatted set of outputs from a data product.

- Notebooks and programs that demonstrate how the data within the product can be used effectively or show the processing logic used within the data product. These programs might include "starter kits" for users of the data product, providing them with a foundational understanding of how to interact with and extract value from the data. These programs might showcase key insights or analyses derived from the data, offering users a head start in their exploration.

- Metadata, or data about the data product, its contents, its fields, and its formats.

- Transformations, including pipelines and other workflow tooling that ingest the data and transform it into a form that is usable and convenient for consumers.

Choosing artifacts to include in a data product is an important decision. It reflects the DPO's understanding of the needs and preferences of their target audience. By carefully curating these artifacts, the owner can significantly enhance the usability and appeal of the data product. This usually requires a deep understanding of both the technical aspects of the artifacts and the user journey within the data product.

Now, what is a modern data product? It is a data product that can evolve beyond "regular" data but recognizes the evolving data landscape and the multimodal data world we live in. It is a data product that contains the full breadth of data and tools that make complex data insights possible, including AI models, notebooks, or programs. It is a data product that showcases the evolution of data management from static storage to dynamic, interactive platforms that empower users to derive greater value and insights from their data.

Defining a Practical Data Product Lifecycle

When you are thinking about a product, you are implicitly thinking about its lifecycle. Let's consider your car (if you don't have a car, you probably know someone who does). It took some time for the manufacturer to design it, develop it, and test it before you bought it. While a certain model is available for sale, the manufacturer continues to develop a new version of it. A great example is the Toyota Camry, introduced as the Celica Camry in 1979; it is still available today, more than 45 years later. Let's keep the Camry in mind as we go through the following examples.

In traditional data engineering, a centralized team is often tasked to build a dataset. The team delivers; either they support the dataset or pass it to an ops team until it is retired, as illustrated in Figure 2-4. In fact, most data projects look like this: after a development period, the projects go into and stay in production until they are retired. Retirement is often impossible as there is no substitution dataset. Thinking back to our Camry, it's as if we were still driving a car from the 1990s.

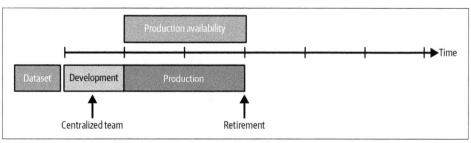

Figure 2-4. Data product lifecycle (early stages)

If a new dataset is built to replace the first version, the transition is often very difficult. Without sufficient time to facilitate the transition, an enormous burden is placed on consuming teams, as illustrated in Figure 2-5, where the dataset is evolving from version 1 to version 2. The transition can be hard, with breaking changes.

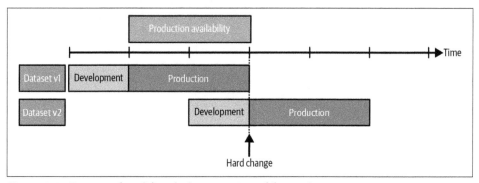

Figure 2-5. Data product lifecycle (new version of dataset)

To soften the transition between two versions of a dataset, teams can include a support or ramp-down period during which two datasets are available simultaneously, as shown in Figure 2-6, where the dataset is evolving from version 1 to version 2.

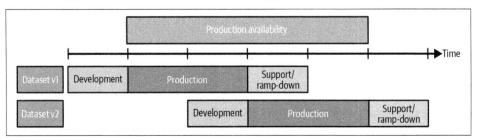

Figure 2-6. Data product lifecycle (with a ramp-down period between dataset versions)

These designs suit an organization with central teams well. After delivering the datasets, the development team might switch to another project. The drawback is that this does not guarantee that the team working on v2 is the same as the team that worked on v1, and therefore it doesn't capitalize on the expertise acquired during the v1 project.

Imagine that you can iteratively improve your product and deliver incremental value rather than big-bang shifts. Going back to the Camry example, there was an incremental shift between the 2014 model and the 2015 model, but it was not a major model change (such as there was between the 2016 and 2017 models). Using semantic versioning, the Camry 2014 could be v50.14.0, and the 2015 could be v50.15.0; however, the 2017 model would be v70.0.0, which indicates a major change.

As Figure 2-7 shows, this methodology does not preclude requiring major (and breaking) changes. Still, you keep your development team focused, on task, and growing their domain expertise. The development team does not have to be as big, but more importantly, you will see benefits in the continued focus, growing domain expertise, and consistent improvement on a single, consistent consumer experience. This process is well in line with all modern (Agile) software development strategies.

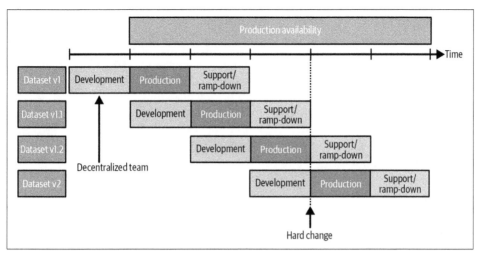

Figure 2-7. Data product lifecycle (incremental and new versions of dataset)

As you build and grow your datasets, they remain aligned to the same domain, providing a similar user experience, as illustrated by Figure 2-8. Once more, the data contract (elaborated upon in Chapter 5) will provide a lot of information for the datasets you are exposing.

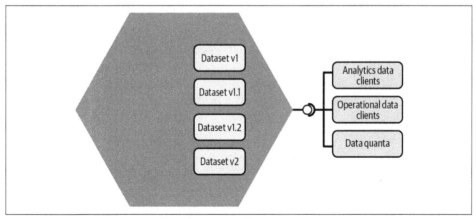

Figure 2-8. User experience of new versions of dataset

Defining a Practical Data Mesh Roadmap

We have now explained the technical aspects of data products—that they adhere to Data Mesh and FAIR principles and have the attributes to be considered enterprise grade. They should be valuable and balanced, and they should be cognizant of the evolving data landscape. But they also must be practical: they need not only a strategy and a vision but also a roadmap and an implementation plan. They need sponsorship and funding, or the data product will not even get started. They need a skilled team suited to the technology and data footprint of the data product, and the way they operate and collaborate with the rest of the organization must be integral to how the data product team operates.

Let's start with translating a strategy and vision for your data products into a practical roadmap. The strategy and vision for the data product should be ambitious yet achievable. It needs to strike a balance between aspirational goals and practical realities. The target state should challenge the status quo but remain grounded in what is realistically attainable given the current technological capabilities and organizational context. A practical data product has a well-defined target state or end goal aligned to its expected contribution to the organization. Much of this is addressed in later chapters.

Clearly linked to the target state is the need for a roadmap: a way to get to the target state, as illustrated in Figure 2-9.

The roadmap is a plan that details the progression from the current state of the data product to its desired future state, addressing the technologies ("technology stream"), processes ("factory stream"), resources and operating model ("operating model stream"), and communication plan ("socialization stream"), as well as the timelines involved, of course. This is clearly a big topic, and much more detail will be available in Chapter 16.

Now, let's tackle sponsorship and funding. A strong level of engagement from senior executives who recognize the long-term nature of a data product is crucial, which is where our sponsor comes in. The sponsor is typically a high-level executive or decision maker within the organization who champions the data product. Their support is crucial for aligning the data product with the organization's broader goals and strategies. The role of the sponsor extends beyond mere endorsement. They are instrumental in navigating organizational hurdles and advocating for the data product across various departments. Their influence can be pivotal in securing buy-in from different stakeholders within the organization, ensuring that the data product is integrated and utilized effectively.

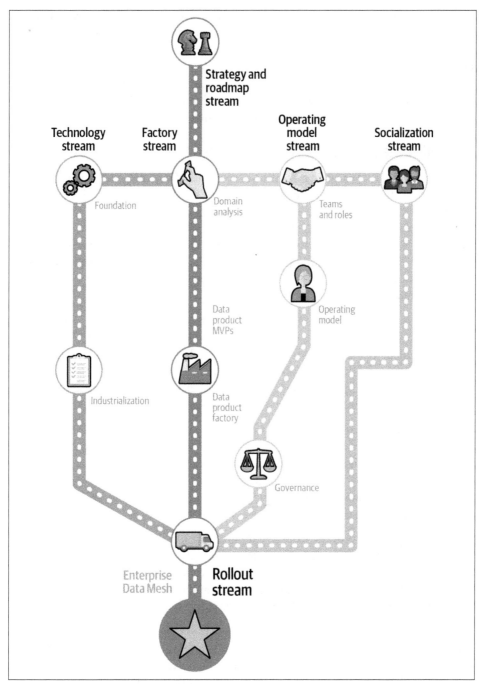

Figure 2-9. A practical roadmap

Having a sponsor with the right level of influence is critical for ensuring that the data product doesn't become sidelined or lost among other organizational priorities. The sponsor's role involves not just securing funding but also ensuring ongoing support for the data product throughout its development and deployment. Presumably with a sponsor comes a sustainable mechanism for funding—and the incentives required—for the creation and operation of a viable and practical data product. This is also addressed in our chapter on operating models (Chapter 15).

A "Good" Data Product Has an Empowered Data Product Owner

An empowered DPO is pivotal to the success and effectiveness of a data product. In this sense, this is not a specific attribute of a valuable data product, but it is still a necessary condition for delivering a valuable data product. In fact, it is the DPO who governs the determination of what is considered valuable. They determine the balance between cost/efficiency and speed/agility. Their local autonomy is fundamental to their decision-making power to influence and guide a data product from its genesis to production. To state the obvious: a viable data product cannot exist without an empowered DPO.

While this is covered extensively in Chapter 14, it is worth digging a bit deeper here. The DPO holds a position of significant responsibility and authority, overseeing the development of the data product, its overall health, its performance, and the strategic alignment of the data product with the business's needs. The DPO's role is multifaceted, encompassing various aspects of data product management, from conceptualization to implementation and ongoing maintenance.

Accountability is a crucial aspect of the DPO's role. They are answerable for the outcomes produced by the data product. This means ensuring that the product meets all quality and compliance standards and that it delivers the expected results. Their accountability extends to all stakeholders, including the technical team, business users, and senior management, requiring them to maintain transparency and open communication about the product's progress and performance.

One of the critical powers vested in a DPO is decision rights. They have the authority to make key decisions regarding the development, deployment, and evolution of the data product. This includes decisions about features, functionalities, and the overall direction of the product. Their decision-making authority is essential for maintaining the product's relevance and effectiveness in a rapidly changing business environment.

With these decision rights, an empowered DPO has a high degree of autonomy. This autonomy allows them to operate independently within the defined boundaries of the data product, making decisions and implementing strategies that foster innovation and agility. The autonomy granted to them is not unfettered but is balanced with the need for alignment with broader organizational goals and strategies.

Let's make this a bit more concrete. A common scenario that illustrates the need for clear decision rights involves the selection of technology tools and platforms for the data product. An enterprise will frequently have a preferred set of tools and platforms that it mandates across its operations. However, the DPO (or the data product engineers) might identify alternative tools that they believe would be more effective for their specific data product.

In such cases, if the principles of Data Mesh are adhered to, the decision rests with the DPO. They have the authority to choose the tools and technologies that best suit the needs of their data product. This autonomy is crucial for ensuring that the data product is built with the most suitable and effective technologies.

However, this decision-making autonomy doesn't mean isolation from the rest of the enterprise. The enterprise, for its part, should focus on making its recommended tools effective, efficient, and user-friendly. The goal should be to create an environment where DPOs see the value in using enterprise-recommended tools, not because they are mandated but because they genuinely meet their needs.

Identifying a Data Product

Probably the first important question you will need to answer is, "How do I get started with building data products?" We would like to give you a really simple answer. But despite having built many data products, we still do not have the magic recipe for a guaranteed successful design. What we can do is share some basic guidelines (Chapter 16 also adds some info).

Talking with your customers is key. You are probably already doing this, but you will need to make sure to ask them about their priorities, which they may not be familiar with. You should determine what data they want by a certain date and if you can spread deliveries over time: v1.0, v1.1, v1.2, and so on. Consider involving multiple customers to widen your use case.

Think about domain-driven design (DDD). This is a popular approach to software design that focuses on modeling software to match a domain according to input from that domain's experts. Under DDD, the structure, language of the software code (class names, class methods, class variables), and data artifacts should match the business domain. If you are interested in learning more about DDD, have a look at *Learning Domain-Driven Design* by Vlad Khononov (O'Reilly).

You will need to identify the person who will become the DPO (you will learn more about the DPO's role in Chapter 14). At this stage, their responsibilities include the following tasks:

Define and prioritize the data product's features
> The DPO aligns the features with business objectives and user needs; adopts Agile methodologies for incremental development, starting with an MVP; and maintains flexibility for ongoing adjustments based on continuous user feedback and performance metrics to ensure the product evolves effectively to deliver maximum value to stakeholders.

Create and manage the product roadmap
> The DPO defines a clear vision and strategic objectives, then translates these into a timeline that prioritizes features and milestones based on their value, technical feasibility, and alignment with business goals.

Prioritize and manage the product backlog
> The DPO continuously refines and ranks items based on their value, feasibility, and alignment with strategic goals.

Validate and accept product increments
> The DPO rigorously tests and reviews each completed feature or enhancement against predefined acceptance criteria to ensure that it meets quality standards and user requirements.

Do not boil the ocean. Aim to bring value fast and be ready to iterate. As you saw in the data product lifecycle, a data product is designed for evolution. You will be able to modify your first data products.

Summary

At this point, we understand what a "good" data product is: it follows Data Mesh principles and is aligned to FAIR principles. It is enterprise grade. It delivers real, tangible value. It balances cost with agility and speed concerns. It is much more than just data. And it has an empowered owner and a lifecycle that can define and deliver on the data product's promise.

The next obvious question is "How do I build a 'good' data product that has all of these attributes?" The next two chapters will kickstart the process. We will first introduce a scenario that is used throughout the book to show how to put these principles and characteristics into practice, and then we will do a deep dive into the architecture components of both a Data Mesh and its constituent data products.

CHAPTER 3

Our Case Study: Climate Quantum Inc.

In this chapter, we will introduce our case study—Climate Quantum Inc.—where we will apply Data Mesh capabilities to an important and pressing need: climate change.

But first some background.

Climate change permeates every aspect of our global society. According to the United Nations (*https://oreil.ly/IM0qT*), "Since the 1800s, human activities have been the main driver of climate change (*https://oreil.ly/-GwX8*), primarily due to the burning of fossil fuels like coal, oil and gas." The article continues:

> Climate change can affect our health (*https://oreil.ly/iplZy*), ability to grow food, housing, safety and work. Some of us are already more vulnerable to climate impacts, such as people living in small island nations and other developing countries. Conditions like sea-level rise and saltwater intrusion have advanced to the point where whole communities have had to relocate, and protracted droughts are putting people at risk of famine. In the future, the number of people displaced by weather-related events is expected to rise.

As businesses grapple with the implications of climate change, they find themselves confronting a new frontier: the complex and constantly changing world of climate data. While the data holds invaluable insights, navigating its intricacies poses significant challenges.

First, climate data is an ever-evolving landscape. Climate data isn't static; it constantly morphs, influenced by countless variables ranging from anthropogenic activities to natural phenomena. Pinpointing the relevant data amid this fluidity is no small feat.

Second, climate data volumes are immense and incredibly diverse. There are thousands of data sources from major government entities (for example, NASA and the National Oceanic and Atmospheric Administration) as well as literally thousands of sensors (for example, there are thousands of weather stations (*https://oreil.ly/MdzAx*)

alone that capture temperature), which offer a stream of constantly changing climate data. Sometimes similar data sources address the same domain but have different formats. And each is governed by its licensing terms, some publicly available and others proprietary. The challenge lies not just in data acquisition but in harmonizing and interpreting all of the data.

Moreover, the regulatory environment is changing fast with its expanding scope, and it mandates businesses to report with precision. Understanding and addressing the demands of Scope 1 (direct emissions), Scope 2 (indirect emissions), and especially the nuanced Scope 3 regulations (all other indirect emissions that are not owned or directly controlled) necessitate robust climate data frameworks.

As if that weren't enough, the axiom upon which foundational decisions are made—that climate change in the past is a solid predictor of climate change in the future—is proving to be false. Historically, the past has been our compass, guiding predictions and decisions. However, the accelerating pace of climate change makes the past an unreliable predictor, thrusting businesses into largely uncharted waters. Consider, for example, insurers in California: they insured properties against wildfire damages based on historical patterns, but rapid and unexpected changes in wildfire occurrences have driven insurers (*https://oreil.ly/2xNx2*) out of the California market. The same has happened in Florida (*https://oreil.ly/8lMnz*), where insurers have pulled out of the market because of unexpected losses due to the unpredicted increase and intensity of hurricanes.

Finally, stakeholder and consumer expectations are also changing: as stakeholders champion transparency and consumers champion sustainability, businesses find themselves under increased pressure to validate their environmental credentials.

The inherent complexity of climate data is compounded by its multidisciplinary nature. It encompasses a wide range of fields, from meteorology to oceanography, glaciology to environmental science. Each of these disciplines generates massive amounts of data, often in different formats and scales, making integration and analysis a daunting task.

Additionally, the accuracy and reliability of climate data are paramount. Decisions made based on this data can have far-reaching consequences, affecting policy, investments, and public opinion. Ensuring data accuracy, therefore, becomes not just a technical challenge but a moral imperative.

Making Climate Data Easier to Find, Consume, Share, and Trust

The need for a more effective way to manage this deluge of data brings us to the concept of Data Mesh. Data Mesh, an innovative approach to data architecture and organizational design, holds immense potential for transforming the way climate data is handled. This paradigm shift proposes a decentralized approach to data management, focusing on domain-oriented data ownership and architecture.

Data Mesh presents a forward-thinking approach to addressing the challenges inherent in managing climate data. This section looks deeper into how Data Mesh transforms the labyrinth of climate data into a more navigable and efficient system.

The central issue with traditional, centralized data platforms lies in their inherent limitations when dealing with the sheer volume and complexity of climate data. In a standard enterprise setting, these systems often struggle with managing internal data effectively. The climate data challenge amplifies this complexity exponentially, rendering centralized systems inadequate. In such scenarios, these systems often become overwhelmed, leading to inefficiencies and data silos.

Data Mesh, with its decentralized, domain-oriented architecture, emerges as a more robust and adaptable solution. By distributing data ownership and conceptualizing data as a standalone product rather than a byproduct of various processes, Data Mesh offers a scalable and responsive framework. This paradigm shift facilitates a network of interconnected data domains, each functioning as a node that enables efficient data sharing and utilization across diverse platforms and sources.

A primary obstacle in harnessing climate data effectively is the disparate nature of its sources. Data Mesh, through its federated approach to data management, addresses this challenge head-on. It establishes a cohesive system that links varied data sources while preserving their individual autonomy. This model is akin to a well-organized library, where books from numerous publishers are readily accessible, yet each retains its distinct identity.

Viewing data as a product under Data Mesh transforms the way data is managed. It assigns clear ownership and responsibility, paralleling a product owner's role in a company. Owners of climate data domains are thus accountable for the data's accuracy, timeliness, and relevance. This shift not only elevates the quality of climate data but also bolsters user trust, as each dataset is meticulously curated and maintained.

Data Mesh recognizes the need for diverse expertise in managing the broad spectrum of climate data. By allocating specific datasets to domain experts or designated entities, the framework ensures that data is handled by those who are best equipped to understand and interpret the data. This decentralized ownership model not only enhances data accuracy and reliability but also expedites decision making. Since domain owners are closer to the sources of the data, they can implement real-time updates and modifications more effectively. This approach draws inspiration from the shift-left (*https://oreil.ly/5ebqJ*) concept in software development where software changes and testing occur much earlier in the delivery lifecycle.

Introducing Climate Quantum Inc.

To address these challenges, we will use a fictional firm called "Climate Quantum Inc.", shown in Figure 3-1, as our case study. This firm uses Data Mesh to address these challenges and, in turn, make climate data easy to find, consume, share, and trust.

Figure 3-1. Climate Quantum Inc.

Climate Quantum Inc., our hypothetical enterprise, has a mission to revolutionize the accessibility, usability, and reliability of climate data by leveraging the Data Mesh framework. This firm stands at the forefront of tackling the challenges associated with climate data, streamlining its management, and enhancing its impact.

The mission of Climate Quantum Inc. addresses critical challenges with climate data management:

Making climate data easy to find
> One of the most significant hurdles in the realm of climate data is its fragmentation. Vital datasets are dispersed across myriad sources, making it hard to find climate data. This dispersion not only leads to inefficiencies but also creates significant gaps in data availability. Climate Quantum Inc. utilizes Data Mesh's discovery capabilities, including a comprehensive set of APIs and a meticulously curated catalog of data products. This approach transforms the search for climate data into a streamlined, efficient process, ensuring that every data product and the information it contains is readily accessible.

Simplifying the consumption of climate data

The complexity of climate data often stands as a barrier to its effective utilization. Researchers, policymakers, and businesses frequently encounter challenges stemming from inconsistent formats, diverse structures, and limited access. Climate Quantum Inc., through Data Mesh, introduces standardized access methods that demystify the process of consuming climate data. These methods provide clarity and consistency, enabling users to extract valuable insights with greater ease.

Facilitating easy sharing of climate data

The sharing of climate data is often impeded by the absence of standardized protocols and overly complex procedures. Traditional centralized models inhibit collaboration, thus hindering a collective response to climate challenges. Climate Quantum Inc. envisions Data Mesh as a solution, offering explicit data contracts that clarify not only the consumption of data but also its sharing. This approach fosters a collaborative environment, which is essential for effective climate action.

Ensuring the trustworthiness of climate data

Trust is a cornerstone in the domain of climate data. Reliability of data sources, consistency in quality, and transparency are crucial to building confidence and maximizing the potential of climate data. Through Data Mesh, Climate Quantum Inc. introduces governance certifications that enhance the verification process, ensuring compliance with enterprise and regulatory policies. This framework elevates the trustworthiness of climate data, making it a more reliable and credible resource.

Climate Quantum Inc. aims to be at the vanguard of transforming climate data management through its innovative use of Data Mesh. This comprehensive solution is designed to enhance the discoverability, usability, sharing, and trustworthiness of climate data. The core components of Climate Quantum Inc.'s Data Mesh framework are constructed to address the unique challenges of climate data:

Global Climate Data Mesh

At the heart of Climate Quantum Inc.'s strategy is a Global Climate Data Mesh. This framework is capable of supporting hundreds of data products required to address the vast landscape of climate data. It is orchestrated by largely autonomous data product teams, each taking responsibility for its specific climate data subsets. This decentralized approach enables these teams to curate, validate, and maintain their data with exceptional efficiency and effectiveness. Such autonomy ensures that the data is not only accurate but also readily accessible.

Climate Data Marketplace

The Climate Data Marketplace functions as a centralized directory for climate data, analogous to the internet's Domain Name System (DNS). It streamlines the process of finding data products, surfacing information from our global set of data products. This user-friendly platform makes it easy to search for climate data, offering users simple access to an extensive repository of information.

Climate data products

Climate Quantum Inc. surfaces data from hundreds of climate data sources, transforming them into data products. Interestingly, there is a design nuance in our data products that the complexity and volume of climate data demand: our data products provide references to the actual climate data because copying or duplicating this data would create redundancies, data management challenges (remember, the amount of data is immense and constantly changing), lineage issues, and governance problems. Rather, we leave the data where it is but provide links to the data.

Climate data consumption mechanisms

To ensure uniformity and make it easier to consume climate data, Climate Quantum Inc. implements consistent data interfaces using commonly available techniques (for example, using RESTful APIs and SQL access). These interfaces provide a degree of consistency across all data access mechanisms within the entire Climate Quantum Data Mesh, allowing for a more streamlined and coherent user experience.

Climate data publication mechanisms

While Climate Quantum aims to make it easy to find climate data, it also makes climate data easy to share. The motivation for this is quite simple: more data publishers means more available data, which in turn leads to more data consumers. And more data consumers means more data publishers will be interested in making their climate data available. Unfortunately, this is a bit of a "chicken and egg" problem—which comes first? Where most solutions focus on the consumer aspect, Climate Quantum is focused on making it very easy for climate data publishers to "publish" their data and make it available in the Climate Data Marketplace. In fact, this is such a crucial issue that Climate Quantum's goal is to allow "anyone to publish their climate data in five minutes or less" (in fact, this leads to specific architecture and design considerations, which are covered in later chapters).

Data trust and verification mechanisms

Recognizing the critical importance of trust in climate data, Climate Quantum Inc. has incorporated robust data contracts that rigorously verify and certify the origination, lineage, and quality of the data. The firm has initiated a certification program, akin to standards set by organizations like ANSI, to provide a seal of trust for data products that meet stringent quality and transparency criteria. This certification not only ensures data integrity but also reinforces user confidence in the data's reliability.

Climate Quantum Data Landscape

Let's explore Climate Quantum's data landscape and Data Mesh, using Figure 3-2 as a blueprint that delineates the relationships among various climate data domains, their respective data products, and the centralized Climate Data Marketplace.

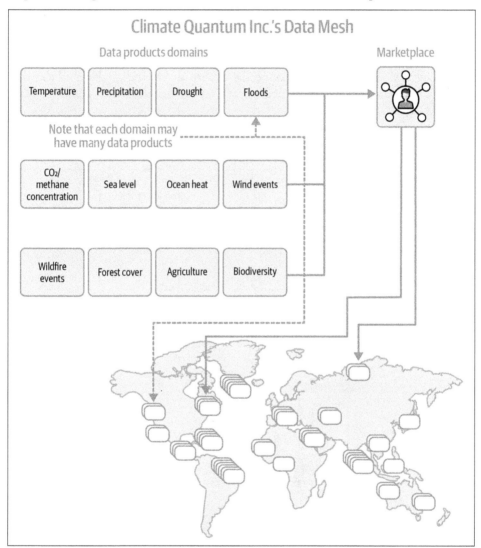

Figure 3-2. Climate Quantum data landscape

The foundation of Climate Quantum Inc.'s Data Mesh consists of various climate data domains, each housing several data products. These domains cover many aspects of climate data, including temperature, precipitation, wind and wildfire events, and others. Each domain could have several individual data products, provided by different data publishers and sources.

Central to Climate Quantum's Data Mesh is the Climate Data Marketplace, which acts as a hub for climate data products. This marketplace provides a "window" into the Data Mesh that facilitates easy discovery of and access to climate data products.

Climate Quantum's data landscape has global scale, with a large set of data products that mirrors the widespread distribution and accessibility of climate events and information across different geographic locations. This global reach is essential for addressing the diverse and interconnected nature of climate challenges, allowing climate data users worldwide to benefit from Climate Quantum Inc.'s comprehensive data offerings.

A reasonably comprehensive (some are simpler, some are more complex) climate data product looks somewhat like Figure 3-3. Let's dig a bit deeper.

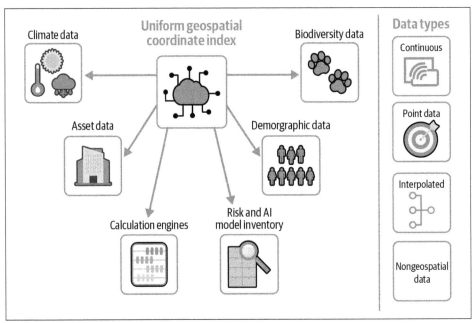

Figure 3-3. Climate Quantum data product

At the core of the diagram is the *uniform geospatial coordinate index*. This central hub functions as a standardized reference system, ensuring that all data points, regardless of their type, are aligned to a consistent geographical schema. (At a technical level, Climate Quantum uses Uber's H3 index schema, which maps hexagons of different scales to all regions on Earth.) This uniformity is critical for integrating and correlating diverse datasets, providing a coherent spatial framework that enhances the usability and accuracy of the data.

Climate Quantum data products reference several different types of data. *Climate data* references essential variables, such as temperature, precipitation, and weather patterns. *Biodiversity data* includes information about species distribution, ecosystems, and habitats. This data is vital for assessing the impacts of climate change on biodiversity and for informing conservation strategies. *Demographic data* provides insights into human populations, including age distribution, population density, and socioeconomic factors. This data is crucial for evaluating the human dimensions of climate impacts, such as vulnerability and resilience. *Asset data* includes information about physical infrastructure, such as buildings, transportation networks, and energy systems. Asset data (as well as demographic data) is typically mapped to climate data to understand risks and impacts to buildings and population centers in the face of climate change.

Each data product also contains processing and transformation capabilities. The *risk and AI model inventory*, for example, includes advanced models and algorithms designed to predict and assess climate risks. These tools leverage AI to generate forecasts and risk assessments, providing valuable insights for decision makers. *Calculation engines* are sophisticated computational tools that perform complex calculations, interpolation, and data transformations, enabling precise, reliable analysis.

Climate Quantum also categorizes the types of data included in data products: *continuous data,* which represents variables that should be continuous across geographic regions (e.g., temperature); *point data,* which provides information with a unique location, such as an asset like a building, dam, or factory; *interpolated data* that has been estimated from other measurements, filling in gaps where direct observations are not available (for example, interpolation would be used to fill in gaps where there is no weather station data); and *nongeospatial data* that does not have a direct geographical reference, such as policy documents or economic reports.

Applying Climate Quantum Inc. to Your Enterprise

Addressing the challenges faced by Climate Quantum in managing climate data offers valuable insights for enterprises looking to navigate similar complexities within their own data landscapes. For this very reason, we have described Climate Quantum in quite a bit of detail: the parallels between and scale of the climate data challenges and those in a large enterprise are similar, and the strategies employed by Climate Quantum can provide a roadmap for effective data management in any organization.

The issue of data fragmentation and discoverability in climate data, for example, mirrors the common enterprise challenge of siloed and inaccessible data. Just as Climate Quantum uses a Global Climate Data Mesh to facilitate data discovery and access across a global, diverse, and federated landscape, enterprises can adopt a similar Data Mesh approach to break down silos.

The complexity and diversity of climate data sources have their counterpart in the varied and often inconsistent data within large enterprises. Climate Quantum's use of standardized data contracts and consumption mechanisms to streamline data structures can be replicated in an enterprise setting. By establishing uniform data formats and access protocols, businesses can simplify the consumption of data across different departments, making data more usable and reducing the time and resources spent on data preparation and interpretation.

The challenge of data sharing, crucial in the realm of climate data, is equally pertinent in enterprises where collaboration across departments and with external partners is essential. Climate Quantum's implementation of simple publishing mechanisms brings "self-serve" to the data producer community, allowing data sharing in a model that enterprises can emulate.

Finally, the need for trust in and verification of climate data is a universal concern in any data-driven decision-making process. Climate Quantum's approach of employing robust data contracts and a governance/certification program to ensure data quality and transparency can be applied to enterprise data management. Establishing similar governance structures and quality standards in an enterprise will build trust among stakeholders, ensuring that decisions are based on reliable, verified data.

Summary

In our exploration of the Climate Quantum case study, we will demonstrate how the principles of Data Mesh can be effectively turned into practice. This will involve an examination of the Data Mesh and data product architecture, showcasing the core components of Data Mesh and the individual data products it comprises. We will detail the structure, interactions, and contributions of these components, illustrating how data is segmented into distinct, manageable units, each overseen by autonomous teams.

Additionally, we will explore the organizational design, operating model, and team topologies of Data Mesh using Climate Quantum as an example. This aspect will focus on the approach to structuring the Data Mesh organization, highlighting how teams are aligned, the roles and responsibilities within these teams, and how they collaborate to maintain the efficacy of the Data Mesh system.

Finally, we will present a roadmap for building Climate Quantum's Data Mesh. This roadmap will outline the step-by-step process for developing and implementing a Data Mesh system on a global scale, tailored specifically to the complex, dynamic nature of climate data. Climate Quantum will be a vehicle for demonstrating strategies for scaling the system, integrating new data sources, and evolving and governing the architecture to meet changing needs and challenges.

PART II

Designing, Building, and Deploying Data Mesh

Now that you understand the basic concepts, you can start your journey of designing and building Data Mesh components. Most of the work might be done by software engineers under the supervision of data engineers and architects. This section will target both groups of engineers (software and data), so terms that may not be familiar to data engineers will be explained.

Chapter 4, "Defining the Data Mesh Architecture", explores the core components of a Data Mesh, focusing on the architecture of data products as well as the broader Data Mesh architecture and highlighting how various artifacts and development, runtime, and operational capabilities come together to create discoverable, observable, and operable data products. The chapter also delves into how these components are integrated through Data Mesh backbone services, marketplaces, and registries, using Climate Quantum Inc. as a case study to illustrate the practical application of these principles for managing complex climate data.

Chapter 5, "Driving Data Products with Data Contracts", discusses the implementation of data products, emphasizing the role of data contracts in establishing trust by ensuring data quality and service levels and using examples from Climate Quantum Inc. to illustrate these concepts. The chapter explores the principles of product thinking, details the elements of data contracts, and introduces the data quality of service (data QoS) framework for combining dimensions of data quality with service-level agreements, which promotes a standardized, reliable approach to data management.

Chapter 6, "Building Your First Data Product", guides you through the steps of creating your initial data product by understanding its components, leveraging data contracts, connecting data sources, and building endpoints while ensuring that observability, discovery, and control services are integrated. The chapter emphasizes the standardization and modularity of data products, facilitated by the use of sidecars and open standards like the ones promoted by the Bitol project to streamline development and operations.

Chapter 7, "Aligning with the Experience Planes", explains how to separate responsibilities across three functional areas in a Data Mesh: the infrastructure experience plane for data infrastructure, the data product experience plane for independent data products, and the mesh experience plane for interconnecting data products and managing enterprise-level tools. Each of these areas has specific capabilities to streamline organization and reduce cognitive load. The chapter also delves into how these planes communicate, particularly focusing on feedback loops, both user and system, which travel across planes to enhance data reliability and inform continuous improvement.

Chapter 8, "Meshing Your Data Products", explains how to register, assemble, and utilize multiple data products within a Data Mesh to enhance their value and ensure data quality and governance. This chapter also focuses on the key concepts of producer-aligned and consumer-aligned data products. Finally, you will learn how Data Mesh can simplify data lineage.

CHAPTER 4

Defining the Data Mesh Architecture

This chapter will discuss the core architecture components within a Data Mesh. The chapter is organized into two major sections. First, we discuss the data-product architecture, including the components required to support a wide-ranging set of artifacts and the components required for developing, running, and operating data products. Second, we focus on the broader Data Mesh architecture that binds all data products together into a unified whole.

Data Product Architecture

Each data product in a Data Mesh is designed to be discoverable, observable, and operable, ensuring that data can be efficiently shared and utilized across different parts of an organization. Figure 4-1 illustrates the data product architecture that we will elaborate on.

There are several key groups of capabilities within the data-product architecture: an architecture for artifacts as well as architectures for development, runtime, and operations capabilities.

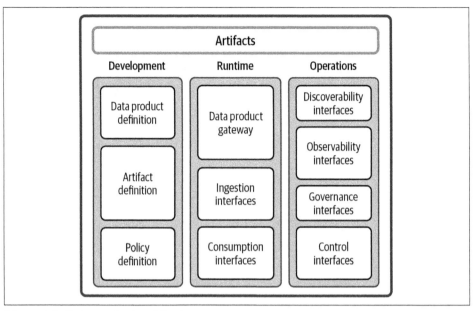

Figure 4-1. Data product architecture

Data Product Artifacts

The contents of a data product—the artifacts—are what make the data product valuable. Artifacts include not just data but also other objects that a DPO wants to make available for consumption.

Artifacts, as shown in Figure 4-2, range from basic datasets to complex programs and models. They add significant value to the data product, making it more than just a data store. They enable a more integrated and user-friendly approach to data management, where the focus is not just on providing data but also on delivering a complete, valuable, and ready-to-use data solution.

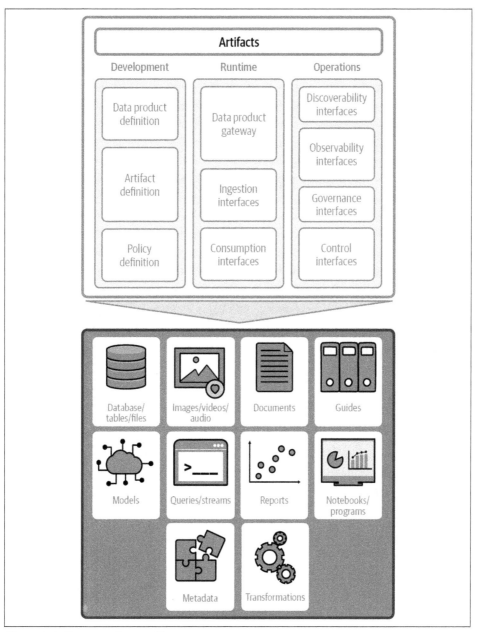

Figure 4-2. Data product artifacts

Let's start with the most common type of artifact, and probably the one that is present in almost all data products today: databases, tables, and files. These fundamental components form the backbone of any data product, providing the core data that users seek for various applications. However, the scope of artifacts goes far beyond these basic elements, embracing a more holistic and integrated approach that is cognizant of the many forms of "data" today. As we discussed in Chapter 2, these artifacts may also include:

- Images, videos, and audio, which are becoming commonplace in our modern multimodal data environment
- Documents, such as PDFs or other text-oriented, unstructured data
- Guides, which may help consumers understand or consume a data product
- Models, including AI and ML models as well as newer generative AI large language models
- Queries and streams that have been vetted (safe, performant, etc.), which simplify consumption of the data product
- Reports, which provide preformatted sets of output from a data product
- Notebooks and programs that demonstrate how the data within the product can be used effectively or show the actual processing logic used within the data product
- Metadata, or data about the data product, its contents, its fields, and its formats
- Transformations, including pipelines and other workflow tooling that ingest the data and transform it into a form that is both usable and convenient for consumers

What architecture capabilities are required to support the varied forms of modern artifacts represented in a data product? We discuss these capabilities in the following three sections:

- Development architecture components support the definition and development of data products.
- Runtime architecture components address the runtime considerations of data products.
- Operations architecture components help make data products discoverable, observable, governable, and controllable.

Development Architecture Components

The first considerations to address when creating a data product are the definition and development of the data product, as shown in Figure 4-3. This encompasses the detailed characterization of the data product, including who owns it, what it contains, and the rules governing its use. This clear and comprehensive definition is essential for ensuring that the data product is not only functional and accessible but also aligns with organizational policies and user needs. By thoroughly defining each data product, organizations can maximize their data's value and utility, which makes this process a foundational aspect of modern strategies for data management.

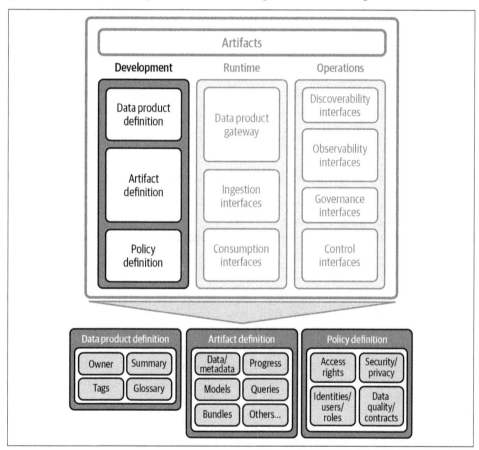

Figure 4-3. Data product definition and development

There are three groups of functionality in the data product development architecture:

Data product definition
Describes the data product

Artifact definition
Describes the artifacts within the data product

Policy definition
Describes the rules and constraints for the data product and/or artifacts

Data product definition

The data product's definition includes a minimum set of attributes:

Namespace
The namespace (or domain) identifies the domain or category for the data product. Namespaces or domains are typically unique across a Data Mesh.

Name
The name uniquely identifies the data product within its namespace/domain.

Description
The description describes the data product's purpose and contents.

Links to endpoints
Links to endpoints are made available by the data product. These typically include references to discoverability, observability, administrative capabilities, and any other information the DPO wants to expose.

Tags
Tags are keywords or labels that help categorize and organize data products within the larger ecosystem. Well-chosen tags can greatly simplify navigation and search processes within a Data Mesh (especially in the marketplace). Tags should ideally reference a broader business glossary, but note that this glossary does not need to start from a clean slate. Rather, many organizations leverage public and/or commercial business glossaries that have been created and vetted by experts.

Owner
The owner (or publisher) plays a pivotal role, acting as the decision maker and primary source of knowledge for the data product. They are the key contact point for any questions, feedback, or problem resolution related to the data product. This information must be easily available and prominently displayed.

Artifact definition

Recall that a single data product can contain many artifacts, each with different and potentially unique form factors, attributes, and security and privacy needs. An artifact definition is more detailed than a data product definition and typically includes the following attributes:

Name
> The name uniquely identifies the artifact within the data product.

Description
> The description describes the artifact's purpose and contents.

Tags
> Tags are keywords or labels that help categorize and organize artifacts within a Data Mesh.

Policies
> Policies reference the set of enterprise, regulatory, security, privacy, or operational rules and constraints that govern the data product's use.

Access rights
> Access rights describe the permissions and roles required to access the artifact. Access rights should be verified before access to an artifact is granted.

License
> The license governs the terms of use for the artifact and should be agreed to when a consumer wants to access the data product.

Links to endpoints
> Links to endpoints made available by the data product typically include references to metadata, sample data, and links to the artifact's data (as well as any other information the DPO wants to expose). Artifact links will probably have to be handled in a creative manner that explicitly recognizes their contents and may even require additional applications to access (for example, a link to a guide in PDF format would require a PDF reader).

Policy definition

The definition of policies for a data product is a critical component that governs the data product's usage and ensures the security and privacy of the data. Policies are enabled through data contracts (addressed in detail in Chapter 5) and delineate the acceptable ways in which the data can be accessed and utilized, taking into account various considerations like access rights, identity management, user authorization, service- and quality-level expectations, and compliance with security and privacy regulations. Establishing clear and comprehensive policies is essential for maintaining the integrity of the data product and for protecting it from unauthorized access or misuse.

Access rights are the primary consideration in policy definition. They determine who can access the data product and what level of access they are granted. This can range from read-only access for some users to full administrative rights for others. Defining access rights involves assessing the needs, purpose, and responsibilities of different users or user groups and assigning access levels accordingly. Effective management of access rights is crucial for ensuring that users can perform their roles efficiently while preventing unauthorized access to sensitive data.

Integration with identity books of record is another important aspect of policy definition. By linking the data product with an enterprise's identity management systems, organizations can streamline the process of user authentication and authorization. This not only enhances security by ensuring that only authenticated users gain access but also simplifies the administrative process of managing user access across various data products and systems.

Runtime Architecture Components

The runtime architecture, as shown in Figure 4-4, describes the components in a data product.

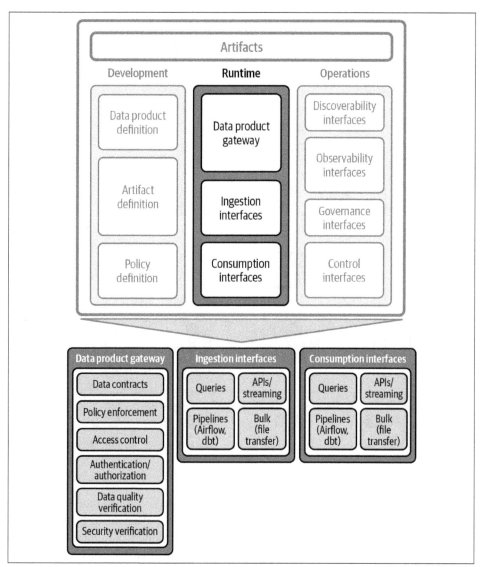

Figure 4-4. Data product runtime components

Data product gateway

All interactions with a data product—for consumers, publishers, and administrators—have interfaces that are implemented using a lightweight *data product gateway*, shown in Figure 4-5, which provides a consistent implementation for all interactions with the data product.

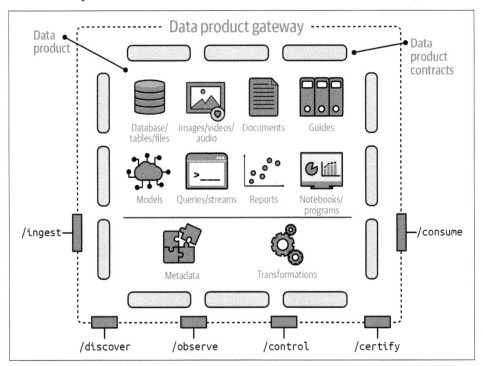

Figure 4-5. The data product gateway

The data product gateway is a lightweight framework and code that implements the various interfaces for a data product. While every data product is different and embodies unique capabilities, the mechanisms by which they interact and the signatures for their interactions can—and should—be made largely consistent.

This is true for ingestion (conceptually, an /ingest interface) and consumption (conceptually, a /consume interface). While these high-volume interfaces may be a simple passthru (passing requests through largely unchanged), the parameters and mechanisms for their interactions can be standardized.

This is even more practical for other core and foundational interfaces for discovery (/discover interface), observability (/observe interface), and control or management capabilities (/control interface). By doing this, all interactions with data products become consistent and standardized—which means that templating and

---

"factories" become a practical consideration for streamlining and speeding up the creation and management of data products.

Since all requests flow through the data product gateway, it becomes the vehicle for implementing cross-cutting concerns that affect or benefit all data products, including access verification, logging, lineage, exception notifications, and many more. The data product gateway also becomes the integration point for data contracts and associated policy-enforcement mechanisms. Data contracts in the data product gateway set policies that all aspects of the data product are expected to adhere to and provide the mechanism for a consistent policy enforcement point. These contracts define the structure and format of data access mechanisms as well as security and privacy needs, data quality and integrity requirements, data lineage and version needs, and any needs related to service expectations. Simply put, they define the policies—and even the enforcement mechanisms—that a data product is expected to meet.

That probably just whets your appetite regarding the power of data contracts—recognizing the importance of data contracts for establishing a Data Mesh that meets user expectations, we have included a full chapter (Chapter 5) to explain the nitty-gritty details of data contracts and their implementation in data products.

Ingestion interfaces

Ingesting data into a data product is a fundamental process that determines how data is collected, processed, and made available for use. The method chosen for data ingestion depends on various factors, such as the volume of data, the frequency of updates, and the specific requirements of the data product. Understanding and selecting the right ingestion method is crucial for ensuring the efficiency and effectiveness of the data product. From APIs to bulk ingestion and pipelines, each technique has its own advantages and ideal use cases.

Queries are a common method for ingesting data and are particularly useful when dealing with real-time or near-real-time data updates. They are ideal for situations where data needs to be pulled frequently and in small amounts. Queries allow for specific data to be selected and retrieved based on certain criteria, making them efficient for targeted data ingestion. This method is especially useful for data products that require up-to-date information and can handle frequent incremental updates.

APIs are another popular method for data ingestion and are especially effective for smaller datasets or when data needs to be integrated from external sources. APIs facilitate a controlled, secure way to import data, allowing for specific datasets to be accessed and transferred. They are particularly useful when the data source and the data product need to communicate in a standardized, consistent manner. APIs are also beneficial when dealing with structured data and when the integration needs to be scalable and maintainable over time.

Bulk ingestion methods, such as file transfers, are suited for scenarios where large volumes of data need to be imported into the data product. This method is typically used for initial data loads or periodic updates where a significant amount of data is transferred at once. Bulk ingestion is efficient in terms of resource usage and time, especially when dealing with large datasets that do not require frequent updates. It is often used in conjunction with data warehousing or when integrating historical data into a data product.

Data pipelines, using tools like Airflow or dbt (data build tool), are designed for more complex data-ingestion scenarios. These tools allow data workflows to be automated, enabling the ingestion, transformation, and loading of data in a more controlled, systematic manner. Pipelines are particularly useful when the data-ingestion process involves multiple steps, such as data cleansing, transformation, or integration from multiple sources. They provide a robust framework for managing complex data flows, ensuring consistency and reliability in the data-ingestion process.

Other ingestion methods include streaming data ingestion, used for real-time data processing, and web scraping, for extracting data from web sources. Streaming data ingestion is ideal for scenarios where data is continuously generated and needs to be processed in real time.

Consumption interfaces

Obviously, once the data has been ingested into the data product, it needs to be made easy to consume. While ingestion is about how data gets into the data product, consumption is about how that data, along with other artifacts created by the DPO, is made available and useful to end users. Consumption focuses on the output and user interaction rather than the input of data into the system. The methods of consumption are similar to ingestion methods, ranging from queries and APIs to bulk transfers and pipelines.

Queries, streaming, and APIs are methods of data consumption that allow users to retrieve specific subsets of data based on their requirements or, in the case of streaming, to be notified when a data event (for example, a new row is added to a database) takes place. These methods support a high level of flexibility, letting users extract precisely what they need when they need it.

Bulk consumption methods, such as file transfers, are used when large volumes of data need to be accessed, often for offline processing or analysis. This method is typical in scenarios where the entire dataset or large parts of it are required, such as for data warehousing or big data analytics. Bulk consumption is less about real-time interaction and more about comprehensive access, making it suitable for use cases where extensive data processing is necessary.

Operations Architecture Components

Within a Data Mesh framework, the operational considerations for data products, shown in Figure 4-6, encompass a spectrum of interfaces and capabilities to ensure that data products not only are functional but also align with an organization's overarching operational standards and expectations. These considerations include discoverability, observability, governance, and control interfaces. Each plays a pivotal role in the lifecycle and utility of a data product.

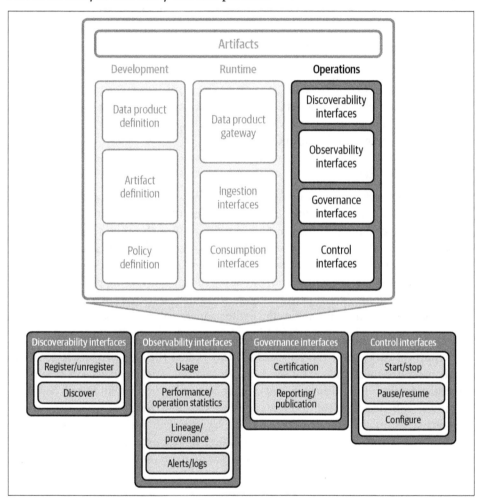

Figure 4-6. Data product operational components

Discoverability interfaces

Discoverability interfaces (conceptually, a `/discover` endpoint, as shown in Figure 4-5) enable data products to be first registered and then located within a Data Mesh, ensuring that the data products are visible and accessible to users.

Registration (conceptually, a `/discover/registration` endpoint) is akin to placing a pin on a digital map, marking the data product's location and existence in the Data Mesh landscape. This registration is vital, as it ensures that the data product is not just a standalone entity but also a recognized part of the larger ecosystem of data products. The information provided during registration typically includes metadata from the data product and artifact definitions (namespace, name, etc.).

Once registered, a data product is made available in the Data Mesh Marketplace and can be found or "discovered" (conceptually, a `/discover/metadata` endpoint) in the ecosystem of data products. The metadata provided during the registration process can be viewed in the Data Mesh Marketplace, making data products and their artifacts easier to find, consume, and share.

Observability interfaces

Whereas data product metadata is relatively stable, the operational characteristics of a data product are constantly changing. Observability interfaces (conceptually, an `/observe` endpoint, as shown in Figure 4-5) monitor the continuously changing operating characteristics of a data product. These interfaces provide a comprehensive view into the various operational aspects of the data product, including usage statistics, performance metrics, and overall operating health. By offering real-time insights into how the data product is performing, observability interfaces allow data product owners and users to monitor and evaluate the product's effectiveness.

One of the most significant benefits of observability interfaces is their ability to track and report on usage patterns. This includes how often the data product is accessed, which parts are most frequently used, and by whom. Such insights are invaluable for understanding user behavior and preferences, allowing for informed decisions on future enhancements or modifications to the data product. This data-driven approach ensures that the product evolves in line with user needs and remains relevant and useful over time while also aiding in resource allocation and scaling decisions, ensuring optimal performance even as demand fluctuates.

Observability interfaces also focus on performance and operating statistics. These encompass everything from load times and response rates to more complex metrics like data throughput and processing efficiency. Monitoring these aspects is crucial for maintaining a high level of service quality and for preemptively identifying potential bottlenecks or performance issues. Surfacing alerts and making logs accessible through observability interfaces are essential for problem diagnosis, enabling quick and effective troubleshooting. This not only minimizes downtime but also ensures that data quality and accuracy are maintained, which is critical for making informed decisions based on the data.

Lineage and provenance tracking exposed in observability interfaces offers traceability of processing within a data product. This feature provides detailed information about the origin and historical changes of the data, all of which are essential for maintaining data integrity and trust. It ensures transparency in how data has been collected, processed, and transformed over time.

Governance interfaces

Governance interfaces are critical for maintaining data integrity and compliance. These interfaces are designed to facilitate the process of certification or verification, whereby owners can assert that their data products meet specific standards of data quality, service-level expectations, regulatory compliance, and even lineage records (many of which can be defined in data contracts).

Viewing these interfaces is typically initiated by the user, who requests the governance or certification status of a data product and receives a report or checklist in response. The following set of interfaces is typically desired (note that the endpoints are conceptual; in practice, they are more verbose):

`/certify`
    Get the data product's certification status or report.

`/certify/subscribe`
    Request to be notified when a governance threshold has been met or not met.

`/certify/publish`
    Proactively publish the data product's governance or certification status on a regular basis.

These interfaces offer transparency into data management practices and standards adhered to by the data product. By providing clear insights into their governance practices, DPOs can build confidence among users, reassuring them that the data is managed responsibly and in accordance with best practices and regulatory requirements.

Control interfaces

Control interfaces in the context of data products are essential tools that give DPOs the ability to manage the operational state of their offerings. These interfaces encompass a range of functionalities, including the ability to start or stop the data product (conceptually, a `/control/start` or `/control/stop` interface) and to configure various settings and parameters (conceptually, a `/control/configure` interface).

This level of control is crucial for ensuring that data products can be managed effectively and can respond flexibly to different operational requirements or situations. In essence, control interfaces act as the command center for DPOs, offering them direct oversight and management capabilities for their products.

Moreover, the configuration aspect of control interfaces plays a significant role in tailoring the data product to specific needs or conditions. Owners can adjust settings to optimize performance, customize features according to user feedback, or dynamically adapt to changing data environments. In a landscape where users' needs and technological environments are constantly evolving, the ability to configure and reconfigure data products swiftly ensures that the data products continue to deliver value and meet the expectations of their users.

Data Mesh Architecture

As defined earlier, Data Mesh is an ecosystem composed of numerous data products, each functioning as a distinct unit with its own purpose and capabilities. However, what makes Data Mesh truly powerful are the components that bind data products into a cohesive and integrated whole. These components, shown in Figure 4-7, specifically address capabilities and components that are used by many, and perhaps all, data products, including the Data Mesh Marketplace, the Data Mesh Registry, and the Data Mesh backbone services. They are the connective tissue that binds all components into a Data Mesh.

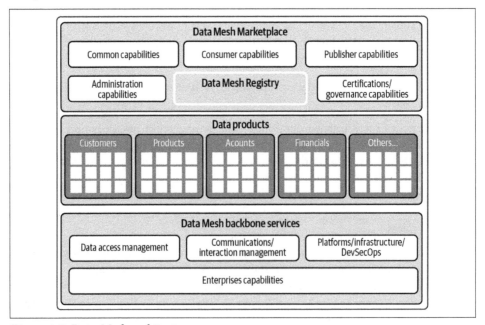

Figure 4-7. Data Mesh architecture

Data Mesh Marketplace and Registry

The Data Mesh Marketplace is a user interface that simplifies the process of finding, consuming, sharing, and establishing trust in data products. This marketplace is a window into a Data Mesh and an interactive space where data becomes more accessible and actionable for consumers, producers, governance professionals, and administrators.

The marketplace's close cousin, the Data Mesh Registry, is a repository for information about a Data Mesh that acts as a phone book for it, much like DNS does for the internet. In many respects, the registry is the backend database for the marketplace, but it also maintains much more information.

We will leave it at that for now. Recognizing the importance of the marketplace and registry to Data Mesh, we have devoted a full chapter (Chapter 11) to these components.

Data Mesh Backbone Services

Data Mesh backbone services integrate Data Mesh components and data products into a cohesive whole, providing the necessary foundation for data products to communicate, interact, and deliver value.

Data access services include a set of common tools and technologies for federated query, data pipelines, and bulk data transfer. These services allow for efficient, flexible access to data across a Data Mesh and its data products, regardless of where they reside. Federated-query capabilities, for instance, enable users to retrieve and combine data from multiple sources without moving the data while pipelines and bulk transfer mechanisms provide efficient ways to move large volumes of data when necessary.

Communication and interaction services are another critical aspect of the Data Mesh backbone services. These services encompass APIs (RESTful (*https://oreil.ly/tkqSS*) and GraphQL (*https://oreil.ly/sa9QK*) APIs are common), streaming technologies (e.g., Kafka (*https://oreil.ly/RtytV*)), and change data capture mechanisms (such as Debezium (*https://debezium.io*)). They facilitate the interaction and exchange of information between different data products, enabling them to communicate and share data in real time. This interconnectedness is essential for creating a dynamic, responsive data ecosystem, where data can flow freely and securely between different data products (and other enterprise applications or external systems).

At the technical foundational layer of the Data Mesh fabric are the platform, infrastructure, and DevSecOps (*https://oreil.ly/kf3S8*) services. Platforms include a range of data management solutions like databases (e.g., PostgreSQL (*https://oreil.ly/HEpeD*)), data marts, data warehouses, data lakes, and data lakehouses (from vendors such as Snowflake (*https://oreil.ly/mrHs1*) and Databricks (*https://oreil.ly/Oct-Y*)).

Infrastructure services provide the foundational compute, network, and storage capabilities that form the core platform supporting almost all components of a Data Mesh. They provide the essential resources required for data processing, storage, and orchestration, ensuring that data products have the necessary computational power and space to operate effectively.

DevSecOps (*https://oreil.ly/YkKQH*) (development, security, and operations) ensures that all services within a Data Mesh are managed—from development through deployment and management in a production environment—in an automated, safe, and reliable fashion. Applying DevSecOps to Data Mesh and data products provides the process and automation that will speed up the development as well as the deployment of data products.

Climate Quantum Use Case Considerations

At this point, we understand the architecture of a data product, how it defines its data and artifacts, its ingestion and consumption capabilities, and its core operational interfaces. We have also seen the constituent components of Data Mesh and how it binds data products into a broader ecosystem.

Now, let's see how we can put the pieces together for a high-level architecture for Climate Quantum, our use case. As you recall, Climate Quantum's mission is to make climate data easy to find, consume, share, and trust using data products and a broader Data Mesh ecosystem. Climate Quantum addresses many domains of climate data; a snapshot of Climate Quantum's Data Mesh addressing specific data domains is shown in Figure 4-8.

Climate Quantum ingests data from raw climate data sources and creates several distinct domains:

Flood data domain
> Captures raw climate data (e.g., from weather stations, sensors, gauges, and satellite images) into more usable forms (e.g., identifying areas subject to flooding from a very large satellite image)

Physical risk domain
> Answers the question "Which of my assets, buildings, and population centers are affected by climate change?"

Disclosure reporting domain
> Responds to the need to disclose physical risks to regulators and stakeholders

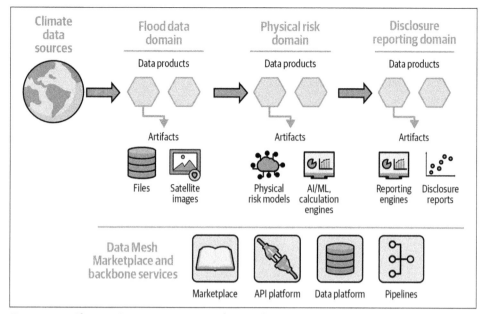

Figure 4-8. Climate Quantum Data Mesh snapshot

Each data product has a consistent definition (namespace, names, and other attributes mentioned previously). And each is both discoverable and observable using a lightweight data product gateway with published APIs. Each artifact is defined in a consistent way (using previously mentioned artifact attributes), making it easy to consume. All of this processing is supported using several core Data Mesh architecture components:

Data Mesh Marketplace
All data products and their artifacts are published to the Data Mesh Marketplace, making them easy to find and consume by users as well as by other data products.

Data Mesh backbone services
All data products interact via pipelines built on a number of common products, including Airflow (*https://oreil.ly/2OsF2*) and dbt (*https://www.getdbt.com*), with data stored in a data platform and accessed via APIs made available through an API platform.

Hopefully, you can see that even in a data landscape as complex and diverse as climate data, Data Mesh can make the data agile.

Summary

Previous chapters described the essentials of a data product. In this chapter, we discussed the various architecture components that make up a Data Mesh, its data products, and the data product's artifacts.

In the next chapter, we will elaborate on data contracts and then apply this architecture to show how to implement data products.

CHAPTER 5

Driving Data Products with Data Contracts

In this chapter, we will start by looking at what Data Mesh is from an implementation perspective, answering the question: what are its main components? We will then draw the parallel with product thinking, explore what a data product is, and finally jump into data contracts. The examples in this chapter follow the theme of our use case, Climate Quantum Inc.

Bringing Value Through Trust

Rooted in Agile methodologies, Data Mesh focuses on bringing value to the enterprise. We know that, from an engineering and technology perspective, it seems strange to talk about value. After all, what is "value" in data engineering?

Don't worry—we aren't switching from an engineering-oriented book to a business book. But we are convinced that, collectively, we need to keep our objectives aligned with Data Mesh, and one of those objectives is trust.

In our many conversations with fellow engineers and scientists, we often tell them that we are not smart enough to know what to do with every piece of data, but we know how to bring them the data they need (and sometimes want). Our teams deliver either the data or the tools to access and process the data. We don't pretend to know our customers' jobs, although we spend time learning about them, and everybody should. Trust is the foundation. *Harvard Business Review* (*HBR*) published a piece on how trust can be materialized (*https://oreil.ly/DlheR*). Let's see how that applies to the data world.

First, we try to nurture an honest and *positive relationship* with our customers. This can be challenging, as you know and have probably experienced in your career.

Trusting Products

When you think about a good product, probably one of the most important consider-ations is that you have trust in it. Maybe you love to take photos with your rather nice Nikon mirrorless camera. When you're out on a hike with your camera, you expect it to be all ready to go as soon as you turn it on, instead of having some long-winded boot time. When you press the actuator, you expect the photo to be available instantly on your CFexpress card and within 10 seconds on your iPhone.

Here, you judge quality by whether the image is saved on the card and matches your expectations for resolution, compression, color balance, and other attributes. The time needed to transfer your photo from the camera to your phone is a service-level objective. When your product works as expected and provides the quality you expect, then your trust in it naturally grows.

The second element of trust is demonstrating *expertise* in our customers' domain. Of course, we can pretend to be experts; however, a data contract is a more tangible way to capture their needs. The data contract will provide the required level of expertise needed to trust the data (for more, see "Navigating the Data Contract" on page 69).

Consistency is the third element of trust described by *HBR*. The data contract will provide this consistency through data quality results and service-level indicators (SLIs). As a result, our customers get access to data they can trust and build upon. Trust is the value you should aim to deliver.

Are we bringing business considerations into a technical book? Everything you do from now will be based on the trust you are going to build, and you are going to guarantee this trust with a series of contracts, as illustrated by Figure 5-1.

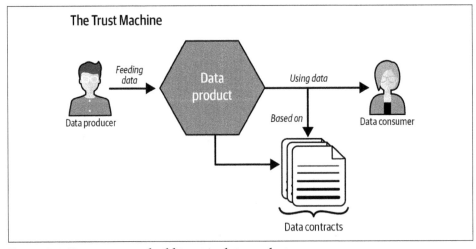

Figure 5-1. Data contracts build trust in data products

Now that we have established the need for trust as the main value, let's look at data contracts and how they build that trust.

Navigating the Data Contract

As you learned in the first section of this chapter, the need for a data contract is pretty obvious: you need an artifact to support the trust you want to build in your data. Let's dive first into the theory to understand the information you want to include in the contract, and then we'll look at a few examples.

Going Through the Theory

Let's start with the boring part: the theory. A contract establishes a formal relationship between two or more parties. We have all signed implicit or explicit contracts: you're working for someone (or you have customers), you most likely have a cell phone, and you probably don't live under a bridge. As you most likely imagined, a data contract is a similar agreement that now involves data (duh). A *data contract* is an agreement between multiple parties, specifically a data producer and data consumer(s).

Let's compare data contracts to real life. The data producer is Volkswagen (VW). The product is a 2013 VW Beetle 2.0L TDI, and the data contract lists the car's specifications. The Beetle's shape is attractive to us, we believe (at times) in diesel, and we think a 2.0L engine for 3117 pounds/1.4T should give us a nicely reactive car. Those features are part of the contract.

In a data contract, those features can be the schema. For example, the dataset contains a customer table with 25 columns, one column being the first name, which is of type VARCHAR and length 32.

The contract includes service-level agreements (SLAs) and functional and nonfunctional requirements (NFRs). For our VW Beetle, these requirements could include the 32 MPG/7.4 L/100 km consumption or when the garage will have it available for pickup. For data, they could include the time to detect an issue or, for a daily batch, the time the data is available.

In some cases, problems can be a total deal-breaker: too many duplicated records, too many NULLs in a required field, or heavier nitrogen oxide (NOx) emissions released in the atmosphere (in the case of the VW scandal a few years ago). The constraints can come from the producer/seller or from the regulator—and this opens the door to federated computational governance, but we won't go there in this chapter.

Stacking Up Good Information

So what do you put in a data contract? We'd say virtually anything that clarifies the production and usage expectations of the data can go into the data contract. In the open source data contract standard (*https://oreil.ly/1GanV*), the community has divided this information into the following eight categories:

Fundamentals and demographics
> This section contains general information about the contract, such as name, domain, version, and the like.

Dataset and schema
> This section describes the dataset and the schema of the data contract. It is the support for data quality, which we detail in the next section. A data contract focuses on a single dataset with several tables (and, obviously, columns).

Data quality
> This category describes data quality rules and parameters. These are tightly linked to the schema defined in the dataset and schema section.

Pricing
> This section covers pricing when you bill your customer for using this data product. Pricing is currently experimental.

Stakeholders
> This important part lists stakeholders and the history of their relationship with this data contract.

Roles
> This section lists the roles that a consumer may need to access the dataset depending on the type of access they require.

Service-level agreements
> This section describes the SLAs.

Custom properties
> This section covers custom and other properties in a data contract using a list of key-value pairs. This section gives flexibility without creating a new template version whenever someone needs additional properties.

The data contract itself uses a YAML file. The choice of YAML was evident as it can be read equally easily by machines and humans. YAML files can live extremely well in GitHub repositories, where source control provides excellent traceability.

> ## Bitol, a Linux Foundation Project
>
> There are many flavors of data contracts; in this book, we will actively follow the *Open Data Contract Standard* (ODCS), which is part of the Bitol (*https://bitol.io*) project supported by LF AI & Data, part of the Linux Foundation.
>
> ODCS is an open standard and as such is superior to closed standards because of its ability to promote interoperability and compatibility across diverse platforms, fostering innovation through broad collaboration. Open standards are cost-efficient, reducing reliance on proprietary solutions and lowering overall expenses. Additionally, open standards enhance security and transparency by allowing collective scrutiny, ensuring higher security standards and quicker issue resolution. They offer greater longevity and sustainability, as they are community driven and don't depend on a single entity, thus avoiding the risk of obsolescence or vendor lock-in associated with closed standards. Overall, open standards create a more dynamic, competitive, and inclusive technological ecosystem.

Let's see how data contracts relate to data products and Data Mesh. This will help you understand how you can optimally use them.

It's All About Proper Versioning

Data can be sold (or consumed) as a product. Like our VW Beetle, it can have functional requirements (four wheels, a steering wheel, etc.), NFRs (the quantity of NOx released in the atmosphere while driving), and SLAs (delivery date, replacement car when stranded, etc.).

However, when we see the NOx problems with the Beetle we've chosen, we may decide to switch to a nondiesel version, like the 2014 2.5L five-cylinder. It's still the same product, but it's not the same version (2014 versus 2013); it's a variation on the original product (gas versus diesel).

It's the same thing with a data product. We can add or remove some information and deal with the changes through versions. We can also have different variations on the product we share, such as raw, curated, aggregated, and more.

To summarize, a data product can have multiple data contracts: at least one data contract per dataset and version, which we will study in the next section. This gives us the required flexibility.

Keeping It Simple and Semantic

Changes follow semantic versioning to guarantee consistency in how data engineers version data contracts. Semantic versioning (*https://semver.org*) relies on patch, minor, and major changes. We'll look at a few examples in "Documenting in a slightly better way" on page 73.

Data Mesh tracks DPOs as stakeholders in any data product. When they move to a new role, we add the new DPO to the contract, keeping a human lineage. This results in a patch version: my data contract can move from 1.0.1 to 1.0.2. A *patch* is a bug fix that provides backward compatibility. It can also be an information change like a new stakeholder in a data contract.

We might add an age column to our prospect table, which is part of our curated customer dataset in our customer data product. The data contract is bumped to a minor version for this dataset, from version 1.0.2 to 1.1.0. A *minor change* maintains backward compatibility; it allows existing downstream apps, solutions, and queries to function with no issue.

Over time, we realize that the prospect and customer tables should be combined. This is a major change, breaking much of the consumer code. This evolution is a reason to bump the updated contract to version 2.0.0. A *major change* is a change that does not provide backward compatibility. Such a change will cause existing downstream apps, solutions, or queries to break.

Changes are not equal in intensity. Table 5-1 lists examples of changes for tables, APIs, and data contracts and describes the severity of the change: whether it is a patch, a minor change, or a major change. These lists are not exhaustive.

Table 5-1. Severity of changes in a data product

Artifact	Patch	Minor	Major
Table		Adding a new column Making a logic change to an existing column	Changing a column's data type Changing a column's name Removing a column
API	A bug fix that is not a minor or major change	Adding a new field in the payload Adding an optional parameter in the HTTP request Changing a required parameter to optional	Changing the format of request or response data Changing the data type of a resource (such as changing from a string to an integer) Removing one or more resources, removing or changing properties or methods for a particular resource, or any other changes to API functionality Adding a new required field for client HTTP requests
Data contract	Updating metadata Changing description fields Changing stakeholders	Revising a data quality rule Adding a new key, given that it is optional or required with a default value Adding a custom property	Changing the data type of a key Changing the name of a key Removing a key

Tracking changes and their consequences on versioning may not sound easy to do, but it will allow data producers and consumers to evolve at their own pace, increasing trust between them and the robustness of our systems.

To make it easier to manage these contracts, Data Mesh needs tooling. For example, the PayPal team developed a comparison service to analyze two contracts and suggest a version number.

A philosophy change may also be needed, as a strict contract does not mean that its consumption should be as uncompromising. Jon Postel, one of the creators of the TCP protocol, said, "Be conservative in what you do, be liberal in what you accept from others." This has become the robustness principle in computer science and is often called Postel's law.

Walking Through an Example: Complementing Tribal Knowledge

You'll find a few examples of data contracts in the GitHub repository (*https://oreil.ly/ 1GanV*), and the team will continue adding more. For now, let's look at a complex business problem that we can solve with data contracts: tribal knowledge. *Tribal knowledge* is when a group of people knows something and this information is relatively hard to get to when you're not part of the group. It's an oral tradition. Tribal knowledge is not wrong per se, but it's hard to scale, it resists organizational changes, and it will create issues in a regulatory environment. You should not get rid of it but learn how to live with it and complement it. Here are two ways of enhancing it:

- Document, document, document.
- Create a human lineage.

Documenting in a slightly better way

Engineers generally don't mind documenting. They are often under- or overdocumenting things, but documentation of some kind usually exists. The problem is documenting change. The data contract provides a solution to documenting at the right level and synchronizing change. For example, you can leverage the description and other informational fields, as shown in Example 5-1. Note: this data contract format focuses for now on table and structured data; extensions are in progress.

Example 5-1. Basic table description in ODCS v3

```
schema:
  - object: tbl
    logicalType: object
    physicalType: table
    description: Provides core payment metrics
    dataGranularityDescription: Aggregation on columns txn_ref_dt, pmt_txn_id
```

```
  properties:
    - name: txn_ref_dt
      businessName: Transaction reference date
      logicalType: date
      physicalType: date
      description: Reference date for the transaction. Use this date in reports
                   and aggregation rather than txn_mystical_dt, as it is slightly
                   too mystical.
      examples:
        - 2022-10-03
        - 2025-01-28
```

But this is an easy example, although sometimes, finding the right field is not as simple as it seems!

Sometimes, fields result from a calculation or have business rules associated with them. The data contract lets you materialize those constraints via authoritative definitions. Example 5-2 shows that the `rcvr_cntry_code` field has both a business definition and a reference implementation.

Example 5-2. Using authoritative definitions

```
schema:
  - table: tbl
    properties:
    - name: rcvr_cntry_code
      description: Receiver country code
      logicalType: string
      physicalType: varchar(2)
      authoritativeDefinitions:
        - url: https://collibra.com/asset/748f-71a5-4ab1-bda4-8c25
          type: businessDefinition
        - url: https://github.com/myorg/myrepo
          type: referenceImplementation
```

Now, it is up to us to define the policies we want to enforce: percentage of completion of documentation, percentage of fields linked to authoritative definitions, and more. No more under- or overdocumentation, no more out-of-sync between your data model and your documentation. The data contract provides a rich single source of truth.

Creating a human lineage

Data lineage applies to following the journey of data. Now, let's understand what a human lineage (instead of a data lineage) can do to share knowledge and track the history. As the story evolves, we'll translate it into code used in the data contract. Let's imagine a scenario where Colin joined Climate Quantum Inc. a few years ago as a DPO (Example 5-3).

Example 5-3. A simple team member

```
team:
  - username: colin
    role: dpo
    dateIn: 2014-08-02
```

Thanks to Colin's intolerant, direct, and fiery attitude, he quickly went exploring other areas and was replaced by Karin (Example 5-4).

Example 5-4. Team evolution

```
team:
  - username: colin
    role: dpo
    dateIn: 2014-08-02
    dateOut: 2014-10-01
    replacedByUsername: karin
  - username: karin
    role: dpo
    dateIn: 2014-10-01
```

Karin's style was a better fit, and she got promoted. She hired Max to replace her as a DPO (Example 5-5).

Example 5-5. Adding Max and replacing Karin

```
team:
  - username: colin
    role: dpo
    dateIn: 2014-08-02
    dateOut: 2014-10-01
    replacedByUsername: karin
  - username: karin
    role: dpo
    dateIn: 2014-10-01
    dateOut: 2019-03-14
    replacedByUsername: max
  - username: max
    role: dpo
    dateIn: 2019-03-14
```

Great things happened, and Max got to his sabbatical. Although he was still going to be the DPO when he returned, he asked Ole to watch it for him during his absence (Example 5-6).

Example 5-6. Finally, Ole joins the team

```
team:
  - username: colin
    role: dpo
    dateIn: 2014-08-02
    dateOut: 2014-10-01
    replacedByUsername: karin
  - username: karin
    role: dpo
    dateIn: 2014-10-01
    dateOut: 2019-03-14
    replacedByUsername: max
  - username: max
    role: dpo
    dateIn: 2019-03-14
    comment: Minor interruption due to sabbatical, will be back by end of April 2021
    dateOut: 2021-04-01
    replacedByUsername: ole
  - username: ole
    role: dpo
    dateIn: 2021-04-01
```

That's when Ole got into trouble and required emergency leave. As we had jinxed Murphy's law too many times, this was when we needed critical information from the DPO. Although Max and Ole were out, thanks to the human lineage described in the contract, we could happily reach out to Karin, who is always helpful anyway.

This example illustrates a fictional situation, but we are pretty sure you have experienced something similar in your career.

What is Data QoS and Why Is It Critical?

Normalizing the way we describe data quality and service levels is key to the success of your data contract. In this section, we'll introduce the notion of data QoS, which is the result of combining data quality with SLAs. We will start by explaining the concept, and then we'll drill down to describe the elements that make up the data QoS, focusing first on data quality and then on SLIs. Finally, we will explain how we grouped them.

 Quality of service is a well-established concept in network engineering. QoS is the measurement of the overall performance of a service, such as a telephony, computer network, or cloud computing service, particularly the performance seen by the network users. In networking, several criteria are considered to quantitatively measure the QoS, such as packet loss, bit rate, throughput, transmission delay, availability, and more. This chapter applies QoS to data engineering.

As your need to observe your data grows with the maturity of your business, you will realize that the number of attributes you want to measure will bring more complexity than simplicity. That's why, back in 2021, Jean-Georges came up with the idea to combine both data quality and service levels into a single table, inspired by Mandeleev's (and many others) work on classifying atomic elements in physics. You can see the result in Figure 5-2. The data QoS table represents the finest elements used for measuring data quality and service levels for data.

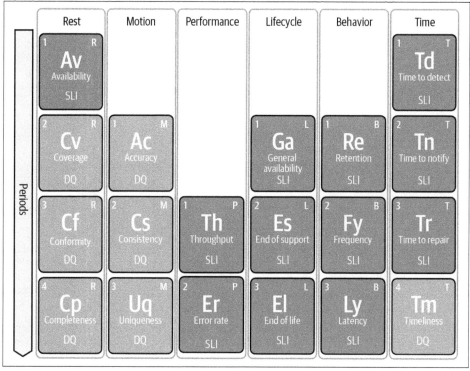

Figure 5-2. The data QoS table

Representation

To represent the elements, it was important to precisely identify each element on two axes:

- Time (or period)
- Group

Each element received additional attributes, as shown in Figure 5-3.

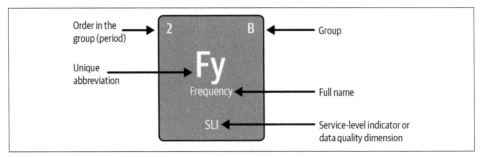

Figure 5-3. The attributes of each element in the data QoS table

Periods

Periods designate time-sensitive elements, or the element's order in its group. Some of these are pretty obvious, as "end of life" definitely comes after "general availability," as illustrated by Figure 5-4.

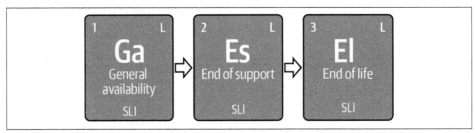

Figure 5-4. The order of elements in group L, or the lifecycle group

Classifying the period of some elements is more subtle: when data comes to your new data store, you will check accuracy before consistency, and you can check uniqueness only when you have significant data. The elements have no chronological link, but they happen in sequence, as illustrated by Figure 5-5.

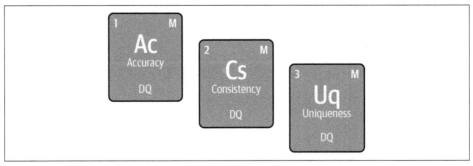

Figure 5-5. Sequential checking of accuracy, consistency, and uniqueness

Groups

The second classification to determine was grouping of elements. Is there a logical relation between the elements that would make sense?

This is what Jean-Georges came up with:

- Data at rest (R)
- Data in motion (M)
- Performance (P)
- Lifecycle (L) of the product itself
- Behavior (B) of the data, including retention, refresh frequency, availability time, and latency
- Time-related (T) indicators

Why Does It Matter?

There are many benefits to the classification and definition of the elements forming the data QoS:

Definitions we can agree on
The first step of developing the Information Technology Infrastructure Library (ITIL) was to set up a common vocabulary among the stakeholders of the project. Although ITIL might not be adequate for everything, this first step is crucial. Data QoS offers an evolutive framework with consistent terms and definitions.

Compatibility with data contracts
As we focus on data contracts, keep in mind that they need to be built on standardized expectations. This is obvious for the data-retention period, as you would probably not see duration, safekeeping, or something else. However, latency and freshness are often interchanged; let's go with latency.

Setting the foundation
Data QoS is not carved in stone. It supports evolution and innovation while delivering a solid base.

Why Data Quality Is Not Enough

Regarding data, the industry standard for trust has often been limited to data quality. Jean-Georges felt this for a long time. In 2017, at Spark Summit (*https://oreil.ly/ d-b04*), he introduced CACTAR (consistency, accuracy, completeness, timeliness, accessibility, and reliability) as an acronym for six data quality dimensions relayed in a Medium article (*https://oreil.ly/YnzAM*). Although there is no official standard, the

EDM Council (*https://oreil.ly/8QBLW*) had a few different ones and added a seventh one. So he decided to align on the EDM Council's list. The seven dimensions of data quality are shown in Figure 5-6.

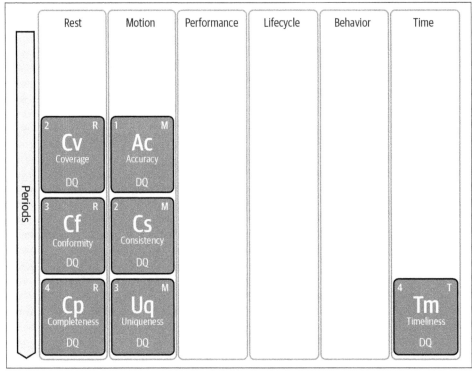

Figure 5-6. The seven data-quality dimensions on the data QoS table

Accuracy (Ac)

Accuracy refers to how precise data is, and it can be assessed by comparing it to the original documents and trusted sources or confirming it against business rules. The veracity of data is compared to its authoritative source to determine if the data is provided but incorrect. Some examples are:

- A customer is 24 years old, but the system identifies them as 42 years old.
- A supplier address is valid, but it is not their address.
- Fractional quantities are rounded up or down.

Fun fact: a lot of accuracy problems stem from the data input. If you have data entry people on your team, reward them for accuracy, not just for speed!

Completeness (Cp)

Data is required to be populated with a value (that is, not null, not nullable). *Completeness* checks if all necessary data attributes are present in the dataset. Some examples are:

- A missing invoice number when it is required by business rules or law
- A record with missing attributes
- A missing expiration month in a credit card number

Fun fact: a primary key is always a required field.

Conformity (Cf)

Data content must align with required standards, syntax (format, type, range), or permissible domain values. *Conformity* assesses how closely data adheres to standards, whether internal, external, or industry-wide. Some examples are:

- The customer identifier must be five characters long.
- The customer address type must be in the list of governed address types.
- The merchant address is filled with text but is not an identifying address (invalid state/province, postal codes, country, etc.).
- The ISO country codes are invalid.

Fun fact: ISO country codes can be two or three characters (such as FR and FRA for France). If you mix up the two in the same datasets, it's not a conformity problem; it's a consistency problem.

Consistency (Cs)

Data should retain consistent content across data stores. *Consistency* ensures that data values, formats, and definitions in one group match those in another group. Some examples are:

- Numeric formats are converted to characters in a dump.
- Within the same feed, some records have invalid data formats.
- Revenues are calculated differently in different data stores.
- Strings are shortened from a max length of 255 to 32 when they go from the website to the warehouse system.

Fun fact: Jean-Georges was born in France on 05/10/1971, but he is a Libra (October). When expressed as strings, date formats are transformed through a localization filter.

So, being born on October 5 makes the date representation 05/10/1971 in Europe but 10/05/1971 in the United States.

Coverage (Cv)

All records are contained in a data store or data source. *Coverage* relates to the extent and availability of data present but absent from a dataset. Some examples are:

- Every customer must be stored in the Customer database.
- The replicated database has missing rows or columns from the source.

Timeliness (Tm)

The data must represent current conditions; the data is available and can be used when needed. *Timeliness* gauges how well data reflects current market or business conditions and its availability when needed. Some examples are:

- A file was delivered too late or a source table was not fully updated for a business process or operation.
- A credit rating change was not updated on the day it was issued.
- An address is not up to date for a physical mailing.

Fun fact: 45 million Americans change addresses every year.

Uniqueness (Uq)

How much data can be duplicated? This supports the idea that no record or attribute is recorded more than once. *Uniqueness* means each record and attribute should be one of a kind, aiming for a single, unique data entry. (Yeah, one can dream, right?) Some examples are:

- Two instances of the same customer, product, or partner with different identifiers or spelling
- A share represented as equity and debt in the same database

Fun fact: data replication is not bad per se; involuntary data replication is!

Let's agree that these seven dimensions are pretty well rounded. As an industry, it's probably time to say: good enough. Of course, this completely ruins Jean-Georges' CACTAR acronym (and its great backstory).

But still it's not enough. Data quality does not answer questions about end of life, retention period, and time to repair when broken. Let's look at service levels.

Service Levels Complement Quality

While data quality describes the condition of the data, service levels give you precious information about expectations for availability, the condition of the data, and more.

Figure 5-7 is a list of SLIs that can be applied to your data and its delivery. You will have to set some objectives (service-level objectives, or SLOs) for your production systems and agree with your users and their expectations (set SLAs).

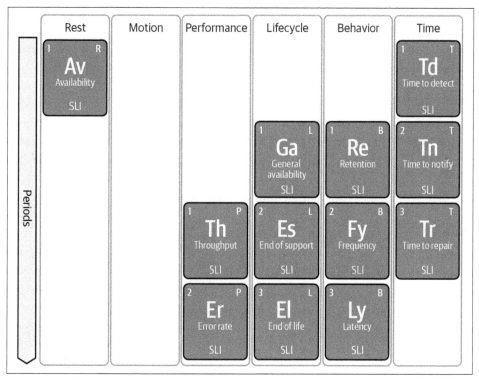

Figure 5-7. The SLIs on the data QoS table

Availability (Av)

Availability is, in simple terms, the answer to the question: is my database accessible? A data source may become inaccessible for various reasons, such as server issues or network interruptions. The fundamental requirement is for the database to respond affirmatively when you use the JDBC's `connect()` method.

Throughput (Th)

Throughput is about how fast the data can be assessed. It can be measured in bytes or records by unit of time.

Error rate (Er)

How often will your data have errors and over what period? What is your tolerance for those errors?

General availability (Ga)

In software and product management, *general availability* means the product is ready for public use, fully functional, stable, and supported. Here, general availability applies to when the data will be available for consumption. If your consumers require it, it can be a date associated with a specific version (alpha, beta, v1.0.0, v1.2.0, and so on). You can also imagine alpha or beta stages as specific SLAs or use version numbers or status to separate between production and development versions.

End of support (Es)

End of support is the date at which your product will not have support anymore. For data, this means that the data may still be available after this date, but if you, as a consumer, have an issue with it, you won't be offered a fix. It also means that you will expect a replacement version.

Fun fact: Windows 10 is supported until October 14, 2025.

End of life

End of life (*El*) is the date at which your product will not be available anymore. No support, no access. Rien. Nothing. Nada. Nichts.

For data, this means that the connection will fail or the file will not be available. It can also mean that the contract with an external data provider has ended.

Fun fact: Google Plus was shut down in April 2019. You could not access anything from Google's social network after this date.

Retention (Re)

How long are we keeping the records and documents? There is nothing extraordinary here—as with most SLIs, this can vary based on use case and legal and regulatory constraints by jurisdiction.

Frequency of update (Fy)

How often is your data updated? Daily? Weekly? Monthly? A linked indicator to this frequency is the time of availability, which applies well to daily batch updates.

Latency (Ly)

Latency measures the time between the production of the data and its availability for consumption.

Time to detect (an issue) (Td)

How fast can you detect a problem? Sometimes, a problem can mean breaking, like your car not starting on a cold morning, or it can mean slow, like your data feeding the Securities and Exchange Commission for publicly traded companies being wrong for several months. How fast do you guarantee the detection of the problem? You may also see this SLI called "failure detection time."

Fun fact: squirrels (or another similar creature) ate the gas line on my wife's car. We detected the problem as the gauge went down quickly, even for a few miles. Do you want to risk driving the car to the mechanic with the car leaking gas?

Time to notify (Tn)

Once you see a problem, how much time do you need to notify your users? This is, of course, assuming that you know who your users are.

Time to repair (Tr)

How long do you need to fix the issue once it is detected? This is a very common metric for network operators running backbone-level fiber networks.

Of course, there are a lot more SLIs that will come over time. Agreements follow indicators; agreements can include penalties. You see that the description of the service can become very complex.

In the next section, let's apply data QoS to the data contract, in the context of Climate Quantum Inc.

Applying Data QoS to the Data Contract

In this section, let's look at three examples of how we apply data QoS, the combination of data quality and service levels, to the data contract.

To demonstrate the use of those dimensions in a data contract, we will use the New York City Air Quality[1] dataset, which could be used by Climate Quantum Inc. Table 5-2 lists the first 10 records of this dataset, and the dataset's metadata looks like Table 5-3.

---

1 Dataset available from *data.gov*.

Table 5-2. The first 10 records of the New York City Air Quality dataset

Unique ID	Indicator ID	Name	Measure	Measure info	Geo type name	Geo join ID	Geo place name	Time period	Start_Date	Data value	Message
216498	386	Ozone (O3)	Mean	ppb	CD	313	Coney Island (CD13)	Summer 2013	6/1/13	34.64	
216499	386	Ozone (O3)	Mean	ppb	CD	313	Coney Island (CD13)	Summer 2014	6/1/14	33.22	
219969	386	Ozone (O3)	Mean	ppb	Borough	1	Bronx	Summer 2013	6/1/13	31.25	
219970	386	Ozone (O3)	Mean	ppb	Borough	1	Bronx	Summer 2014	6/1/14	31.15	
164876	383	Sulfur Dioxide (SO2)	Mean	ppb	CD	211	Morris Park and Bronxdale (CD11)	Winter 2008-09	12/1/08	5.89	
164877	383	Sulfur Dioxide (SO2)	Mean	ppb	CD	212	Williamsbridge and Baychester (CD12)	Winter 2008-09	12/1/08	5.75	
219971	386	Ozone (O3)	Mean	ppb	Borough	2	Brooklyn	Summer 2009	6/1/09	26.27	
219972	386	Ozone (O3)	Mean	ppb	Borough	2	Brooklyn	Summer 2010	6/1/10	33.83	
164878	383	Sulfur Dioxide (SO2)	Mean	ppb	CD	301	Greenpoint and Williamsburg (CD1)	Winter 2008-09	12/1/08	4.33	
164879	383	Sulfur Dioxide (SO2)	Mean	ppb	CD	302	Fort Greene and Brooklyn Heights (CD2)	Winter 2008-09	12/1/08	4.41	

Table 5-3. Metadata of the NYC Air Quality dataset

Column name	Description	Type
UniqueID	Unique record identifier	Plain text
IndicatorID	Identifier of the type of measured value across time and space	Number
Name	Name of the indicator	Plain text
Measure	How the indicator is measured	Plain text
MeasureInfo	Information (such as units) about the measure	Plain text
GeoTypeName	Geography type; UHF stands for United Hospital Fund neighborhoods. For instance, Citywide, Borough, and Community Districts are different geography types.	Plain text
GeoJoinID	Identifier of the neighborhood geographic area, used for joining to mapping geography files to make thematic maps	Plain text
GeoPlaceName	Neighborhood name	Plain text

Column name	Description	Type
TimePeriod	Description of the time that the data applies to; this could be a year, a range of years, or a season, for example.	Plain text
StartDate	Date value for the start of the TimePeriod, always a date value; this could be useful for plotting a time series.	Date and time
DataValue	The actual data value for this indicator, measure, place, and time	Number
Message	Notes that apply to the data value; for example, if an estimate is based on small numbers, we will detail here.	Plain text

Checking Conformity of Measurements

Let's make sure that the information around measurements conforms to our expectations. As a reminder, here are some conformity examples:

- The customer identifier should be eight characters long, and it is not.
- The customer address type must be in the list of governed address types (home, office).
- The address is filled with text but is not an identifying address.
- There are invalid ISO currency codes.
- The temperature contains letters.

In the data contract, Example 5-7 shows how you could add a conformity data quality rule. In this scenario, the measurement identifier requires a minimum value of 100,000; if not, the error is considered to have an operational business impact.

Example 5-7. A data contract for the air quality of New York City

```
schema:
  - name: Air_Quality
    description: Air quality of the city of New York
    dataGranularityDescription: Raw records
    properties:
      - name: UniqueID
        primary: true
        description: Unique identifier
        logicalType: number
        physicalType: int
        quality:
          - rule: rangeCheck
            description: This column should not contain values under 100000
            dimension: conformity
            severity: error
            businessImpact: operational
            mustBeGreaterThanOrEqualTo: 100000
```

Completeness

Data is required to be populated with a value: you don't want NULL values. Here are some examples:

- A missing customer identifier, phone, or more
- When NULL values are not allowed (required fields)
- A field that must be populated per business rules
- A record with missing attributes

Example 5-8 shows how you can represent completeness in a data contract: UniqueID is a required field. If this rule is not valid, it is an error with an operational business impact.

Example 5-8. Adding more data quality rules

```
schema:
  - name: Air_Quality
    description: Air quality of the city of New York
    properties:
      - name: UniqueID
        primary: true
        description: Unique identifier
        logicalType: number
        physicalType: int
        quality:
          - rule: nullCheck
            engine: ClimateQuantumDataQualityPackage
            description: This column should not contain null values
            dimension: completeness
            severity: error
            businessImpact: operational
            mustBeLessThan: 1
            unit: percent
```

Accuracy

Accuracy ensures that the provided data is correct. Here are a couple of examples:

- A customer is 12 years old, but the system identifies them as 32 years old.
- A supplier address is valid, but it is not the actual supplier's address.

In the data contract, you can specify that the value of the air quality should be between 0 and 500. As you can see in Example 5-9, it is the same application (rangeCheck) used for the validity dimension. The same tool can be used for multiple data quality dimensions.

Example 5-9. Adding an accuracy rule to the air quality data

```
schema:
  - name: Air_Quality
    description: Air quality of the city of New York
    dataGranularityDescription: Raw records
    properties:
      - name: DataValue
        description: Measured value
        logicalType: number
        physicalType: 'float(3,2)'
        quality:
          - rule: rangeCheck
            engine: bitol
            description: 'This column should contain positive values under 500'
            dimension: accuracy
            severity: error
            businessImpact: operational
            mustBeGreaterThanOrEqualTo: 0
            mustBeLessThan: 500
```

Engaging Service Levels

Service levels usually apply to the entire data product. You will not have a table with a retention of six months and another with a retention of three years.

Describing service levels in the data contract needs to be flexible, as more SLIs can be created over time. Example 5-10 shows what the definition of the service levels would look like, assuming the end of support is January 1, 2030, the retention period is one hundred years, the dataset was released on October 23, 2014, and the latency is clearly undefined.

Example 5-10. Adding service levels for additional information

```
slaDefaultElement: StartDate
slaProperties:
  - property: endOfSupport
    value: 2030-01-01T04:00:00.000Z
  - property: retention
    value: 100
    unit: 'y'
  - property: generalAvailability
    value: 2014-10-23T04:00:00.000Z
  - property: latency
    value: -1
    unit: As needed
```

As you can see, SLIs are properties, leaving room for extensibility.

You can see many other contract examples at GitHub (*https://oreil.ly/kLa9s*), including excerpts and full ones.

Summary

In this chapter, you learned that trust is fundamental when it comes to data. It is achieved through three qualities: having a positive relationship, showing expertise, and being consistent.

Data contracts are key to enabling this trust and building reliable data products. They can also be used outside of the scope of data products—for example, for documenting data pipelines.

Data contracts should follow a standard such as ODCS of the Bitol project.

Compared to a non–Data Mesh approach, creating and maintaining the data contracts are additional work, but they simplify a lot of the data engineering team's burden, such as documentation and implementation of data quality. Data contracts can help with documentation, and they complement tribal knowledge.

Data QoS combines the seven dimensions of data quality, as recognized by the EDM Council, with an extensive list of service levels. They can be grouped and organized through a timeline, like a periodic table. Data QoS is an extensible framework that defines the values you can use when implementing data contracts.

CHAPTER 6

Building Your First Data Product

Once we have the requirements, we are ready to build the first data product (or first data quantum), and this is what you are going to do in this chapter. You will first learn what a data product is. After that, you will see that the data contracts are going to help you immensely with your task. You will then switch to connecting the data sources to your product. You will then create the different endpoints. Finally, we'll look at the considerations for building and packaging the data product.

 What is the difference between a data product and a data quantum? We wish we had a savant answer for you, but they are basically the same. The term *quantum* comes from the architecture world, where a quantum is the smallest deployable element that brings value. By extension, the *data quantum* is the smallest deployable data element that brings value. The plural of *data quantum* is *data quanta*. Although there is a slight difference between the two terms, we will continue to use *data product* throughout the chapters to avoid confusion.

The data products will be assembled to make a Data Mesh; you will read about this in Chapter 8.

Anatomy of a Data Product

Let's first look at the different elements that make up a data product. This will ensure that you have a good list of the components to build.

From the outside, as suggested by Figure 6-1, a data product has many connection options.

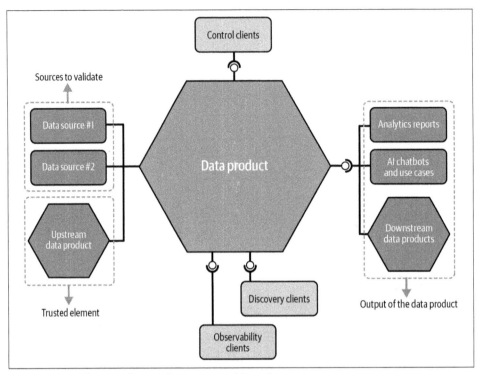

Figure 6-1. A data product with its external interfaces

On the left, you can see the data that is coming into the data product. In our experience, there is always at least one data source. Of course, the data product can manage some of its own transformations, but it is not a producer per se like an application is. The data product does not have to make a copy of the data. It can rely on views or federated data to avoid copying data. Sources can be databases, files, streams, or other data products.

On the right, you will find the consumers. In this case, it can be a bunch of analytics reports, AI chatbots, deep learning models, and other use cases, but it can also be one (or more) downstream data products.

So far, this looks like a data pipeline, right? Let's see what makes this different.

On the top are control clients who communicate via a REST API to the data product. We will talk more about this endpoint in "Enabling Operability and Control" on page 102.

On the bottom, we added both observability and discovery clients. Observability has the responsibility of enhancing trust, while discovery has the ambition to reduce the time needed for data discovery. They are described more thoroughly in the sections "Ensuring Higher Data Quality with Observability" on page 98 and "Getting Faster Data Discovery" on page 101.

 Why are data products represented by a hexagonal shape? Hexagonal shapes were used by Zhamak Dehghani in her book *Data Mesh*. Her inspiration is rumored to be from the hexagonal architecture aimed at creating loosely coupled components of an application. Hexagonal architecture is often seen as a predecessor to microservices architecture. Alistair Cockborn, the inventor of hexagonal architecture, gives more details on his website (*https://alistair.cock burn.us/hexagonal-architecture/*).

Let's look at the internals of our data product, shown in Figure 6-2.

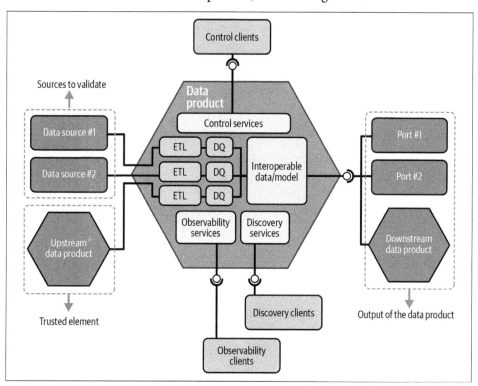

Figure 6-2. A data product with its internal components

In this scenario, we have two data sources, which could be databases, files, and streams but are not governed as a data product. We also have a data product as a source, which is a trusted element. In this scenario, we have three ETL pipelines that are getting the data from the sources. We could have one pipeline; it doesn't really matter. The next step is executing data quality (DQ) rules and measuring before the data is made available in the interoperable data or model (as in a data model, not an AI model). The interoperable model or interoperable data is the destination (or sink) within the data product. There are three consumers: two different output ports and a trusted downstream data product (which has its own output port).

The most interesting part is the inside of the product. As you can see, the data is flowing in, through the ETL, followed by the execution of DQ rules (or during the transformation); then it is stored in the interoperable model.

Observability tasks are monitoring the processes, data quality rules, data store(s) behavior, and more. This information is gathered at the product level and exposed via the observability services, through REST APIs, or published in a Kafka topic. Observability also includes the feedback loop where users can share their opinion and ratings of the data product.

Better discovery is a key benefit of a data product, hence its dedicated services. Each data product can publish its extended dictionary information, similar to observability.

The control services are slightly different from the discovery and observability services, as they are used for operating your data product.

Table 6-1 summarizes the roles of each service, illustrated in Figure 6-3.

Table 6-1. Summary of shared services for data products.

	Observability services	Discovery services	Control services
Role	Access to observability, data quality, and feedback loop	Access to the dictionary	Operate the data product
Data	Share read-only data	Share read-only data	Receive control orders
Payload	Based on the upcoming Bitol Open Observability Results Standard (OORS)	Based on the Bitol Open Data Contract Standard (ODCS)	Based on the upcoming Bitol Open Control and Orchestration Standard (OCOS)
Link	*https://abea.cx/oors*	*https://abea.cx/odcs*	*https://abea.cx/ocos*

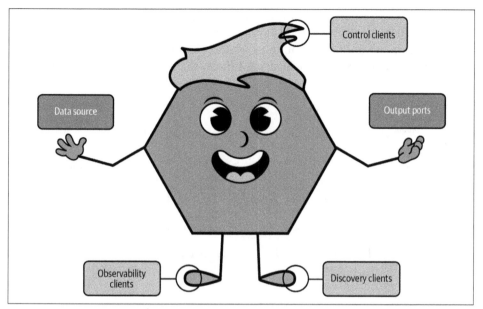

Figure 6-3. Data Quanto is a sweet little guy who will always be there to remind you of the key elements of a data product

The Data Contract to the Rescue

In Chapter 5, you learned a lot about data contracts. They will come in handy in this section as we are composing them to build a data product. Because we are going to use UUIDs, which are not great for reading, we will reference only the last four digits, so `fbe8d147-28db-4f1d-bedf-a3fe9f458427` will be 8427. In source code, we will use the full value.

 Bitol (*https://bitol.io*) is a project from the Linux Foundation with the mission of fostering a set of standards to define data contracts, data products, and more in order to tackle multiple challenges in data engineering, such as normalizing data, ensuring the relevance of documentation, establishing service-level expectations, simplifying data and tool integration, and promoting a data product–oriented approach.

Data contracts can be leveraged as resource descriptors. They contain all the necessary information for defining the data sources: the expected quality, ownership, and SLAs. The contract itself does not know whether it is used in an input or an output context; the data product knows. Figure 6-4 shows their location from a high level.

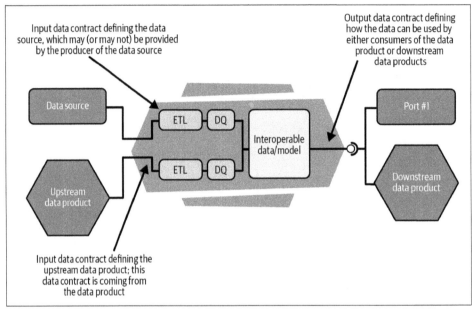

Figure 6-4. Data contracts' roles in a data product

How does this look from an implementation perspective? In this applied example, you can see that this particular data product, identified by the UUID ending in 8427, has two data sources and one output port. The two input data sources are identified by two data contracts, whose IDs are 838e and 97d2. The output port is governed by another data contract identified by d95b. Figure 6-5 illustrates this scenario. Your data product is a composition of those data contracts.

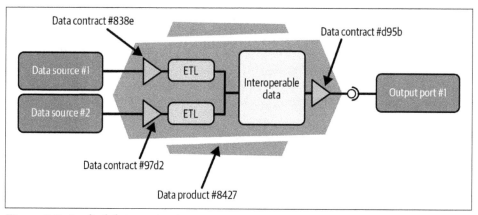

Figure 6-5. Applied data contracts

Although the standard has not been made official yet, the future Bitol ODPS could look like the following listing. Example 6-1 shows an attempt to create a simplistic definition of a data product using ODPS.

Example 6-1. A very basic data product defined by ODPS

```
name: my data product
id: fbe8d147-28db-4f1d-bedf-a3fe9f458427
kind: DataProduct
apiVersion: 1.0.0
versions:
- version: 1.0.0
  in:
  - contractId: 560525a6-0bd3-4aff-905f-39589c8c838e
    version: 1.2.0
  - contractId: 341b02d1-5e52-4186-a20e-74ffc31997d2
    version: 1.0.0
  out:
  - contractId: af12347d-b730-48e5-a369-33a2c70fd95b
    version: 1.0.0
- version: 2.0.1
  in:
  - contractId: 560525a6-0bd3-4aff-905f-39589c8c838e
    version: 1.2.0
  - contractId: 341b02d1-5e52-4186-a20e-74ffc31997d2
    version: 1.0.1
  out:
  - contractId: af12347d-b730-48e5-a369-33a2c70fd95b
    version: 2.0.0
```

Consider the group of input data sources and data output ports as a single set. The data product can have multiple versions of those. This example shows a data contract with two versions: version 1.0.0 and version 2.0.1. In this scenario, your data product relies on the same data contracts, but this could be different based on the evolution. The major benefit is that this allows concurrent use of multiple versions to ease the evolution of the data product.

Connecting Your Data Sources

Data sources are critical to your data product. Let's find out how data products integrate them.

Your data sources can be anything: a JDBC connection, a Parquet file in an S3 bucket, and so on. The connection information is available in the input data contract and in the ETL tool.

Once more, that's where the data contract comes into action, as it will contain the connection information to your data source. Bitol's ODCS has all the necessary information to establish a connection to your data source, including user and password, which can be sourced from a value in the contract (not the best idea) or the environment (a better idea). The Bitol ODCS working group is working on extending the security aspect.

Ensuring Higher Data Quality with Observability

As one of our goals is to increase trust in data, one way to achieve that is to make sure that both data quality and data observability are integrated within your data product.

The observability API is connected to the observability services. Those services monitor the data coming in and flowing in the pipelines and store it in the interoperable model.[1] They oversee data quality and data/system observability, as illustrated by Figure 6-6. The services source their configuration and parameters from the data contracts while they collect results.

---

1 In some situations, the data is not "moved" into the data products: the data could be federated or accessible via views. These are not the most common cases, but they exist.

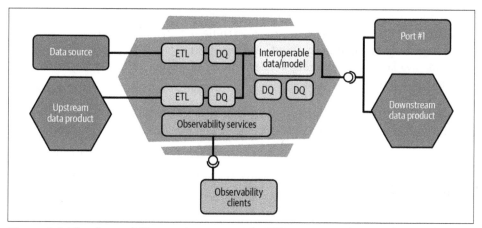

Figure 6-6. The observability services oversee the ETL processes, data quality, and data observability of the data product

To monitor the components of your data infrastructure, you have probes that collect information about the behavior of those components. Once more, a standard makes sense to ensure that the communication between the probes and the services matches what is expected. Let's look at Figure 6-7.

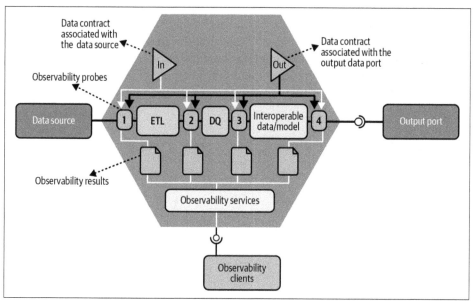

Figure 6-7. Flow of observability messages from the probes to the services

To simplify the illustration, we kept one data source, one pipeline, and one output port. You have two data contracts, one governing the input ("In" on the illustration) and one governing the output ("Out" on the illustration). Those two data contracts are made available to four probes. The number of probes will vary based on your installation, but in this scenario:

- Probe 1 measures that the incoming data is as it is expected. It could check that the data source's schema did not change or that the data source is available.

- Probe 2 checks that the ETL was run or measures the number of processed rows.

- Probe 3 ensures that the data quality rules were executed and that the results match the expectations.

- Probe 4 measures that the data in the interoperable data store matches the expectation of the output data contract. For example, it could check the latency of the data or any other SLA we discussed in Chapter 5.

Of course, the number of probes is highly variable, ranging from zero to many depending on how critical or complex the pipeline is. They might be situated at various other points of the flow, too. Not all probes will use all data contracts. As an example, if one of your probes monitors changes in the data source, it will not need the output data contract.

The four probes send their results to the observability services, which are the brain that will process the results. The services can compute an index, send notifications to users, or more. The results should follow a standardized format such as Bitol's future OORS, as exemplified in Examples 6-2 and 6-3. These examples are sample payloads that could be sent from the probes to the observability services. For consistency, we use YAML.

Example 6-2. A sample payload coming from the probe in charge of measuring latency

```
id: 078079d4-dbf2-4656-a37c-5119789d20ad
kind: ObservabilityResult
apiVersion: 1.0.0
timestamp: 2024-10-08T20:24:21+0000
emitter: com.abeadata.LatencyMeasurer
criteria: sla
property: latency
value: 2
unit: d
element: tab1.txn_ref_dt
```

```
id: 8d89606f-8ad3-4875-8086-0a83b9e52ecd
kind: ObservabilityResult
apiVersion: 1.0.0
timestamp: 2024-10-09T20:24:21+0000
emitter: com.abeadata.NullCheck
criteria: dq
property: NullCheck
value: 0.00314
unit: percent
element: tab1.rcvr_id
```

Getting Faster Data Discovery

Data discovery is expensive as it is a labor-intensive process, as shown by the proliferation of tools and solutions on the market. Although Data Mesh is not designed as a data discovery tool, its domain orientation makes it a very good add-on to the tooling you (will) use.

As Figure 6-8 illustrates, the dictionary services gather their information from the output data contract(s) and the interoperable data store. The discovery clients can access those services. The payload is either the full output data contract, a set of those contracts (when you have multiple output ports with different contracts), or a subset of the contracts (as you may want to limit the distribution of some sections).

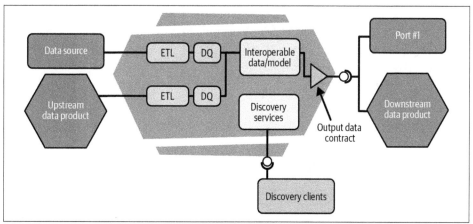

Figure 6-8. Discovery clients leverage the dictionary services, which are tightly linked to the output data contracts

Enabling Operability and Control

When operating your data product, you will use the control services. Since the API is the same across all your data products, it is easy to control all of them in a uniform fashion.

Control services cover modification of the internal components and tools, adding new versions of datasets or deprecating some, stopping or restarting the ETL processes, and more. In terms of your development priority, the control services may come later, as these operations can be done directly at the tool level. If you are using Apache Airflow to orchestrate your pipeline, the need to do that from the control clients may be less of a priority than the dictionary services. Bitol, the Linux Foundation project that focuses on modern data engineering standards, has the ambition to offer a standard here as well.

Figure 6-9 shows where the control services fit in the data product, overseeing any ETLs, data quality, data observability, and the data store.

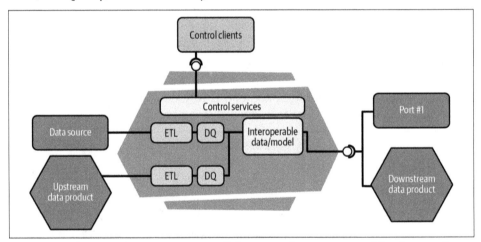

Figure 6-9. The control services operate all the internal components of the data product

Building and Packaging

You are now ready to build the services. Let's make sure you follow the correct pattern from the ground up.

As you have probably guessed by now, you will not have to redevelop the code for each data product. The only moving parts from one data product to another are the interoperable data store, the data contracts, and the ETL process, as is the case with most data pipelines anyway (if you replace data contract with data documentation).

The active code resides in a sidecar: a "running" library. A library is linked to an array executable (either statically or dynamically), but a library does not run by itself. It sits in a repo and is eventually loaded by an application. With a sidecar, the library becomes an active (or running) component.

The sidecar runs all the services: observability, discovery, and control. It also manages its local infrastructure needs.

Summary

In this chapter, you learned about building your first data product.

All the APIs are the same for all data products: you will not have to learn another API when you switch from one data product to another.

The implementation is isolated in a sidecar. The sidecar is comparable to a running library.

Payloads are standardized and, when possible, match an open standard like the ones Bitol is offering:

- ODCS (Open Data Contract Standard)
- ODPS (Open Data Product Standard)
- OORS (Open Observability Results Standard)
- OCOS (Open Control and Orchestration Standard)

And last but not least, Data Quanto is a cool little guy.

CHAPTER 7

Aligning with the Experience Planes

In this chapter, you will learn how to separate the responsibilities between different functional areas in your Data Mesh. You will discover the infrastructure experience plane, data product experience plane, and mesh experience plane. You will also find out how communication between planes works. Each experience plane has its own set of capabilities, and we will describe the most popular ones. Finally, we will walk you through one of these capabilities, feedback loops, which include the user feedback loop and the system feedback loop.

The Three Planes

Let's first look at the three planes stacked together: infrastructure experience, data product experience, and mesh experience. Then, we'll drill down deeper into each one.

Splitting the implementation into three groups will drastically simplify the organization and cognitive loads of your team. As you'll see throughout this chapter, each plane will focus on a different aspect:

Infrastructure experience plane

> The *infrastructure experience plane* focuses on the data containers, producers, warehouses, and so on.

Data product experience plane

> Data products live in their own plane of existence (the *data product experience plane*) to ensure isolation and evolutivity without interference.

Mesh experience plane

> The *mesh experience plane* allows the meshing (or interconnection) of the data products as well as mesh-level tooling.

Figure 7-1 shows the three planes stacked together. In the next section, we'll explore each plane individually.

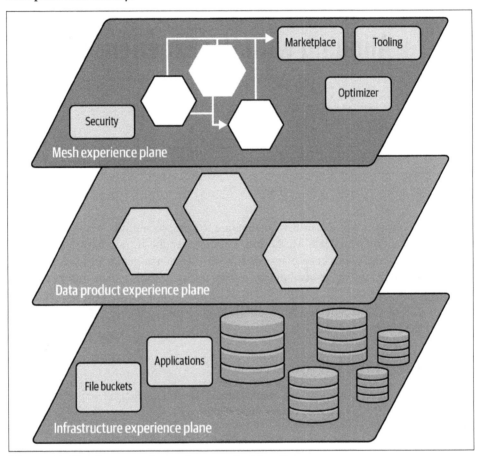

Figure 7-1. The three experience planes stacked together

The Infrastructure Plane Remains Key

The infrastructure experience plane contains all the elements you would consider to be your data infrastructure (pre–Data Mesh). As a data person, you are naturally aware of these elements: databases, data marts, and other applications that produce data. This plane also contains lower-level elements like compute, storage, orchestration, networking, operating systems, and more. Figure 7-2 represents this plane.

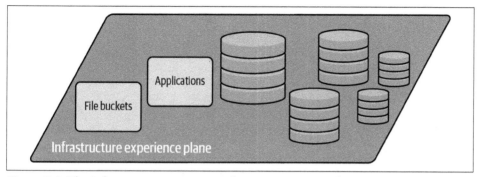

Figure 7-2. The infrastructure experience plane contains your data stores

Users of the infrastructure experience plane are your traditional system administrators (or system reliability engineers), database administrators, security engineers, and so on. You will build your data product and Data Mesh capabilities in other planes on top of this plane.

The Data Product Experience Plane Is Independent

The data product experience plane is the home of your unlinked data products. Let's have a look at how this plane interacts with the infrastructure plane.

You build and deploy your data products independently of one another. They live on the data product experience plane, as illustrated in Figure 7-3.

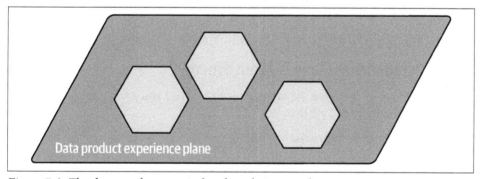

Figure 7-3. The data products are isolated on their own plane

As you saw in Chapter 6, a data product can feed itself from any source of data. This data product uses three data sources, illustrated in Figure 7-4: two databases and one application. The link between the planes is guaranteed by data contracts.

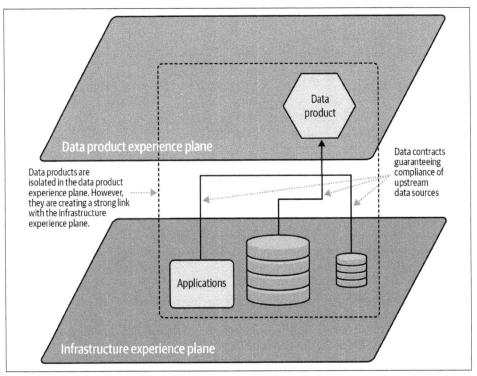

Figure 7-4. In the data product experience plane, data products communicate with the infrastructure plane via data contracts

The typical users of this plane are the data product engineers and data engineers.

The Mesh Experience Plane Is About Synergy

As you can imagine, the mesh experience plane is where you are going to connect all the components together. Let's dive in.

Figure 7-5 shows the enterprise-level components that the mesh experience plane will offer. Your enterprise data catalog (or data marketplace) sits here. You will also find a variety of tooling, monitoring, security management, and more. This is where you see the data products meshing.

Let's analyze two data products. Data product B uses data from data product A. Both report their information to a marketplace. Figure 7-6 focuses on data product A. The way B can leverage information from A is through the data contract shared by A. A shares the same data contract with the marketplace.

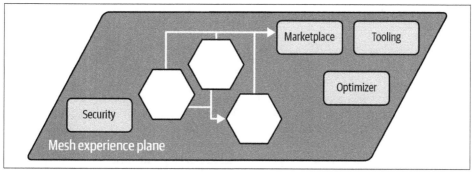

Figure 7-5. In the mesh experience plane, data products talk to one another as well as with mesh-level tooling

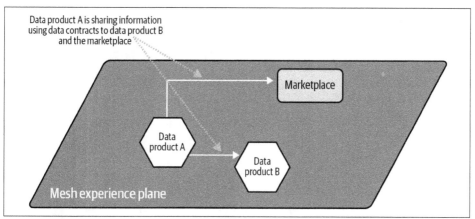

Figure 7-6. How data products share information in the mesh experience plane

For example, data product A could contain temperatures of all cities in France, while data product B contains only the temperatures of metropolitan areas (with a population between 500,000 and 1.5 million). Data product A exposes, through a data contract, its metadata (including its SLOs) to the marketplace where a user can find it. The same contract is shared with data product B so that it knows, for example, when the data in data product A is updated, the units that are used, and so on.

Data contracts can be transmitted in a number of ways. The most common way is in a source control manager like GitHub, but it can also be in a Kafka topic, accessible via a set of REST services, or through other technology.

Building a Capability Model for Each Plane

The *capability model* illustrates what features (or set of features) your planes offer. Let's look at the most important of them.

 What is a capability model? Imagine you're a superhero, and you have different powers like flying, super strength, or invisibility. These powers are like your capabilities—they're the things you can do because you're special. In the same way, each plane has its own special abilities or capabilities. It's like having a toolbox full of tools, each one helping you do different things. The capability model is the guide to your superpowers.

Now that we've established the content of the three planes, let's have a look at the different capabilities of each plane. Figure 7-7 shows the capabilities per plane.

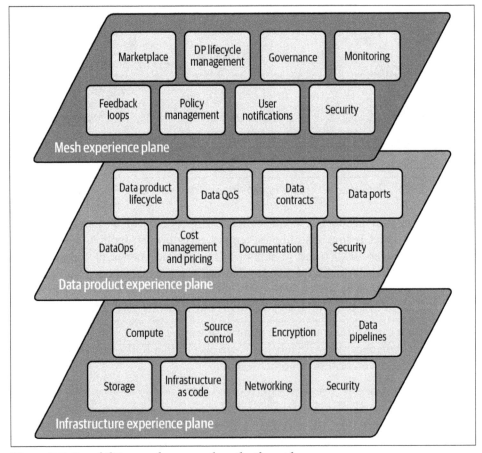

Figure 7-7. Capabilities can be mapped on the three planes

Capabilities of the Infrastructure Experience Plane

Figure 7-8 shows the capabilities in the infrastructure experience plane.

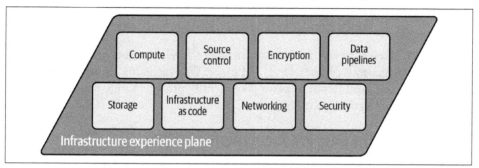

Figure 7-8. Capabilities of the infrastructure experience plane

Let's have a look at these capabilities:

Compute
> The compute resources associated with your Data Mesh. These can be used for the data transformations or analytics needs (including AI) that your data products will require.

Storage
> The storage and its management associated with your Data Mesh. This could be a database, a data warehouse, buckets on cloud storage, and so on.

Source control
> Many artifacts in the Data Mesh operations are source controlled: data contracts, definitions of data products, infrastructure as code, and the like.

Infrastructure as code
> One of the Data Mesh principles is self-service, so you will need a way to provision resources automatically. This is what infrastructure as code (IaC) is all about. You can imagine Terraform tooling, for example.

Encryption
> Encryption is a part of security and deserves a dedicated capability focusing on encryption on the wire and encryption at rest.

Networking
> A lot of networking is involved with Data Mesh as data flows or is federated from various instances.

Data pipelines

In the infrastructure plane, the data pipelines are more the tooling available to the data engineers rather than the instances of the pipelines themselves that live within the scope of the data product.

Security

Security is everywhere: at the infrastructure level, it relies on access control, token mechanisms, physical keys, and more. This capability focuses on the infrastructure you need to put in place, like identity providers, role management and policies, audit systems, and so forth.

Capabilities of the Data Product Experience Plane

Figure 7-9 shows the capabilities in the data product experience plane.

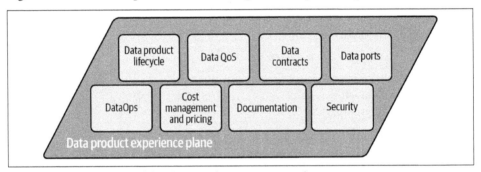

Figure 7-9. Capabilities of the data product experience plane

Let's learn about these capabilities:

Data product lifecycle

Each data product has its own lifecycle, which involves some capabilities linked to the product. Data contracts can help describe the essential lifecycle information as part of the service levels and data QoS (see Chapter 5).

DataOps

The DataOps capabilities include the instantiation of the pipelines (building the pipelines for this specific data product). They also include organization, continuous integration, and deployment.

Data QoS

The data QoS defines both the data quality and the service levels you are expecting from your data product. Data QoS is described in Chapter 5.

Cost management and pricing

In many organizations, the cost of making data available falls on the data producers, which is not fair as the benefits will be for the consumers. The data product needs to be aware of how to deal with those costs, either through chargeback or showback.

 Chargeback and showback are two ways to manage costs within an organization. They have gained more popularity in recent years with the popularity of the cloud. Showback reports the cost of cloud usage for transparency, while chargeback involves billing users, departments, or business units for their actual consumption. Both can be used to incentivize data producers to share their data.

Data contracts
As you have seen in Chapters 5 and 6, data contracts play an essential role at the data-product level: data products need to fully support them.

Documentation
Each data product is responsible for its own documentation. It is not responsible for rendering it (allowing users to see it) but rather for sharing it with a component that will enable discovery, like the marketplace (see the next section).

Data ports
Data products share data via ports: the data ports.

Security
Security at the data-product level focuses more on role attribution and information.

Capabilities of the Mesh Experience Plane

Finally, let's discover the capabilities in the mesh experience plane, as shown in Figure 7-10.

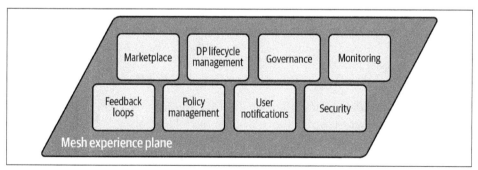

Figure 7-10. Capabilities of the mesh experience plane

When you combine data products in a mesh, you can see many new services and possibilities. Here are eight of them:

Marketplace

Data discovery is a pain. The data marketplace is essential in Data Mesh: it is the entrance door. A marketplace can expose the data product's lineage, represent the data product as a knowledge graph, allow search using metadata, and more.

Feedback loops

One of Data Mesh's major advances is its integration of feedback loops. The user feedback loop allows any type of user to report incidents or suggest improvements. The system feedback loop captures system events. The data product owns the data, but the management of the loops is at the mesh experience plane. The next section provides more details about feedback loops.

Data product (DP) lifecycle management

Each data product is responsible for its own lifecycle; however, the management of the lifecycle is done in the mesh experience plane. It consists of basic activation of data products within the mesh as well as advertising new versions, optimizing duplicates, and more.

Policy management

One of Data Mesh's principles is federated computational governance. Governance includes enterprise-level policies as well as line-of-business (business units) and country-specific policies. Their management takes place at the mesh level since you will need consistency across your data products.

Governance

Here both the mesh and its data products are governed. The mesh's governance includes reporting, monitoring, and auditing SLAs, data quality, and usage at the mesh level compared to individual data products.

User notifications

Another benefit of Data Mesh is facilitating communication with users. Notifications can be sent via email, Microsoft Teams, Slack, or any way you want (including ham radio).

Monitoring

Although each data product knows its state, you are not going to ask yourself individually about the state of each data product. Monitoring is brought up at the mesh experience plane to simplify your 360-degree view of Data Mesh.

Security

Security at the mesh level involves global policies, access control, integration with DevSecOps tools, reporting, alerting, and more.

Gathering Key Metrics Through Feedback Loops

Feedback loops are an essential feature of Data Mesh. They allow users to become more informed and provide relevant information to DPOs. Information feeding the loops comes from both users and the system. They are one of the few mechanisms that require traveling across planes. In this context, feedback loops are slightly different from those used in systems thinking.

In this section, we will use UML-originated sequence diagrams, which allow us to visually represent the interactions between objects or components in a system over time in a normalized way. This temporal aspect is crucial because it enables you to see the exact sequence of events and the dependencies among various components.

Figure 7-11 illustrates the principle of a feedback loop from a high level. It is based on the principle of "if you see something, say something." A user sees an issue and reports it to the management tool in the mesh experience plane. The management tool then notifies the various users of the issue.

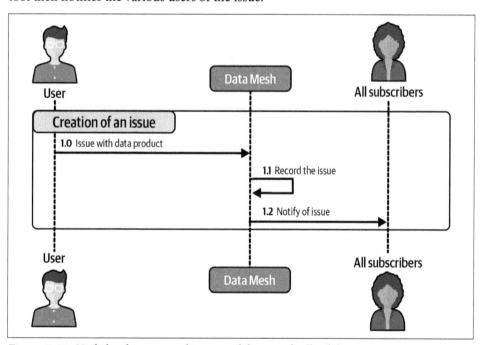

Figure 7-11. High-level sequence diagram of the user feedback loop

In reality, as Figure 7-12 illustrates, the Data Mesh management tool does not know how critical the issue is. Therefore, it shares this information with the data product, which reports on the gravity of the issue. The rest of the process is similar to the high-level sequence described in Figure 7-11.

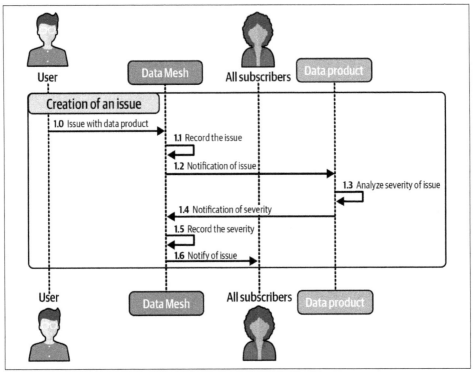

Figure 7-12. Looking at the details, you see that the services communicate across the planes

When it comes to the system feedback loop, as shown in Figure 7-13, the infrastructure experience plane tells the data product (or more likely, the data product finds out) and then follows a similar process.

The feedback loop is an essential part of Data Mesh: it increases trust in the data by showing its potential weaknesses and allowing people to act on it. Feedback loops are allowed to cross the experience planes.

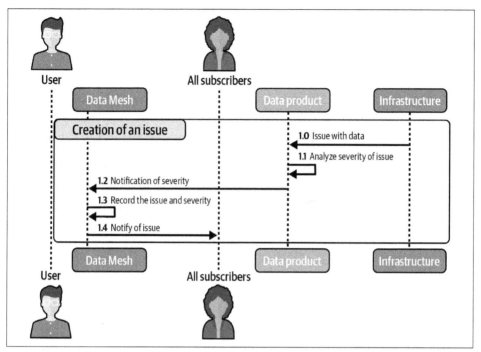

Figure 7-13. When an issue arises at the infrastructure experience plane, it is propagated to all planes

Summary

This chapter emphasizes the importance of separating concerns and responsibilities across different experience planes in a Data Mesh, ensuring efficient and secure data management:

- The infrastructure experience plane focuses on the data infrastructure (databases, data marts, compute, storage, orchestration, etc.) and is managed by system administrators, database administrators, and security engineers.

- The data product experience plane houses independent data products, allowing them to evolve without interference. Data product engineers and data engineers are the primary users.

- The mesh experience plane connects data products and includes enterprise-level tools like data catalogs, monitoring, and security management. It ensures that data products can interconnect and share data efficiently.

Each plane has its own capabilities:

- The infrastructure experience plane includes essential resources for data operations, such as compute for analytics, storage management for databases and cloud, and networking for data flow. It also manages data contracts and provisioning through tools like Terraform and ensures security with encryption and infrastructure for data pipelines and security.
- The data product experience plane oversees the development and operations of individual data products, ensuring quality and managing costs. It supports data contracts and documentation for transparency, provides interfaces for data sharing, and maintains security measures at the product level.
- The mesh experience plane connects and manages the entire Data Mesh ecosystem. It facilitates data discovery, integrates feedback loops for continuous improvement, and oversees data product lifecycle and policy compliance. It ensures governance, user notifications, monitoring, and security for comprehensive data management.

Data products interact with the infrastructure plane through data contracts.

The mesh plane integrates components and manages their interactions, such as data sharing between products and centralizing capabilities like marketplaces and feedback loops.

The user feedback loop allows users to report issues and suggest improvements. Information is shared across planes, enhancing data reliability. The system feedback loop allows infrastructure issues to be communicated to data products and managed similarly to user feedback.

CHAPTER 8

Meshing Your Data Products

Now that you have several data products, let's discover how we can use them.

Registering your data product is a crucial first step to ensuring its availability and usability within your data ecosystem. This process involves formalizing and publishing your data product so that it can be discovered and used by others. Central to this task are data contracts, which are text files based on the ODCS and ODPS, as we discussed in Chapter 5.

Once the necessary data contracts are built and stored in source control, the DPO assembles the data product and initiates its registration to a data marketplace. This process, often automated through a continuous integration and continuous delivery (CI/CD) pipeline, involves several collaborative steps. Data engineers and architects create initial data contracts based on existing assets, refine them with input from the DPO, and push the finalized contracts to source control. The DPO then compiles these contracts into a complete data product and triggers its registration. This workflow ensures that the data product meets quality standards and is ready for consumption by data users, with thorough documentation and governance in place to support its lifecycle.

Let's dive into this exciting part of the process!

Registering Your Data Product

Once your data product is ready, you must register it to make it available. Let's examine how this process works.

Your data product relies on data contracts. All those artifacts are text files (YAML) in your source control. In Figure 8-1, you can see where those artifacts are. In a typical data product, you will have 0–n data contracts defining your input (although 0 is an edge case, and we would not recommend it as you need to control what is coming in). You will have at least one data contract for the output. In this example, we use the ODCS for describing data contracts and the ODPS for defining data products. Both standards are defined by the Bitol project (*https://bitol.io*) of LF AI & Data, part of the Linux Foundation.

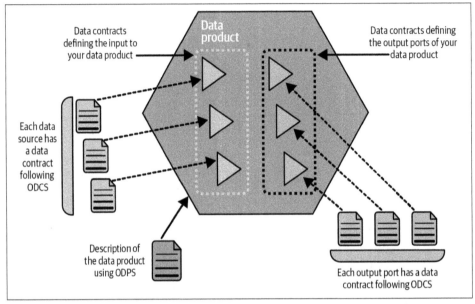

Figure 8-1. Resource artifacts in a data product: data contracts (ODCS) and data product descriptors (ODPS)

As you learned in Chapter 5, a data product is a collection of data contracts. So your energy should be spent on building those first; then you can assemble them under the supervision of the DPO. Figure 8-2 details the sequence of events.

The first step is to build all the data contracts you need. The data engineers and architects create initial versions, usually based on existing data assets (brownfield) like databases, file buckets, and so on. The DPO adds their requirements, which can be detailed on the transformation, including references to authoritative sources, service levels, and more. In step 1.2, the engineering and product teams collaborate on building the final contracts and the software artifacts, such as the data pipelines. In the end, they push the final version of the data contract to their source control manager (step 1.3). They will repeat this process for as many data contracts as they plan to have in their data product.

The next major step (2.0 on Figure 8-2) is for the DPO to assemble the data product with all the data contracts and push it to the source control. When everything is ready, the DPO can trigger the registration (you may also see the term *publication* in some documentation) of the data product to the data marketplace (step 3.0 in Figure 8-2).

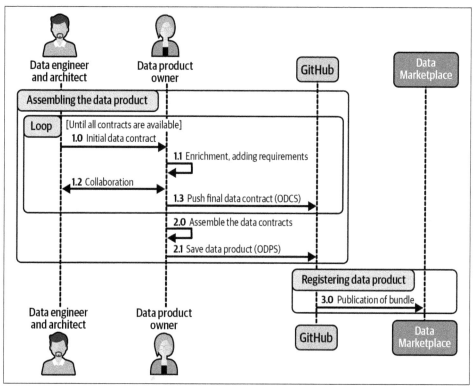

Figure 8-2. Sequence diagram for publishing a data product in the registry/marketplace

Of course, this is a simplified version of all the interactions. The DPO will interact heavily with their customers (the data consumers), and the decision to publish will definitely go through a deployment process that involves other stakeholders and validation tasks. However, most of those operations can be automated as part of a CI/CD process, increasing the quality of the deployment process.

Connecting to Your Products in the Mesh

Let's study three use cases where you can mesh data products, see the benefits, and understand how the implementation will work. In this section, we will use *mesh* as a verb or noun to mean combining data products or adding data products to Data Mesh. The first use case is basic meshing to produce better and trusted data. The second focuses on lineage. Finally, we will look at the notification system.

Meshing Data Products Together

Let's start by meshing a few data products together to understand the benefits and mechanisms of doing that.

There is already a lot of value in using individual data products: you can find the data more easily, and as a data consumer, you can trust the data product based on its service levels (both the objectives and the measured values). The natural question is, why mesh them, then? The answer is pretty straightforward: it's simple to do and unlocks a lot of value. Follow the story with us.

You are a data scientist for Climate Quantum Inc., and you are trying to gain a global view of precipitation in North America and Europe. You have access to datasets from the National Oceanic and Atmospheric Administration (*https://www.noaa.gov*) (NOAA), the US agency in charge of climate, as well as from Météo France (*https:// oreil.ly/WsAiO*), the agency for France. For simplification purposes, we won't list all the other European agencies.

If you used only data products, like in Figure 8-3, you would have multiple data sources. If you are tempted to compare that to multiple databases or tables, remember that data contracts following the OCDS standard come with data quality and SLAs.

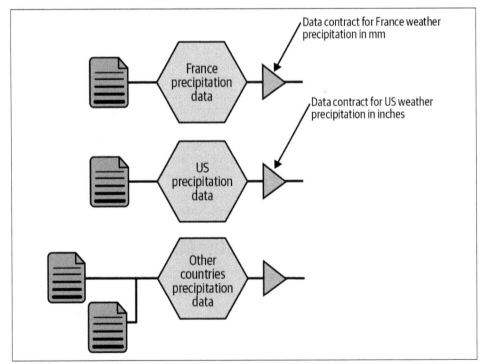

Figure 8-3. Multiple data products to access data

However, you will have multiple SLAs. You can imagine that the data is not updated at the same time, that the units are not the same (mm in Europe, inches in the US), and other discrepancies.

One solution is to mesh your data products into a new one, consolidating the data in a single data product, as illustrated by Figure 8-4.

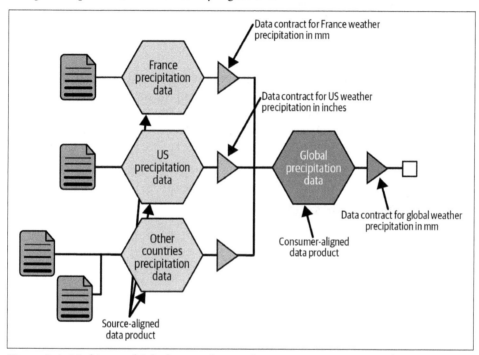

Figure 8-4. Meshing multiple data products to have consistent output and SLAs

There are different types of data products: the data products closer to the source are often called *source-aligned* data products while the one next to the consumer is *consumer-aligned*.

Building this architecture is easier than building a new data product from scratch. In this scenario, the global precipitation data product reuses the output data contract of each data product, simplifying the development of the internals of the global precipitation data product, such as the data pipelines. Figure 8-5 illustrates this process.

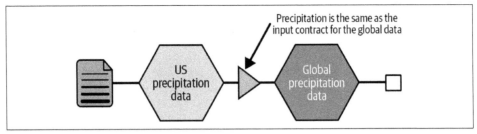

Figure 8-5. Sharing data contracts

When you look at the structure of the data product description using ODPS, you see that the output contract of the US precipitation data product has a UUID ending in e778 in Example 8-1. The same ID is used in Example 8-2 for the input of the global precipitation data product. Of course, the version (1.0.0 here) should match as well.

Example 8-1. The US precipitation ODPS file

```
name: US precipitation
id: da6025e9-695b-4022-85ee-695fc2aa0004
kind: DataProduct
apiVersion: 1.0.0
versions:
- version: 1.0.0
  in:
...
  out:
  - contractId: 06648f07-b3d9-4eb9-a990-6065fccce778
    version: 1.0.0
```

Example 8-2. The global precipitation ODPS file

```
name: Global precipitation
id: 303dc6c6-3763-4e71-9ecb-7df268720de7
kind: DataProduct
apiVersion: 1.0.0
versions:
- version: 1.0.0
  in:
  - contractId: 06648f07-b3d9-4eb9-a990-6065fccce778
    version: 1.0.0
  out:
...
```

You now have a clear lineage between your two data products in your Data Mesh.

Describing Your Data Lineage

Data Mesh can simplify data lineage in many ways. Let's take a closer look at lineage: what it is, why it's complex, and how Data Mesh can help.

Data lineage is the process of tracking data as it flows from the source (or producer) to the consumer. This should include all transformations that the data underwent along the way. It answers the questions of how the data was transformed, what changed, and how. It gives precious information about the data, and it is compulsory in some regulated industries.

Data lineage is hard because it involves tracking complex and dynamic data flows across diverse sources and systems, each with unique formats and processes. The continuous evolution of data environments coupled with the extensive manual effort required for accurate documentation add to the difficulty, as does integrating lineage information from various tools and maintaining up-to-date records.

Figure 8-6 illustrates a simple scenario where an application dumps a file, an ingestion pipeline takes it and stores it in a database in its raw form, and then a data quality and transformation process puts it in its consumable form so that an application can use it. In this scenario, data is transformed twice. The transformation itself is hidden in the code.

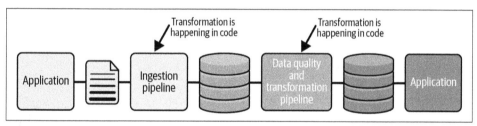

Figure 8-6. Simple scenario to illustrate data lineage

A similar scenario, illustrated by Figure 8-7, uses data contracts and data products. First, you have the lineage for the data product, as described in the previous section. You can track what is coming in and out of each data product. If needed, data contracts can provide a detailed description of the transformation that can be used in a very thorough lineage.

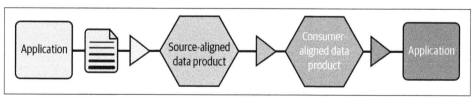

Figure 8-7. Simple scenario to illustrate data lineage using data contracts and data products in a simplified example of Data Mesh

Second, data contracts can track the transformation field by field, as shown in Example 8-3, using ODCS v3.0. For a given column, you can define its source tables, the transformation logic, and a description. You can also leverage external definitions and references (aka authoritative definitions) through the `authoritativeDefintions` block to track additional information. As the Bitol Technical Steering Committee (TSC) works on future versions of ODCS, lineage will be enhanced.

Example 8-3. Focus on transformation in an ODCS file

```
schema:
  - name: tbl
    properties:
      - name: txn_ref_dt
        transformSourceObjects:
          - table_name_1
          - table_name_2
          - table_name_3
        transformLogic: >-
          sel t1.txn_dt as txn_ref_dt from table_name_1 as t1, table_name_2 as
          t2, table_name_3 as t3 where t1.txn_dt=date-3
        transformDescription: Defines the logic in business terms.
        authoritativeDefinitions:
          - url: 'https://example.com/asset/742b358f-71a5-4ab1-bda4-dcdba9418c25'
            type: businessDefinition
          - url: 'https://github.com/myorg/myrepo'
            type: transformationImplementation
```

As you can see, Data Mesh will easily provide a better lineage.

Notification Through the Mesh

Let's look at another benefit of using data products: user notifications. You'll also learn how to implement these, as you'll see in Figure 8-8. The mechanism for notifying your users about a problem (email, Slack, SMS, carrier pigeons, or even Teams) is outside the scope of this book, but we'll focus on how to identify who needs to be notified.

Figure 8-8 shows an implementation of Data Mesh. We have eight data products using four data sources and, in this scenario, only one application consuming from data product H.

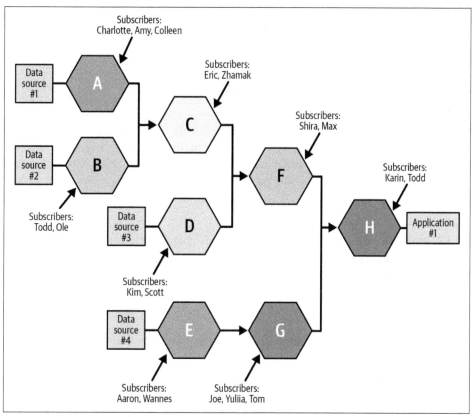

Figure 8-8. An implementation of Data Mesh with its subscribers

Imagine the scenario where data source #3, which is feeding data product D, has an issue. The issue could be nonavailability (like a database being down) or an SLA not being matched (for example, the data arrived too late). The users subscribe to the data products as they find them through the marketplace, so the system knows who to talk to. Figure 8-9 illustrates the fault lineage with the appropriate subscribers to notify when an issue with data source #3 occurs: Kim, Scott, Shira, Max, Karin, and Todd will be notified.

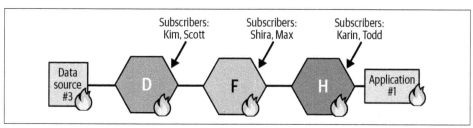

Figure 8-9. The faulty lineage with its subscribers

In a traditional system, only the direct users of data source #3 would be aware of the issue.

Reporting Issues

We recently worked with a company that is expected to make monthly reports to a US agency. A problem appeared in early September: the August report was not sent with the proper values. The problem was quickly fixed after the discovery, and the September report was delivered correctly. The forensic analysis showed that a data source had not been behaving as expected since July 4. By using data contracts and data products, this problem—and potentially many others—would have been avoided.

In a Data Mesh implementation, users are known and identified. This also applies to applications: users can subscribe in the same way to applications and be notified when the data is not as expected.

Summary

Data products are fantastic, but with little effort, you can multiply their value by assembling them in a mesh.

There are two main types of data products: the ones closer to the source are called *source-aligned* data products while the ones next to the consumer are *consumer-aligned*. Data Mesh can normalize data from source-aligned data products to consumer-aligned data products. This will normalize SLAs, data quality, and more.

Data Mesh simplifies data lineage. In addition to the nice-to-have information that lineage provides, some regulated industries require it, which alone may justify a Data Mesh implementation.

Finally, by enabling notifications, Data Mesh can warn users and applications early of the data's unavailability or subpar quality.

PART III

GenAI, Teams, Operating Model, and Roadmap for Data Mesh

Once you have a basic Data Mesh in place, how do you successfully use generative AI (GenAI) and set up the teams, operating model, and roadmap required to establish, nurture, and grow your Data Mesh? This part details the processes for making data products discoverable, observable, and secure to foster a more agile and efficient data ecosystem; proposes a dynamic platform for data discovery and sharing while minimizing metadata duplication; explains decentralized, agile governance through self-serve capabilities and certification; describes creating efficient "data product factories"; explores how combining Data Mesh with GenAI enhances decision making; focuses on the sociotechnical aspects of implementation; outlines a decentralized, domain-centric approach; and provides a structured, multistream plan for implementation.

Chapter 9, "Running and Operating Your Data Mesh", explores how to make data products discoverable, observable, and secure, highlighting the dynamic nature of data within Data Mesh, the crucial interfaces and processes involved in ensuring seamless operation, and the opportunities for enhanced data management through standardization and self-serve capabilities, all of which ultimately foster a more agile and efficient data ecosystem.

Chapter 10, "Creating a Data Mesh Marketplace", addresses the challenge of finding data products in a growing Data Mesh ecosystem by proposing a Data Mesh Marketplace, which, unlike traditional data catalogs, provides a dynamic, user-friendly platform for data discovery, consumption, and sharing that leverages self-serve capabilities and minimizes metadata duplication.

Chapter 11, "Establishing Data Mesh Governance", explains how the self-serve capability and embedded agents within dynamic data products facilitate a more agile, federated approach to data governance, emphasizing certification for compliance, which decentralizes policy enforcement to DPOs while maintaining centralized policy definition.

Chapter 12, "Understanding Data Product Supply Chains", explains how the embedded services and self-serve capabilities of data products enable the creation of consistent, efficient, and repeatable "data product factories" and establish a dynamic data supply chain ecosystem analogous to modern manufacturing supply chains.

Chapter 13, "Integrating Data Mesh and Generative AI", reveals that by combining the decentralized wonders of Data Mesh with the mind-blowing capabilities of GenAI, organizations can turbocharge their data-driven decision-making processes, creating a future where even your data products have the brains to make your business smarter!

Chapter 14, "Establishing Data Mesh Teams", emphasizes that successful Data Mesh implementation relies 20% on technology and 80% on winning over people, with data product teams acting like autonomous "data product factories" within a sociotechnical ecosystem while interacting with platform and enabling teams to create a flourishing data-driven environment.

Chapter 15, "Defining a Data Mesh Operating Model", explains how Data Mesh requires a shift from traditional centralized data management to a decentralized, domain-centric approach, involving the creation of an operating model that aligns people, processes, and technology to manage, share, and utilize data products efficiently across an organization.

Chapter 16, "Establishing a Practical Data Mesh Roadmap", outlines a pragmatic roadmap for Data Mesh implementation, emphasizing the need to balance technology, organizational culture, data product creation, and governance, structured into parallel work streams (technology, factory, operating model, and socialization) to build a scalable and efficient Data Mesh ecosystem.

CHAPTER 9

Running and Operating Your Data Mesh

At this point, you have read the chapters on data product and Data Mesh architecture as well as on how to define data products using data contracts, how to build data products, and how to bind your data products into a broader Data Mesh. In this chapter, we'll explore how to run and operate your data products: how to make your data products discoverable, observable, and secure. And then we suggest that Data Mesh and data products make data "dynamic"—that data is not just inert bits on a storage medium but rather that the Data Mesh principles of clear boundaries and a self-serve capability introduce a whole new set of opportunities.

Making Data Products Discoverable, Observable, and Secure

Adopting a Data Mesh model brings unique challenges and opportunities, requiring a comprehensive reevaluation of how data is approached, handled, and leveraged within an organization. At its core, the Data Mesh philosophy views data not merely as a static resource but rather as a dynamic, valuable product with its own lifecycle. This perspective demands a holistic understanding of various key themes: observability, operability, security and identity management, performance management, and day-to-day governance. Each of these themes plays a pivotal role in ensuring that a Data Mesh operates efficiently, securely, and in alignment with the organization's broader objectives.

Observability within Data Mesh is essential for gaining deep insights into data usage and quality management. This theme emphasizes the need for comprehensive monitoring and analytics capabilities, enabling organizations to understand and optimize the flow and utilization of data across various domains. In parallel, operability focuses on Data Mesh's ability to rapidly detect, notify, and resolve operational issues, ensuring minimal downtime and maximum efficiency. It involves creating a responsive system capable of identifying and addressing outages and anomalies swiftly.

Security and identity management in a Data Mesh context are critical, involving stringent measures to ensure that data access is both authenticated and authorized. This theme underscores the importance of robust security protocols and identity management systems, safeguarding sensitive data against unauthorized access and breaches. Performance management, another key area, revolves around understanding and enhancing Data Mesh's capabilities, focusing on scalability and efficiency to meet evolving organizational needs. Finally, day-to-day governance is integral to maintaining compliance with regulatory and enterprise policies, requiring continuous monitoring and adaptation to ensure that Data Mesh aligns with established standards and practices.

As we explore these themes in the following sections, we aim to provide a comprehensive guide for effectively running and operating an enterprise Data Mesh. By integrating technology, process, and people considerations into each aspect, the goal is to unveil a pragmatic approach that not only addresses the immediate operational needs but also paves the way for future scalability and adaptability in the ever-evolving world of data management.

Data Product Discovery Interface

In terms of consumption, once a user locates their desired data product in the Data Mesh Marketplace, they can directly access its "discover" feature, shown in Figure 9-1. (Note that the discovery interface is depicted as /discover, which is illustrative since a real discovery interface will be more complex.) This interface is implemented in the data product gateway mentioned in Chapter 4. Since the /dis cover interface usually does not convey sensitive information, it is typically accessible without special authentication and authorization requirements (although this isn't always the case).

This interface is more than just a gateway to the data; it's an intuitive guide that provides a comprehensive overview of the data product. It offers essential details (or links to this information), such as data structure, data contracts, usage guidelines, any relevant metadata, and even data lineage. This level of detail is invaluable for users, particularly those who may not have deep technical expertise but need to understand the data for practical applications.

The /discover interface enhances the consumption of data by providing not just metadata but also contextual insights. This means that users see the ingested data as well as descriptions, references to guides, tutorials, and any other information about how the data product can be applied in various business scenarios. This context is particularly important for users who may be exploring data outside their immediate area of expertise. By offering metadata, sample data, or other information related to your data products, the /discover feature helps users see the broader implications and potential uses of the data, thereby expanding the utility and impact of the data across the enterprise.

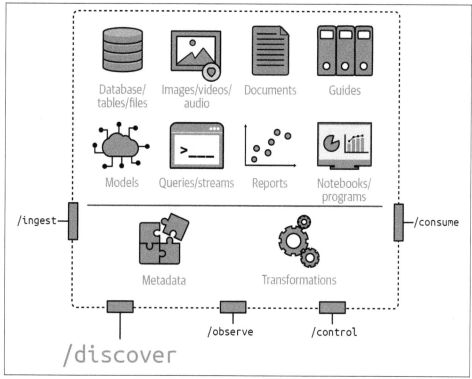

Figure 9-1. The /discover interface

In essence, the /discover feature addresses the challenge of making complex data understandable and usable for a broad spectrum of users. By providing a user-friendly, informative, and context-rich interface, the /discover feature not only democratizes data access but also enhances the overall quality of data-driven decision making within organizations. As such, it is a key component in realizing the vision of a data-empowered enterprise where all members can effectively harness the power of data for their specific needs.

Data Product Observability Interface

A data product is made observable, which means that its operating state is made visible via an /observe interface, shown in Figure 9-2. (This is a conceptual interface, as it will be more complex in an actual environment.) This interface is implemented in the data product gateway mentioned in Chapter 4. Since the /observe interface usually doesn't convey sensitive information, it is typically accessible without special authentication and authorization requirements (although this isn't always the case).

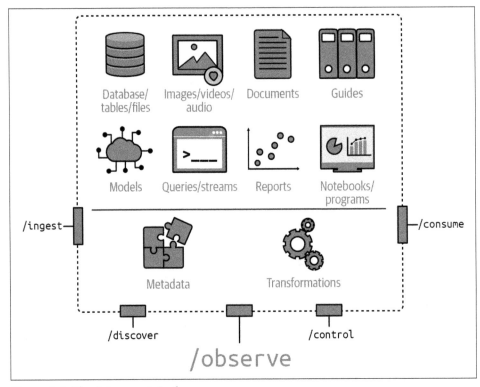

Figure 9-2. The /observe interface

Making data products "observable"[1] is a multistep process that involves capturing, normalizing, and consolidating a wide range of operational information about a data product and then making that information accessible. However, the distributed nature of data products in a Data Mesh requires a nuanced approach to observability, one that accommodates the autonomy of different domains while maintaining a cohesive view of the entire system.

This is achieved through the integration of advanced monitoring tools and analytical frameworks within the Data Mesh architecture. These tools must be capable of capturing a wide array of data points—ranging from usage statistics to performance metrics—thus offering a granular view of the data product's health, usage, and operating characteristics.

---

1 To learn more about observability, we recommend *Fundamentals of Data Observability* by Andy Petrella (O'Reilly).

Observability offers insights into the operating characteristics of data products. These encompass a range of information types, including usage statistics, performance metrics, and service-level compliance. The parameters and methods for observing these characteristics are typically outlined in a data contract. The contract specifies which aspects of the data product can be observed and how they can be monitored, whether through APIs, notifications, logs, or other means.

Still, the core of observability is to capture events relevant to the data product. Let's start with Figure 9-3 and explore what this means.

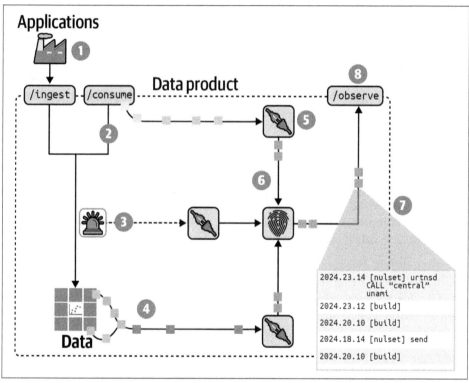

Figure 9-3. Data product observability

The process of observability begins with the fundamental interactions that applications have with data products. These interactions (step 1 in Figure 9-3) occur through two primary interfaces: /consume and /ingest. (Note that these interface endpoints are illustrative and real endpoints will be more complex.) At this point, relevant information or events regulated to data ingestion or consumption characteristics are captured (step 2), including metrics such as the volume of data ingested and its adherence to quality objectives (as measured against a data contract, for example). This data can reveal insights into user behavior, peak usage times, and potential bottlenecks in data access.

Alongside access requests, all alerts or operating exceptions that occur within the data product are also captured (step 3). These alerts can indicate issues such as service disruptions, problems with data integrity, or security breaches. By tracking these exceptions, administrators can quickly respond to and resolve issues, minimizing their impact on the data product's operation and users.

Another critical component of observability is capturing data changes (step 4). This step involves monitoring any modifications to the data within the product (for example, via a "change data capture" capability or transactional requests against data) as well as messages generated by applications interacting with the data. This information is useful for diagnosing data-product errors while also vital for tracking the evolution of the data over time and understanding how interactions with the data product might affect its content and structure.

The next step in the observability process involves normalizing the captured data—access requests, alerts, exceptions, data changes, and application messages—into a harmonized observability event format (step 5). This harmonization provides a consistent event format that simplifies monitoring and analysis of the data product's operation.

After normalization, all observability events are consolidated (step 6). This consolidation involves aggregating the events into a centralized repository or system where they can be accessed and analyzed collectively (step 7). This step is essential for providing a comprehensive view of the data product's operational state, as it brings together diverse data points into a cohesive whole.

The next step in the process is making all normalized observability events available through the /observe endpoint (step 8). This endpoint serves as the primary interface for accessing observability data. It gives users the ability to query and retrieve information about the operational characteristics of the data product, offering insights into its performance, usage, and any issues that may have arisen.

The /observe endpoint can be implemented in a couple of different ways, depending on the needs of the users and the design of the data product. One common implementation is as an API that operates on a request-response model. Users can send requests to the API to retrieve specific observability data, and the API responds with the requested information. This model is suitable for scenarios where users need to pull specific data points on demand.

Another implementation of the /observe endpoint is as a subscription service. In this model, users subscribe to receive notifications about observability events. Whenever an event occurs that matches the user's subscription criteria, the user is notified automatically. This approach is particularly useful for real-time operational monitoring, as it allows users to be promptly informed of operational changes or issues as they happen.

The benefits of observability in Data Mesh are clearly multifaceted. With a clear, real-time view of data dynamics, organizations can make more informed decisions, enhance data quality, and optimize system performance. Observability supports the agile, responsive nature of Data Mesh, allowing organizations to adapt quickly to changing data needs and market conditions. Furthermore, it plays a crucial role in governance and compliance, as the visibility it offers ensures adherence to data policies and regulatory requirements. In essence, effective observability transforms Data Mesh from a mere architectural model into a dynamic, intelligent system that continuously evolves and adapts, driving the organization toward data-driven excellence.

Data Product Control Interface

Controlling a data product is implemented in a /control interface, shown in Figure 9-4. (This is a conceptual interface, as this is expected to be more complex in an actual environment.) This interface is implemented in the data product gateway mentioned in Chapter 4.

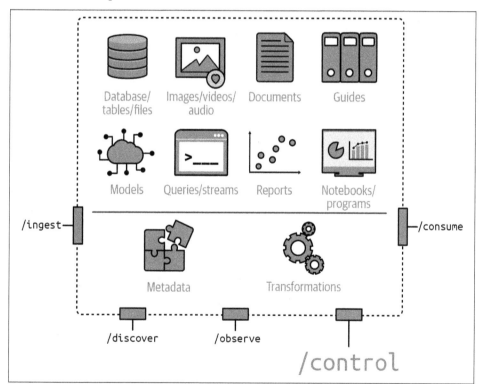

Figure 9-4. The /control interface

Control interfaces in the context of data products let DPOs manage the operational state of their data products. This interface addresses a range of functionalities, including the following:

- Start the data product (conceptually, a `/control/start` interface), which marks the data product as available in the Data Mesh Marketplace
- Stop the data product (conceptually, a `/control/stop` interface), which marks the data product as unavailable in the Data Mesh Marketplace
- Configure a data product by facilitating changes to various settings and parameters (conceptually, a `/control/configure` interface)

Since the control interface can change the state of the data product, it is usually accessible only with appropriate authentication and authorization.

Data Product Security

Security and identity management in a Data Mesh environment is a complex yet critical area that requires a multifaceted, comprehensive approach. In a Data Mesh, where data is decentralized and distributed across various domains, the challenge lies in maintaining a cohesive security posture while allowing for domain-specific requirements and autonomy. More specifically, the data product's data contracts define data product service levels and quality characteristics and are implemented at the boundary of the data product, as shown in Figure 9-5. We have a full chapter on data contracts (Chapter 5), so we won't repeat what we have already written, but rather we'll provide a more detailed view on the security and privacy considerations of data contracts within a data product.

The security and privacy of data within data products are crucial, driven by various factors that include regulatory compliance, competitive advantage, and protection of proprietary knowledge. Data contracts—which can be defined at the data-product level or for an individual artifact within a data product—play a crucial role in facilitating security and privacy measures in data products. But these contracts are not just administrative documents; rather, they are active components that directly influence the security posture and privacy standards of a data product.

In fact, data contracts are embedded within the data products themselves. This integration ensures that the security and privacy policies defined in the contract are inherently linked to the data product. Whenever a data product is accessed, the access rights and permissions are governed by the stipulations laid out in its data contract, ensuring that every interaction with the data product is evaluated and managed in accordance with the predefined security and privacy standards.

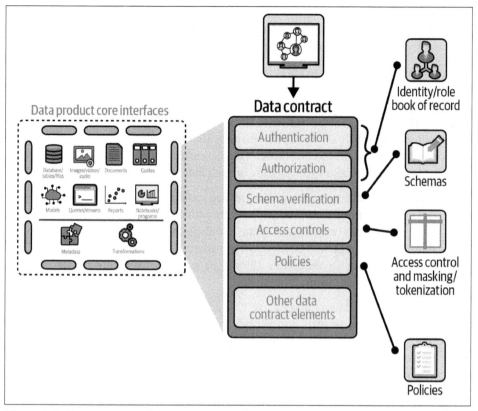

Figure 9-5. Data contract–driven security and privacy

Clearly, the scope of data contracts extends beyond simple access rights. Data contracts encompass a variety of elements, including service-level expectations and usage norms. For the purposes of security and privacy, data contracts define specific policies and standards that must be adhered to when interacting with the data product. These policies cover a wide range of security aspects, ranging from the overall architecture and data-handling processes to specific technical, governance, and/or privacy and regulatory safeguards.

A fundamental requirement for ensuring the security and privacy of data products is a robust authentication and authorization mechanism. The data product's security profile maintains links to an identity book of record, which lists authorized users and their respective roles. This linkage is crucial to ensure that only authenticated and authorized individuals can access the data product, and even then, only in ways that align with their defined roles and permissions.

The structure of the data within the data product, defined through schemas, is also a critical component of security and privacy. These schemas, which are part of the data contract, specify which attributes are available to data product consumers and producers. This level of control helps enforce data governance policies and ensure that sensitive data is not exposed unintentionally.

Granular control over data access is now a fundamental requirement when accessing sensitive or confidential data. Data contracts enable this by allowing for a variety of security policies, including, for example, role-, row-, or attribute-level security policies. They can also specify methods for obfuscating data, such as masking or tokenization, to protect sensitive information. By defining these policies within the data contract, organizations can enforce tailored security measures that align with the specific characteristics and requirements of each data product.

Finally, data contracts in concert with related policy-enforcement capabilities are instrumental to aligning data products with broader enterprise, regulatory, and privacy constraints. They ensure that data handling within the product adheres to applicable laws and regulations as well as internal organizational policies. This is particularly important in industries subject to stringent regulatory requirements, such as finance and health care.

It is safe to say that data contracts are a key facet (although not the only one) of the implementation of security and privacy in data products. They ensure that every interaction with the data is governed by well-defined rules and standards, offering a comprehensive framework for managing access, protecting sensitive information, and complying with regulatory requirements. By embedding these contracts within the data products and aligning them with industry best practices, organizations can achieve a high level of security and privacy assurance.

That being said, there are still other security techniques available within a data product that do not rely on the data contracts and should be seriously considered for all data products: techniques such as implementing strong encryption protocols for data at rest and in transit and ensuring that sensitive information is shielded from unauthorized access. In terms of artifacts generated by data products, access logs and authentication protocols are indeed cornerstones of security in a Data Mesh. Access logs provide an audit trail of who accessed what data and when, which is invaluable for detecting and investigating unauthorized access or data breaches.

The process and organizational component of security and identity management involve regular security audits and compliance checks tied to suitable governance and certification mechanisms (which are addressed in more detail in Chapter 11). Given the distributed nature of data in a Data Mesh architecture, these audits must be comprehensive and frequent, ensuring that each domain adheres to the established security standards. Compliance with relevant data protection regulations, such as GDPR or HIPAA, is not optional but rather a mandatory aspect of these processes. Organizations must establish clear guidelines and procedures for handling data, including protocols for responding to security incidents. This ensures a standardized approach to security across all domains while allowing for the flexibility needed to address domain-specific challenges.

Climate Quantum Use Case Considerations

Climate Quantum implements a variety of discover, observe, and control interfaces, as shown in Figure 9-6.

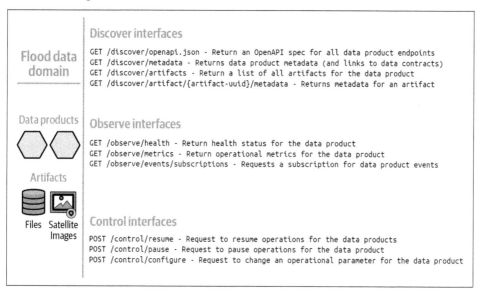

Figure 9-6. Climate Quantum interfaces

The discover interfaces retrieve information about the data product (listed with the HTTP verb and then the path):

GET /discover/openapi.json
> Returns an OpenAPI specification for all data product endpoints

GET /discover/metadata
> Returns data product metadata (and links to data contracts)

GET /discover/artifacts
> Returns a list of all artifacts for the data product

GET /discover/artifact/{uuid}/metadata
> Returns metadata for an artifact

The observe interfaces retrieve information about the data product's operating characteristics:

`GET /observe/health`
Returns health status for the data product

`GET /observe/metrics`
Returns operational metrics for the data product

`POST /observe/events/subscriptions`
Requests a subscription for operational events for the data product (subscriber endpoints are in the POST body)

The control interfaces manage the data product's operating characteristics:

`POST /control/pause`
Requests pausing of data product operations (the data product gateway stops processing requests)

`POST /control/resume`
Requests resuming data product operations (the data product gateway once again accepts requests)

`POST /control/configure`
Requests changing an operating characteristic for the data product

Toward Dynamic Data Products

We have discussed key interfaces related to discovery, observability, and operability and shown them to be crucial to successful data products. But their benefits do not stop there—in fact, data products make data "dynamic." The point in naming it this way is that there is a stark contrast between data products and their consistent embedded capabilities for facilitating understanding and interaction among many diverse data products. In comparison, a typical multivendor enterprise environment would have many inconsistent—and probably proprietary—interfaces, making it difficult to offer discover, observe, and control interfaces and capabilities.

Data Mesh principles provide a path to dynamic data products: clear boundaries for data, owners empowered and accountable to make decisions on the bounded data, and a delegated, federated governance model providing a level of trust. These principles create the necessary conditions for data products that make data discoverable, observable, and operable, and the standardization offered through these interfaces makes it easy for data products to interact and be assembled like building blocks into larger solutions. In a word, data products allow data products to make data dynamic.

But there's more. The catalyst for "dynamic data products" lies in the self-serve capability that makes it easy to find, consume, and share data products, facilitating a level of interaction and transaction that goes beyond traditional data management techniques.

The discovery capability "self-describes" how data—through a data product—can be understood and consumed. It offers contracts that "self-describe" quality and service-level expectations but also provide a built-in mechanism of "self-enforcing" those data contracts. The boundary of a data product offers a single "self-enforcement" point for security and privacy. The observability capability offers a "self-describing" mechanism to understand the data product's health and operating characteristics. And the operability capabilities offer a "self-publishing" mechanism to issue alerts when the data product recognizes it is not within operating characteristics or when important events (security violations, for example) occur.

The Power of Dynamic Data Products

So it's probably clear that the "dynamic" nature of data products offers benefits, but by abstracting away from the underlying (varied and at times proprietary) technology, it also fosters consistency and standardization, which are crucial for creating a unified, efficient data ecosystem. Consistency across data product interfaces (discovery, observability, and operability as well as ingestion and consumption) provides the uniformity needed to simplify many aspects of data management—such as integrating into pipelines, querying data, governing data, and training users—and lays the groundwork for creating composable data solutions.

Standardization facilitates the creation of templates for data products, significantly easing the process of building and deploying new data assets. These templates act as blueprints, ensuring that new data products are developed with consistency in quality and functionality. Using templates streamlines the development process, reducing the time and resources required to bring new data products to fruition.

Uniform interfaces, a product of standardization, enable seamless interaction between different data products. This interoperability is crucial for building integrated data systems that are more than the sum of their parts. Moreover, standard interfaces allow for implementing consistent security policies across the data ecosystem.

Summary

Hopefully, you agree that the dynamic nature of data products provides, among other things, a set of consistent and standard building blocks. But what can we build with them? For starters, dynamic data products make it easy to build lightweight marketplaces that are a window into your Data Mesh. Dynamic data product–powered factories transform custom, bespoke software-delivery processes into streamlined, manufacturing-style operations. And dynamic data products upend traditional centralized governance into a federated "certification" process. We will elaborate on each of these topics—marketplace, factories, and certification—in the next few chapters.

CHAPTER 10

Creating a Data Mesh Marketplace

As Data Mesh matures in enterprises, we see data products grow from proofs of concept and MVPs into a flourishing ecosystem of interacting data products. But with this success, enterprises face another set of challenges. Although the proliferation of data products is a sign of a healthy, vibrant Data Mesh ecosystem, it also brings the problem of finding data products in this growing ecosystem. Perhaps this is obvious, but without effective ways to find data products, the benefits of Data Mesh cannot be fully realized.

In this chapter, we discuss the challenges with traditional data catalogs and then illustrate how Data Mesh offers new opportunities in what we call a *Data Mesh Marketplace*. We will explain how the Data Mesh Marketplace is a window into your Data Mesh that makes data products (and the data within them) easy to find, consume, and share.

Challenges with Traditional Data Catalogs

We find that as organizations try to make data discoverable, they fall back on older practices, which is all fine and good except when the older practices are flawed and when there are obvious opportunities to change. So not surprisingly, we see "traditional" data catalogs being considered to maintain and manage data products, as shown in Figure 10-1. (To be clear, the use of the term *traditional* is not meant in a pejorative manner. Rather, these catalogs serve an especially important role for data governance and even data engineering in non–Data Mesh environments.)

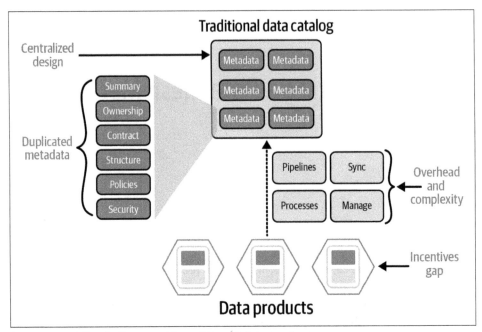

Figure 10-1. The challenges with traditional data products

Traditional data catalogs have a centralized design that requires metadata to be shipped to them and duplicated in a central repository. This introduces overhead and complexity as metadata is moved from its source—in the data (or database)—into the catalog.

Next, let's consider issues arising from centralized ownership, the typical model for traditional data catalogs. The central group must coax the actual owners of the data—those in distributed groups or business units—to provide the data in a timely fashion and fix migration issues when they occur. This creates a gap in incentives (and hence, priorities), as somewhat disengaged third parties (the distributed groups and business units) are encouraged to get engaged in this migration exercise.

According to Conway's law (*https://oreil.ly/Iu1aU*), an organization's systems will reflect its communication and organizational structure. This centralized approach creates an incentives gap that leads to a clash at the crossroads of different organizational domains, with issues around control, incentives, priorities, and funding cropping up, complicating an already challenging landscape. Now, if there is minimal investment and processes are simple, then there are fewer issues—funding, support, and timeliness of fixes—but, as stated earlier, this is rarely the case.

Perhaps most important, these challenges foster a costly, slow, bureaucratic, and complex approach that stands in stark contrast to business's demand for speed and agility. This alone is a nearly insurmountable challenge!

We humbly suggest that the traditional data catalog architecture, predicated on a central repository and at times complex data-migration needs, does not take advantage of the dynamic, self-serve, discoverable, and observable nature of data products. But what type of "catalog" can take advantage of this dynamic capability? Is there a solution that does not duplicate metadata but rather goes directly to the source (the data product) when it is needed? Is there a solution that takes advantage of a standard, consistent set of discovery capabilities that gets metadata from the source rather than requiring complex (and costly) data migration?

Enter the Data Mesh Marketplace.

The Data Mesh Marketplace

The Data Mesh Marketplace is a platform that simplifies interaction with data products for all users within an enterprise—it makes data easy to find, consume, share, and trust. The Marketplace is a full participant in an enterprise's Data Mesh and acts as a "window" into your Data Mesh. It is one of the primary ways to interact with your Data Mesh and caters to a wide range of users, from data scientists to business analysts to data product owners and administrators.

Let's explain this a bit more. Data products—or more specifically, "dynamic" data products, as we see them—by definition incorporate a consistent, self-serve set of interfaces for discovery, observability, and operability. These interfaces shape the user's interaction with Data Mesh, acting as standardized touchpoints for accessing and managing data.

The discovery and self-registration interfaces in particular play a crucial role. The discovery interface enables users to find relevant data products easily, making navigation through the vast data landscape straightforward and efficient and significantly enhancing the user experience. The self-registration interface allows data producers to register their products, making them available to be found.

The combination of these interfaces creates a "two-sided marketplace" (going forward, we will just call this a "marketplace"). To better understand our proposed marketplace, consider Amazon, a large online store. Amazon provides a platform (the portal, or online storefront): a centralized location to browse, search, and purchase a wide array of products. This centralized location offers a similar experience to all consumers. Amazon also provides a consistent experience for product sellers, making it easy for sellers to create and update product information (metadata) within the Amazon store. And it offers an "observability" interface that lets sellers understand their sales and other characteristics of the consumer's buying experience.

To be sure, this marketplace is not a new concept. While Amazon may be one of the most well-known examples, digital marketplaces are becoming commonplace. For example, as shown in Figure 10-2, Uber is a ride-sharing platform with a mobile app that is a two-sided marketplace enabling those who want a ride (consumers) to find, interact, and transact with those who want to offer rides (producers). Another example is Airbnb, which provides a marketplace that lets those who want to rent a place to stay (consumers) find, interact, and transact with those who want to offer their places for rent (producers). Perhaps the most famous example is Apple's App Store, where software developers (producers) publish their apps and then people (consumers) pay for and use the apps.

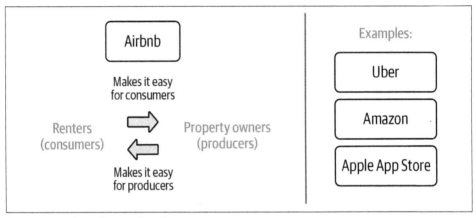

Figure 10-2. Popular marketplaces

Our Data Mesh Marketplace offers similar capabilities—a two-sided marketplace—for data products. It makes it easy for consumers to find data products, understand how to consume them, and, ultimately, consume them. And it makes it easy for producers to publish data products that are made available in the Data Mesh Marketplace.

A Window into Data Mesh

We suggest a two-sided marketplace, modeled on the same high-level capabilities and model as Airbnb, as the right approach for a Data Mesh Marketplace.

The Data Mesh Marketplace, as shown in Figure 10-3, sits on your Data Mesh's communication backbone and is accessible by any consumer or producer (subject, of course, to your organization's security posture). At the heart of the Data Mesh Marketplace is a user-friendly graphical interface designed to make the process of finding data as intuitive and straightforward as possible (note, however, that in most cases the Marketplace has a corresponding CLI as well as a standard set of APIs that make it accessible to administrators and other applications as needed).

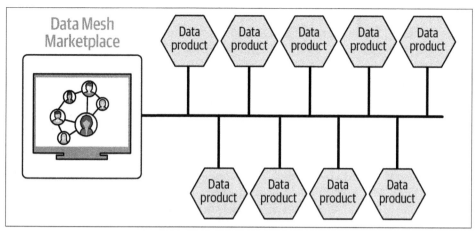

Figure 10-3. The Data Mesh Marketplace: a window into Data Mesh

This interface is more than just a static directory of data products; it incorporates advanced search functionalities, leveraging the power of natural language processing and semantic search technologies. These technologies allow users to conduct searches in a way that mirrors human communication, making it easier for them to find the data products that best match their requirements.

Let's dig a bit deeper into its design, starting with Figure 10-4.

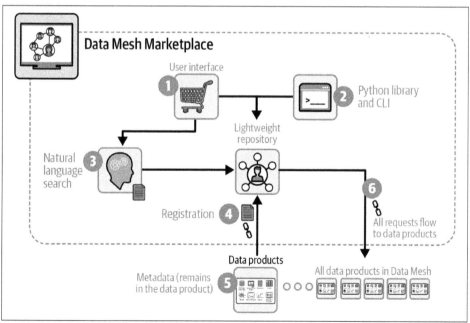

Figure 10-4. The Data Mesh Marketplace design

The design of the Data Mesh Marketplace centers on providing a seamless, intuitive user experience, reminiscent of familiar online marketplaces (step 1). This approachability is critical for ensuring that the Marketplace is accessible to a wide range of users within an enterprise, regardless of their technical expertise. The interface is designed to be simple and user-friendly, enabling users to navigate it easily and find the data products they need. This simplicity plays a vital role in fostering a self-serve consumer experience. Users can independently explore and interact with the data products available in the Marketplace, facilitating a more efficient and empowered approach to data utilization.

For administrative and advanced users who require a more robust interaction with the Data Mesh Marketplace, the platform offers command-line and Python library interfaces (step 2). These tools cater to users who are more technically proficient, allowing them to execute more complex operations and automate tasks. This level of access, combined with the user interface, is crucial for enabling a truly "self-serve" approach for all users, as it provides the flexibility to interact with the Marketplace in a way that best suits each user's skills and needs. By offering both a user-friendly interface and more advanced tools, the Marketplace ensures that it meets the diverse requirements of its user base.

Integrating natural language search capability into the Marketplace experience marks a significant enhancement in how users find data products (step 3). This technology allows users to search using conversational phrases and questions, making the process more intuitive and aligned with natural human communication. Additionally, data product summaries are "vectorized" and stored in a vector database, which supports the natural language search by providing more accurate and relevant search results. This advanced search functionality considerably reduces the time and effort required to locate the right data products, making the Marketplace experience both efficient and user-friendly.

The Marketplace is designed to make the job of the DPO (the "publisher" in marketplace lingo) as easy and simple as possible. Owners are required to provide only short, two-paragraph summaries of their data products and artifacts (although they can add more if they choose), along with relevant links (step 4). This minimal requirement is intentionally designed to enable a self-serve DPO experience. By reducing the burden of registration, the Marketplace encourages a wider range of data products to be shared, enhancing the diversity and richness of the data available to users.

This design choice is intentional to ensure that the Marketplace remains streamlined and easy to navigate. Users are presented with just enough information to understand what a data product entails and how it might be relevant to their needs, without being overwhelmed by excessive detail while making it easy to navigate when more information (about artifacts, for example) is needed. It should be pointed out that when requests are forwarded to data products and responses are received (step 5), this information is rendered in the Marketplace using a consistent look and feel, leading to a simpler and better user experience. And this approach avoids the duplication of metadata (as well as the overhead and issues that it creates).

When users request more detailed metadata or want to acquire data from a data product, the Marketplace facilitates this by providing direct links (step 6) to the actual data product (via the previously mentioned discovery interface). This design ensures that the Marketplace itself remains uncluttered and focused on discovery and initial evaluation while still providing easy access to more detailed information and data retrieval. This streamlined approach respects the user's time and attention, guiding them efficiently to the resources they need.

We believe that the implementation of a Data Mesh Marketplace represents a different and, we think, much more effective method of publishing and consuming data products in a Data Mesh. By addressing the core challenges of finding, consuming, sharing, and trusting data, the Data Mesh Marketplace not only enhances efficiency but also reinforces the integrity and usability of data within an enterprise.

The Consumer User Journey

The goal of the Data Mesh Marketplace for consumers is to make the data products in a Data Mesh easy to find and use. This consumer journey map, shown in Figure 10-5, presents a structured pathway that data product consumers—from analysts to data scientists—navigate in order to locate, understand, and consume data products within their own domains of expertise.

To remove obstacles to the user of the Marketplace, all consumers are typically able to get access to the Marketplace site with few-to-no restrictions (step 1). The user begins with an introductory screen that provides an overview of the Marketplace. At this point, users are encouraged to explore guides and tutorials that help them understand how to use the Marketplace (step 2).

The next set of steps allow users to interact with the Marketplace and data products, which typically requires user authentication and authorization. A simple login (step 3) is offered that asks a user to provide their credentials. In many cases, this aligns with an enterprise's single sign-on posture.

After the consumer logs in, the interface offers a personalized dashboard (step 4), containing information about data products that the user has indicated their interest in or is consuming or observing. This dashboard reflects a commitment to delivering a tailored experience that values the user's time and the unique context of their data requirements.

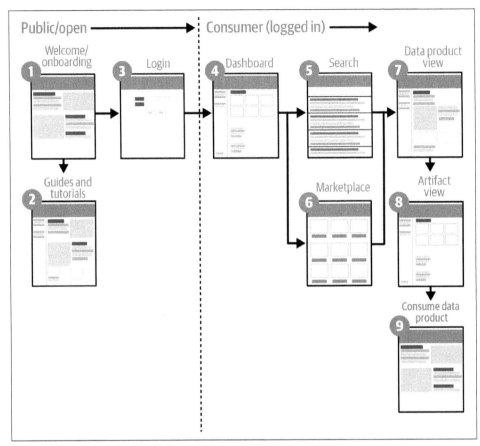

Figure 10-5. The Data Mesh Marketplace: consumer user journey

At this point, the consumer is able to search for data products. This is accomplished in two ways: through a search capability (step 5) or via a user-friendly Marketplace experience (step 6). With search, the user can enter a natural language expression (we see GenAI LLMs and vector databases providing this capability), which will return a list of data products that match the search request. Users are presented with a list of data products in the Marketplace interface, each with a tile containing summary information. In organizations with many data products, a basic hierarchical filter mechanism can be used to narrow the larger list of data products into a more manageable list based on topic areas.

At this point, the consumer can select a data product (from either the search list or the Marketplace tiles) and view information about the data product (step 7). Depending on how the data product is defined (for example, it may represent many files, many tables, or many images), the user can view artifacts and examine detailed information about data (for example, metadata, sample data, etc.) within the data product (step 8).

Once the user has confirmed their interest in a particular data product's artifact, they can consume the artifact (step 9). What it means to "consume" an artifact is actually a DPO's decision. In some cases, we see consumers actually download data; in other cases, especially with large amounts of data (such as satellite images in the climate data landscape), consumers "order" data much like in an online store, with the data being delivered asynchronously to a designated storage area; and in other cases, where data is in a database, the consumer is permitted to query the data via SQL.

The Producer User Journey

The goal of the Data Mesh Marketplace for producers is to make data products easy to share. The producer journey map, shown in Figure 10-6, starts like the consumer journey: they are presented with a public, open marketplace (step 1) overview and are provided access to guides and tutorials (step 2).

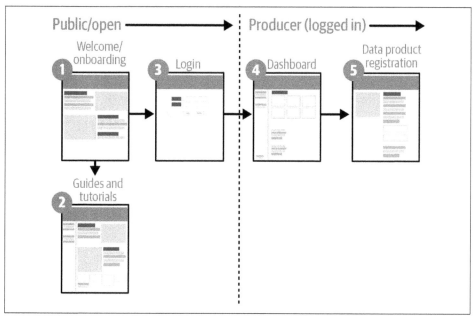

Figure 10-6. The Data Mesh Marketplace: producer user journey

Once the producer has logged in (step 3), they see a dashboard (step 4) listing only their data products. (Note: a user may be both a consumer and a producer, but depending on the role they play, they see different dashboards.) At any point, the user can drill down on one of their individual data products and view information about it (step 5), including, for example, usage statistics, consumer feedback, and so on.

The key differentiator in the producer journey is that producers are able to publish their data products, which makes the data products available in the Marketplace.

Let's dig a bit deeper into this core capability.

Self-Publishing of Data Products

The Data Mesh Marketplace has been designed with a fundamental focus on simplifying the data-sharing process within an enterprise. One of its most notable features is the streamlined system it provides for data owners to share their data products. This system is engineered to be user-friendly, allowing even those with limited technical expertise to navigate the process with ease.

Data owners can create a data product configuration through a simple, guided process. This involves defining the parameters of the data product, such as its scope, access permissions, and any relevant metadata. The interface is intuitive, making the configuration process straightforward, efficient, and quick.

The rapid publication capability of the Marketplace is another key characteristic that facilitates easy data sharing. Once a data product is configured, it can be published and made available in the Marketplace in a relatively short time frame—often within minutes. This rapid turnaround is significant, as it ensures that data can be shared and accessed quickly, fostering a dynamic and responsive data environment.

Let's take a look at the self-registration, or data product publishing process, enabled by the Data Mesh Marketplace, as shown in Figure 10-7.

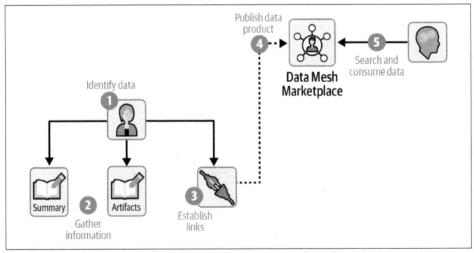

Figure 10-7. Data product self-registration

The self-registration process is owned end-to-end by the DPO. The process starts rather simply with the identification of a data product (step 1), its purpose, its boundaries, and the data within those boundaries.

With this basic information in hand, data product team members gather basic information about the data product (step 2):

- A list of artifacts, or data elements, within the data product, including databases, tables, files, images, guides, and any other type of content that may be relevant to the data product

- A basic summary description of the data product that makes the data product not only searchable but, when found, useful to the consumer

- Links to "discoverable" information (step 3) about the data product, including (but not limited to) metadata

The data product summary and the discoverable links are registered in the Data Mesh Marketplace (step 4). These discoverable links are crucial since they are registered to the Marketplace and provide a way to actually retrieve information about the metadata. It is important to note that links to the metadata, not the actual metadata, are registered.

A related but very important point is that only a simple data product summary is registered. Why? Well, a two- to three-sentence summary will rarely change. Hence, the registration not only is simplified but, in many cases, is a one-time event. Obviously, should this basic summary change, the DPO can reregister their data product.

Once the data product is registered, a consumer can find and consume it (step 5).

The Power of Discoverability

The dynamic nature of data products—more specifically, their discoverability—allows us to provide a new and different way of opening a window into our Data Mesh. Where traditional data catalogs duplicated metadata extensively across the enterprise into a central repository, the Data Mesh Marketplace keeps metadata at its source—in the data products. When a data product is "registered," the Data Mesh Marketplace knows where its metadata exists and reaches out, as and when needed (typically, when a user views the Marketplace). There are no duplications of data, no costly pipelines for keeping a central metadata repository updated, and no stale data.

In its design and functionality, the Data Mesh Marketplace bears a closer resemblance to real-world marketplaces like Airbnb or Uber than to traditional data catalogs. And like these real-world marketplaces, the Data Mesh Marketplace has consumers (those who find and consume data products) and producers (those who create data products). In some implementations, we have seen this extended to allow data products to be "purchased" via a shopping cart and ordering-checkout process similar to real-world marketplaces.

Since Airbnb is so well known, we will use this real-world example to draw an analogy to the Data Mesh Marketplace. Let's start with making properties known to Airbnb or, in our terminology, the "publishing" process. The secret ingredient to Airbnb's success is that it delegates almost all operational capabilities—selling rentals, updating information about rentals, and so on—to property owners. It offers a relatively simple "publish" experience to get properties onto the Airbnb platform.

But Airbnb also makes it easy for those rental publishers to understand their sales and the buying experience, and it provides the tools they need to market their properties. It has a "self-serve" platform where almost all of the sales activities are completed without intervention from Airbnb. And it provides the "observability" required to allow rental property owners to understand their sales and the customer feedback needed to be successful.

Now, let's examine the consumer experience. In Airbnb, it's all about search. The platform lets users search for rental units, and it returns properties that match the customer's needs. It also offers hierarchical categories that make it easy for customers to narrow their search.

Airbnb doesn't stop there. It encourages reviews to help customers find high-quality properties. It also offers tons of information about each product, making it easy for customers to be confident in their purchases. And it provides a simple shopping experience and feedback mechanisms that make it easy for customers to find ideal properties and trust that they will get what they pay for.

Finally, Airbnb has strategically placed incentives in the right place: rental property owners are motivated to keep their info updated and highly reviewed, and consumers rent properties with better information and reviews.

But what does the Airbnb platform look like? It is first and foremost a user interface for both consumers and producers, but it is also a platform that delegates or federates the end-to-end sales process. It works because Airbnb has deployed a unique technique and platform that makes it easy for consumers as well as producers to find one another, interact, and transact. All the while, it provides the tools that deliver an outstanding consumer and producer experience while keeping the incentives aligned properly.

Now, let's map this example to our Data Mesh Marketplace. Our marketplace is composed of, minimally, the following components, as shown in Figure 10-8:

- Data products (obviously) and a communication backbone that lets them (and users) interact

---

- A two-sided marketplace that makes it easy for data consumers and producers to find, consume, share, and trust data
- A registration mechanism to let producers register and publish their data
- A discovery mechanism to let consumers find data

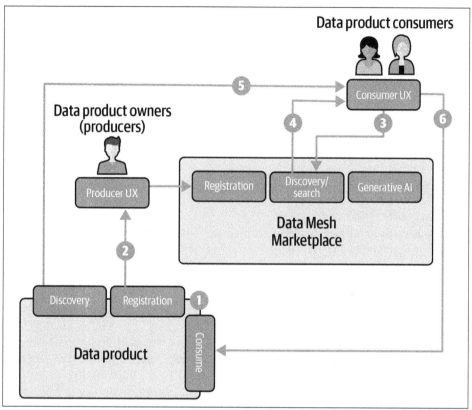

Figure 10-8. The Data Mesh Marketplace architecture

Let's walk through the marketplace information flow:

1. DPOs define the data product's scope and boundaries and provide standard discovery and registration services (as well as consumption services).

2. DPOs register the data product as well as a link to its discovery service endpoint using a simple user interface offered by the marketplace. Once the data product is registered, consumers can search for and find it in the marketplace.

3. A data consumer searches for a data product and finds one of interest.

4. The marketplace returns the discovery endpoint link.

5. The marketplace issues a request to the data product discovery service, which then returns metadata about the data product, including links to other services (for example, consumption services).

6. The user now has the consumption endpoint (and presumably, links to consumption documentation) and can consume the data product.

Bootstrapping Your Marketplace

Building a marketplace from scratch is not necessarily trivial, but it is not that complex and, until commercial or open source products become available, it can be built relatively quickly from relatively common components. In fact, we have built these marketplaces several times with small teams (two to three people) in about three to four months, and they are well worth the effort. But if you have to prioritize, we suggest an approach that will allow even the smallest firms to build a Data Mesh Marketplace.

Mandatory capabilities should include the following:

Consumer user experience
A basic frontend can be built from React (*https://react.dev*) and Material UI (*https://oreil.ly/APSBB*) (pick your favorite framework), which provides the consumer user experience. You can get something built quite easily and quickly using modern AI tools such as ChatGPT (*https://chatgpt.com*). This makes data products easy to find and consume.

Publisher user experience
Some might say that the publisher user experience would be an optional component. This is a mistake—in fact, the power of the marketplace is the fact that it addresses both consumer and publisher needs, and it focuses on making data products easy to publish and share. Building this capability can be done using the same approach as the consumer user experience, but we have also seen success with offering a command-line publisher user experience that can be developed very quickly and cost-effectively.

Registry
The registry keeps track of data products. For this, just about any database will do, but simple database tools such as SQLite (*https://sqlite.org*) and DuckDB (*https://duckdb.org*), or any cloud native database, can maintain information about data products.

An optional capability might be natural language search using vector databases (and even LLMs), which would not be necessary for environments with a modest number of data products.

Climate Quantum's Data Mesh Marketplace

Let's now apply the Data Mesh Marketplace to the scenario we are using in this book: Climate Quantum's Marketplace.

In this scenario, our challenge is to create a marketplace for literally thousands of distinct data sources, each consisting of different formats, structures, and versions as well as varying volumes that change daily and are owned by thousands of unrelated data owners. Fundamentally, this is a *discovery* as well as an *integration* challenge. However, the complexity is increased because of the volume, versioning (in some cases, data formats change and schema versions need to be maintained to be able to read older data), and variability of climate data. And with no overriding standard data format, the cost and effort required to harmonize this data makes this a nearly impossible challenge.

The first step in addressing this challenge is discovery. Assuming that discovery can be addressed, then integration can follow. So our solution is composed of, minimally, the following components:

- Climate data that has a boundary, owner, and self-serve capability, or more specifically, climate data products

- A two-sided marketplace that makes it easy for climate data consumers and producers to find, consume, share, and trust climate data

- A registration mechanism to enable producers to register and publish their climate data

- A discovery mechanism to let consumers find climate data

Let's start with our climate data products. Since almost all climate data is available on the internet, we have a basic "self-serve" (via a website) capability. And since each website and its associated data has a boundary and the owner has dictated the scope of its website, we can probably safely make the case that we already have real climate data products.

Next, it is not overly complex to build a two-sided marketplace. We need a user interface for climate data producers to register and share their data products and a user interface for consumers to find and consume the data products. The key design challenge is how to get federated, potentially uninterested parties to register their data products and make them discoverable. We need a solution that makes it simple, extremely low cost, and easy to provide discovery and registration services that connect to and surface data products for our marketplace.

There are probably two approaches to doing this. First, we could get the thousands of climate data providers to adopt a common data standard, but this is highly unlikely. In an enterprise, this would be like expecting all data providers (database vendors, file formats, images, etc.) to adopt a single standard—and as much as some vendors say they have this, to date there is no widely adopted standard or product that implements a standard.

Or we could try a second approach: provide a lightweight service on top of climate data that is extremely simple (and low cost) and, importantly, must not require any changes to existing data and related services. Rather, we need only provide an interface to surface metadata that is general enough for many use cases but is also simple and lightweight enough that it is easy to implement. This is the essence of what we mean by a "self-serve" data product platform.

This is a relatively simple solution to implement and does not require consensus from thousands of climate DPOs. It can be deployed quickly, incrementally, and cost-effectively as a single lightweight microservice. The beauty of this is that while we haven't fully overcome the incentive challenge, we have dramatically reduced obstacles to connecting data producers and consumers by offering a simple, easy-to-use marketplace, with no need to change or modify data, that provides a low-cost, consistent, standard service that makes it easy for a motivated data curator to cheaply and quickly add innovative services on top of a common set of climate data.

The culmination of all this—Climate Quantum's Marketplace—is shown in Figure 10-9.

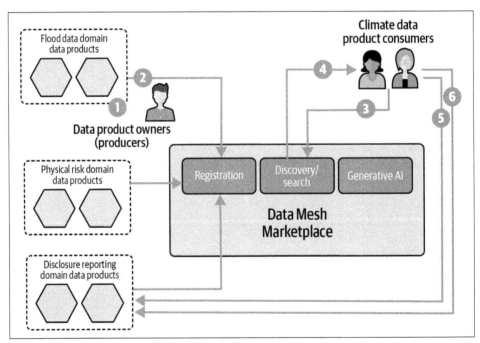

Figure 10-9. Climate Quantum's Data Mesh Marketplace

Let's walk through the information flow for Climate Quantum's Marketplace:

1. Climate DPOs from various domains define their data products' scopes and boundaries and provide standard discovery and registration services (as well as consumption services).

2. Climate DPOs register/publish their data products, along with a link to the data product's discovery service endpoint, using a simple user interface offered by the marketplace. Once the climate data product is registered, consumers can search and find it in the marketplace.

3. A climate data consumer searches for a climate data product and finds one of interest.

4. The marketplace returns the discovery endpoint link.

5. The marketplace issues a request to the climate data product's discovery service, which then returns metadata about the climate data product, including links to other services (for example, consumption services).

6. The user now has the consumption endpoint (and presumably, links to consumption documentation) and can consume the data product.

Summary

In this chapter, we addressed a particular challenge confronting a successful, growing Data Mesh: how to find data products using a Data Mesh Marketplace. But this marketplace is not a traditional catalog, where metadata needs to be migrated into a central repository and thus incur the overhead and synchronization challenges. Rather, it is a lightweight window into your Data Mesh that capitalizes on the "dynamic" nature of data products by fully taking advantage of their self-serve nature while also providing a compelling experience for the consumer as well as the data producer, thereby making it easy to find, consume, and share data.

CHAPTER 11

Establishing Data Mesh Governance

In Chapter 9, we highlighted that there is a fundamental difference between data and data products: data requires an external agent to make the data usable, and data products have an embedded "agent" (the data product gateway introduced in Chapter 4)—their discoverability, and observability, supported by a self-serve capability—that allows them to interact on their own. We have suggested that this capability makes data products "dynamic."

Dynamic data products are equipped with a self-serve capability, including interfaces for discovery, observability, and control. These interfaces provide capabilities that aid in governance of Data Mesh and data products. In this chapter, we will extend this self-serve capability with an additional "certification" interface that makes the data-governance process much more agile.

Data Governance

Data governance is responsible for defining and enforcing data policies across an organization. It addresses many topics, typically implemented as policies, that include (but are definitely not limited to):

- Data privacy and security
- Data provenance and lineage
- Data service levels and quality
- Data pricing and licensing

Data governance is a set of processes, roles and responsibilities, and policies that ensure the effective, efficient, and safe use of information within an organization in a fashion that adheres to the organizational strategy, goals, and objectives.

The implementation of data governance leads to several key outcomes that benefit an organization. One of the primary advantages is improved decision making. Access to high-quality data enables business leaders and professionals to make more informed and effective decisions. It also significantly reduces the risks associated with data management, particularly those related to compliance with legal standards, thereby avoiding potential financial and legal repercussions. Additionally, effective data governance fosters operational efficiency by streamlining the management processes and ensuring data transparency, allowing all stakeholders to have a clear understanding of data-related practices and policies.

It is important to note that data governance as a discipline is wide-ranging and comprehensive, and Data Mesh will not be able to influence the entire scope of data governance. But which parts of this discipline can Data Mesh affect? What can be made more agile and fast?

We will see that core Data Mesh principles lead to clear data boundaries, empowered data owners, self-serve capabilities, and—importantly—a federated governance capability, all of which establish an agile mechanism for data governance.

Data Product Certification

Data Mesh delegates responsibility for ensuring compliance with policies to the individual data products. Here, the DPO plays a crucial role—they are responsible for the data product's functionality and performance and also for automating its governance in code.

The owner "certifies" (we will elaborate on this term later) the compliance status of the data product, a process that involves determining, publishing, and regularly refreshing this status. This certification ensures that governance is not an afterthought but rather an integral part of the data product's lifecycle. Certification is:

- A proactive declaration of the data product's compliance with organizational policies and standards
- An automated approach that makes it easy to capture a data product's governance status (is it compliant or not) as well as to publish its status to interested parties
- An ability to query a data product's governance status at any time, by anyone (within the organization's security and privacy posture, of course)

This approach to certification realizes modern governance capabilities by balancing policy definition (centralized) with policy implementation and enforcement (federated). By decentralizing the responsibility and embedding it within each data product, organizations can realize the goal of data governance organizations everywhere: to create a more dynamic and responsive governance model.

We differentiate our approach by calling it *certification* instead of *governance* (although, strictly speaking, it is still data governance). This emphasizes how Data Mesh's federated nature allows data products to become self-contained units of governance that are continuously monitored and updated with their governance status published to reflect the latest compliance status.

To contextualize this concept, consider Figure 11-1, where we show existing "certification" capabilities for real-world products. UL Solutions (*https://www.ul.com*) and ANSI (*https://www.ansi.org*) in the US, CSA (*https://oreil.ly/Lw_Kf*) in Canada, and various agencies in the European Union (most countries or regions have something like this in place) all provide real-world product-certification services.

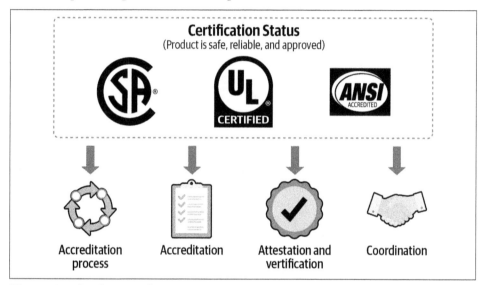

Figure 11-1. Product certification

These organizations define, in participation with industry, fully delegated "certification" models in which standards are described, organizations are identified to participate in the certification process, product owners attest to and publish their certification statuses, and, in some cases (for critical data), groups verify their attestation through rigorous testing for compliance with safety and quality standards. Perhaps just as important, these organizations work with other global governance organizations to coordinate international standards, which simplifies the sales and use of products in other markets. After certification, product owners can attest to their compliance (the certification brand/label) as not just a simple indicator of compliance but also a badge or label that makes an explicit claim for a product's conformance to standards and expectations.

Similarly, for Data Mesh, the automated data product certification model delegates the responsibility of adhering to governance standards for each data product. This delegated certification model ensures a consistent level of compliance across all data products, akin to how certified electrical appliances assure a standard level of safety and quality so that you can plug in a certified device anywhere that meets a designated specification. This analogy helps illustrate how intelligent data product certification can standardize governance across a Data Mesh, ensuring that each data product meets the set enterprise policies and standards.

Federated Data Product Certification

In a federated governance model, policy definition remains centralized to ensure that broader organizational and regulatory visibility is required. However, the enforcement of policies is decentralized and delegated to DPOs.

Data Mesh principles empower this model. The federated governance model—in particular, its near-complete delegation of responsibility to the DPO—is aligned to the concept of domain ownership. DPOs have full responsibility for and autonomy over policy enforcement for their data assets. This autonomy enables teams to define, produce, and serve their data products while aligning with organizational policies. The self-serve data infrastructure principle supports this by providing teams with the tools and platforms to govern their data independently.

The shift to federated governance empowered by Data Mesh is marked by a change in how data products are accredited and how to attest to a certification status. The coordination process for accreditation is shown in Figure 11-2.

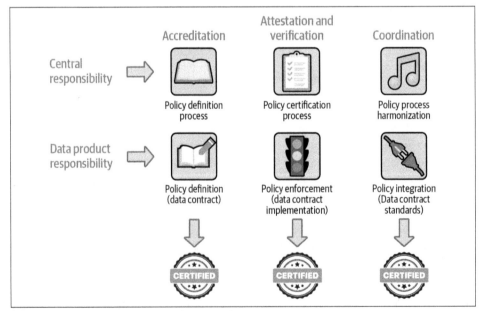

Figure 11-2. Delegated data product certification

Nevertheless, while Data Mesh delegates the enforcement of policies to DPOs and their teams, a central group still defines and manages the accreditation process, attestation groups, and related coordination process (and defines global policies and standards).

A data product team is responsible for self-certification of its data product by:

- Participating in the accreditation process (defining policies via data contracts)
- Implementing, attesting to, and publishing the certification status (via implementation of data contract enforcement and publication of certification results)
- Integrating policies with the broader enterprise (participation in data contract standardization)

This self-certification empowers data product teams, giving them both the responsibility and the autonomy to ensure that their data products meet the required standards. One of the significant benefits of this approach is the increased agility and responsiveness it brings to data governance. In a rapidly changing data landscape, the ability of individual teams to certify their products places the burden of quality on producers and reduces the time and bureaucratic overhead typically associated with centralized governance models.

Another advantage is the heightened sense of ownership and accountability among teams. When teams are responsible for certifying their data products, they are more likely to be diligent in adhering to standards and policies. This sense of responsibility leads to higher-quality data products, as teams understand that they are directly accountable for the trustworthiness and reliability of their data.

Certification also fosters a culture of transparency in data governance. By having clear, automated, and rigorous processes for certification, all stakeholders within the organization gain visibility into how data products are validated against established standards. This transparency builds trust not only within the organization but also with external parties who rely on the organization's data.

For data consumers within and outside the organization, certification provides a clear indication of the trustworthiness of data products. Just as (Canadian) consumers trust a CSA-certified electrical appliance, stakeholders can trust a certified data product, knowing that it meets established quality and compliance standards. As regulatory landscapes evolve, especially concerning data privacy and protection, having a robust certification process enables organizations to swiftly adapt and ensure that all data products remain compliant with new regulations.

Implementing Data Product Certification

To implement data product certification, we have added a "certify" endpoint (conceptually, /certify, but this will likely be different in a realistic scenario), as shown in Figure 11-3. This interface is implemented in the data product gateway mentioned in Chapter 4.

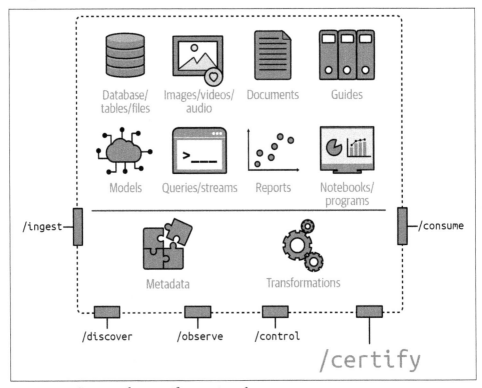

Figure 11-3. Data product certification interface

The certification interface lets DPOs manage the certification status of their data product. The interface addresses a range of functionalities, including the following:

- Publish the data product certification, which sends a report describing the certification status (i.e., its compliance to policies) to a designated recipient
- Automatically execute policy enforcement checks at regular intervals and store the status and reports for further publication or review
- Get the certification status of the data product (conceptually, a /certify/status interface), which returns a simple "OK" or "NOT COMPLIANT"
- Get the certification report for the data product (conceptually, a /certify/ report interface), which returns a detailed report outlining full compliance for

the data product (for example, individual policies would be marked as certified or not)

Data Contracts and Certification

Things get interesting (at least from a certification perspective) when we inject data contracts between the interface and the actual data, as shown in Figure 11-4: we get a natural policy enforcement point.

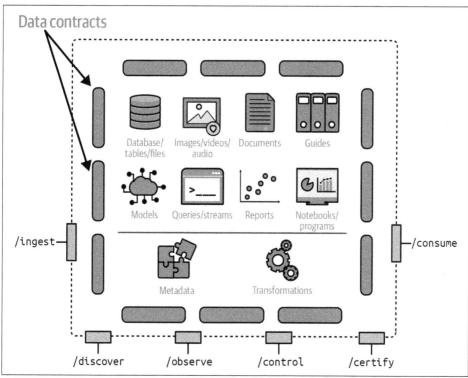

Figure 11-4. Contracts as policy enforcement points

Data contracts essentially set the ground rules for how a data product should function and how it should be interacted with. As outlined in previous chapters, a comprehensive description of these elements forms the backbone of a data product's operational framework. In this context, our data contracts—as part of the ingestion and consumption flow—intercept or at least have visibility into each request going into and coming out of the data product. This gives data contracts their superpower: they provide the foundation for assessing each and every interaction with a data product through the lens of policies defined in the data contract.

They don't just assess the requests, though. Minimally, they can log requests that deviate from data contract policies: perhaps data in a request did not fit the profile expected for it, or maybe a nonnullable field was presented as null. In some cases, the deviation is material enough that a request is rejected, awaiting future diagnostics before being processed. Or maybe a user requested data that required elevated privileges that the user did not have, in which case the request was rejected.

The information collected through these data contract policy enforcement points is stored and then made available using the /certify interface.

Climate Quantum's Certification Approach

Climate Quantum addresses several aspects of data governance, implemented using our certification approach:

Data service levels and quality
Ensure that climate data is available, reliable, and timely

Data provenance and lineage
Ensure that there is a "chain of evidence" between interacting data products that demonstrates where data came from and how it has been transformed

Data pricing and licensing
Ensure that users can access data while respecting climate data licensing and pricing schemes

Data privacy and security
Ensure that only authenticated and authorized users can access climate data

The policy definition, accreditation, and harmonization processes as well as macro-level policies are defined by the Climate Data Authority, a central group that dictates broad climate data guidelines ("use open data licensing schemes") and policies ("proprietary asset data must be obfuscated"), as shown in Figure 11-5. This group also determines how to define *certification* and establishes a third-party group that verifies certification claims and formally attests to data certification status.

In keeping with the federated and delegated nature of our certification approach, DPOs must implement data contracts and any other mechanisms required to enforce and report on policies defined by the central group. The DPO publishes their certification status regularly to the central group but also makes it available via the certification interfaces to anyone who wants to review it. Climate data attestation and verification firms are assigned by the Climate Data Authority to verify claims made by the DPOs, thereby providing an independent perspective regarding the trustworthiness of a climate data product.

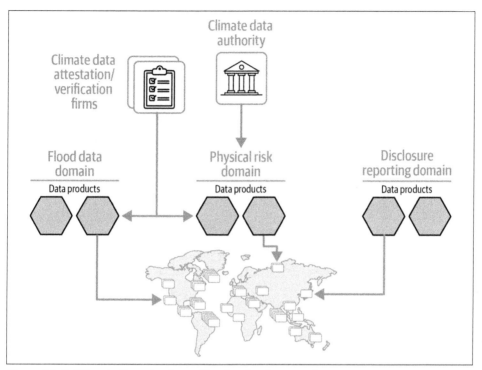

Figure 11-5. Climate Quantum's certification implementation

Summary

In this chapter, we highlighted that the self-serve nature of data products coupled with the local autonomy and authority invested in DPOs permits a new way of approaching data governance. We introduced an approach that we call *certification*, which uses the power of Data Mesh principles in a way that makes data governance agile.

CHAPTER 12

Understanding Data Product Supply Chains

In Chapter 9, we showed that data products have embedded services that make them discoverable, observable, and certifiable. These services are supported by a self-serve capability, which allows data products to interact in a consistent and trusted fashion on their own. In this chapter, we will demonstrate that this capability enables "data product factories" that can create data products in a consistent, efficient, and repeatable fashion. Then, we will explain how the embedded services in data products enable the interaction needed for a modern software supply chain.

The Modern Manufacturing Supply Chain

The assembly line became the symbol of a new era of manufacturing, epitomizing efficiency and standardization. Pioneered by the likes of Henry Ford in the automobile industry, it revolutionized production by breaking down the manufacturing process into simple, repetitive tasks. This system enabled the mass production of goods at unprecedented speeds and significantly reduced costs. Products that were once luxury items, accessible only to the affluent, became available to the general public.

The assembly line also introduced a new level of precision and uniformity in products, eliminating the inconsistencies that are a natural part of handcrafted goods. This shift not only changed production methods but also had profound social and economic impacts, leading to the rise of consumer culture and the modern industrial economy.

The integration of multiple individual factories into a modern manufacturing supply chain, shown in Figure 12-1, created a highly integrated, complex network to manage the flow of materials, information, and finances from raw material acquisition to the delivery of finished products. This involves a sequence of steps: sourcing of raw materials, fabricating parts, assembling final products, and distributing products to consumers. Basic parts and raw materials are offered by specialized "Tier 3" suppliers. Then, multiples of these suppliers supply further specialized suppliers ("Tier 2" suppliers), which, in turn, supply "Tier 1" suppliers, until major components arrive at a Final Assembly Plant where they are assembled into a product offered directly to consumers or to dealers/distributors (who then offer the final product to consumers).

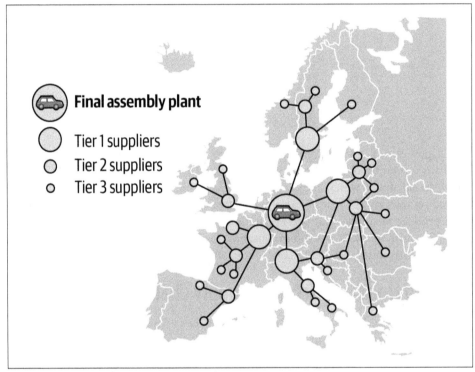

Figure 12-1. The modern manufacturing supply chain

There are several obvious benefits of this sophisticated supply chain. It allows for significant cost reduction through economies of scale and efficient resource use. At the same time, it enhances market responsiveness, enabling adjustments in production based on fluctuations in consumer demand. And we experience its benefits every day: the chain supports higher product quality and consistency, facilitates globalization by opening access to new markets and materials, and fosters innovation through technological integration.

Consequently, the modern manufacturing supply chain is not just a logistical framework but also a dynamic ecosystem of suppliers collaborating to efficiently create the goods that drive our economy.

The Modern Software Factory

The software development industry is shifting ever so slowly from a predominantly artisanal to a manufactured process. Traditionally, software development was approached in a manner akin to craftsmanship, with developers working on unique, bespoke projects. This method, while allowing for customized and specialized software solutions, was often slow and labor intensive, with a high degree of variability in quality and performance. As the demand for software grew, along with its complexity, this approach became increasingly unsustainable. The need for a more systematic, scalable approach became evident, leading to the adoption of principles akin to those of industrial manufacturing.

This necessity gave birth to the software factory (*https://oreil.ly/aZhtN*) model, a concept that draws heavily on the efficiencies of the industrial manufacturing process. Just as standardized parts and assembly lines revolutionized the production of physical goods, standardized coding practices, frameworks, and development tools have transformed software production. In this model, software is no longer crafted as a one-off artisanal product but rather is produced using standardized processes and components.

While the modern software factory emphasizes automation and tools, it does so to free individuals from repetitive tasks, allowing them to focus on creative problem solving and collaboration. Agile practices, defined in the Manifesto for Agile Software Development (*https://oreil.ly/a3xr5*), brought innovations in team size (smaller), individual empowerment (more), and collaboration (much more) to facilitate the local autonomy required for high-performing teams.

But where does Data Mesh fit in? How can the software-factory concept be applied to data products? What attributes of Data Mesh enable a more consistent and standard development of data products? Is there a natural analogy between the manufacturing supply chain and an ecosystem of data products? Let's explore deeper.

The Data Product Factory

Standardization enables the "mass production" of data products with consistent quality and functionality, allowing organizations to rapidly scale their data-product creation and management capabilities in a controlled, efficient manner. The factory model epitomizes the shift from artisanal, one-off data solutions to a systematic, industrial approach to data-product creation and management.

Our data product factory process, shown in Figure 12-2, is modeled on a simplified manufacturing factory process. The key superpower introduced by Data Mesh, and data products in particular, is the encapsulation of the data contract within the data product. The data contract becomes the glue that binds all stages of construction of the data product.

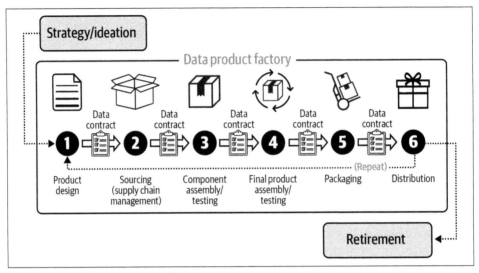

Figure 12-2. The data product factory

The preconditions for our data product factory are that a value proposition has been established based on the firm's strategy and that the data product has gone through an initial ideation phase. At this point, we have the basic inputs for our data product factory process:

Product design (step 1)
Our objective is to define a data product, including its boundaries, owner, and team structure. At this point, we create our initial data product definition, which explicitly includes a data contract that governs our data product's behavior, service levels, quality, and expected interactions.

Sourcing (step 2)
In this step, our objective is to identify the data sources, or our data product supply chain, and understand their formats, structures, and, if available, data contracts. The source's data contract defines all inputs, their formats, and service-level and quality expectations.

Component assembly and testing (step 3)
At this point, we want to build (and test) the component parts that will transform our raw source data into a more useful form (for example, we may aggregate fields or run data through a model to create derived data). The source data contracts inform how the components in our data product are built to adhere to

our data product's own data contract. Data contracts, especially the parts related to the consumer experience, inform how our interfaces are built.

Final product assembly and testing (step 4)
Here, we assemble (and test) the individual components into a set of capabilities that can be offered to our data product's customers. Our data contract becomes one of the foundational elements that enables the testing of our data product.

Packaging (step 5)
This is the step where we package our data product into a deployable unit that can be pushed into our production environment. Data contract elements that touch consumer-facing capabilities are once again verified, after which our data product is available for consumer usage.

Distribution (step 6)
In this step, the product is consumed by the data product customers. At this point, the data product is operational, capturing usage metrics and other performance statistics, which are made available through the data product's observe interfaces. These metrics, as well as any other relevant operational characteristics, are defined by our data contracts, assessed against the data contracts, and then surfaced with our "certify" interfaces.

As a last step, after the usefulness of our data product has diminished, our data product may be retired and decommissioned.

The Data Product Supply Chain

At its core, a manufacturing supply chain is an ecosystem of product suppliers, each responsible for delivering a component or service that together result in a final product. Similarly, a Data Mesh "supply chain" is an ecosystem of data products. Each data product, managed by a specific team or department, contributes to the overall data landscape of the organization, akin to how each supplier in a manufacturing chain contributes to the final product.

In the manufacturing supply chain, each supplier has a clear responsibility for the quality and integrity of its product. This ensures that the end product meets the desired standards of quality and functionality. In our case, each data product team is responsible for the quality and reliability of the data it provides. This responsibility extends to ensuring that the data is accurate, up to date, and relevant. We know from experience that, just as a defective component from a supplier can compromise the quality of a final product in manufacturing, poor-quality data can undermine decision making and analytics in an organization.

Now let's apply these principles to our data product's "supply chain":

- The data product supplier owns product quality. While the supplier and consumer jointly define product-quality metrics, once these are agreed to, no data leaves the data product until there is confidence that quality and service levels meet expectations.

- All data products make data available based on published data contracts. All data made available by the data product is governed by a published data contract, which ensures that all interactions are defined by well-known structures and formats as well as predetermined service-level and quality expectations.

- All data product shipments are tracked, or at least observed and/or logged (and probably tracked financially as well).

- The data product supplier tests product quality (hopefully using statistical processes) and publishes transparent quality and service-level attainment metrics.

Now we can see why Data Mesh is so powerful: it provides the principles, and thus lays the foundation, for consistent, bounded, owned, discoverable, and observable data products that bring our supply chain to life! Once again, the data contract becomes the glue that binds all data products to one another.

Climate Quantum's Data Product Supply Chain

Climate Quantum has data products that span the globe, as shown in Figure 12-3. Flood data domain data products are typically located in countries and regions that experience flooding events. Physical risk domain data products reside in financial centers where assets under risk are managed. Disclosure reporting domains reside in financial institutions that operate in each country and are subject to local regulations but own assets (in our case, those in the physical risk domain) that span the globe.

The unique aspect of Climate Quantum's supply chain is that it is almost 100% federated. This is perfectly adapted to Data Mesh principles that explicitly take into account the distributed ownership of data products. And it recognizes that each DPO needs explicit local autonomy to meet the needs of its shareholders, stakeholders, and local and regional regulators.

Climate Quantum uses data contracts to bind these discrete and largely independent data products. Data contracts are negotiated between individual data products to meet their individual needs. In fact, it is these contracts that bind data products, forming the web of interactions in a complex climate data ecosystem.

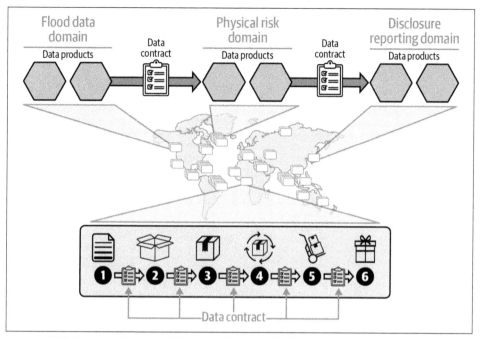

Figure 12-3. Climate Quantum's data product supply chain

Summary

In this chapter, we explained how Data Mesh principles, implemented in data products, enable powerful capabilities. Data product factories use data contracts to create data products in a transparent and efficient fashion. Data contracts streamline the communication between data products and efficiently bind data products together to create an end-to-end data product supply chain—an ecosystem of data products that we call Data Mesh.

CHAPTER 13

Integrating Data Mesh and Generative AI

Generative AI (GenAI) is emerging as a new foundational technology that is driving a wave of innovation throughout business and IT. By leveraging the capabilities of GenAI within the decentralized framework of Data Mesh, organizations are poised to unleash a torrent of innovation that has the potential to revolutionize their data-driven decision-making processes!

In this chapter, we explore how GenAI and older-style AI and machine learning (referred to collectively as "AI") can supercharge Data Mesh capabilities. We explain how Data Mesh, data products, and data contracts offer new capabilities to improve the quality of the data required to create accurate and useful AI models. We show how AI models can be offered as data product artifacts that complement the data already provided by data products. We illustrate how AI can be components of data products that permit transformation of ingested data into a form that drives value for data product consumers. Finally, we discuss how AI is used to complement the basic capabilities of data products.

Generative AI Background

Wikipedia defines *generative AI* (*https://oreil.ly/jTlRC*) as "artificial intelligence capable of generating text, images, videos, or other data using generative models, often in response to prompts." Wikipedia also states that GenAI "models learn the patterns and structure of their input training data and then generate new data that has similar characteristics."

GenAI has many uses today. It is used to create content, such as articles and reports. Models such as DALL-E (*https://oreil.ly/SdxRg*) can generate new images from textual descriptions, allowing artists to develop unique visuals and concepts quickly. GenAI is also used to create short videos or to enhance videos, with products such as

Sora (*https://oreil.ly/d02-T*) making it quite useful in filmmaking and advertising (although, at the time of writing this chapter, video capabilities were still early in their evolution).

But GenAI is not limited just to content creation. In health care, we see its use spanning many applications: models such as Google DeepMind's AlphaFold (*https://oreil.ly/6eKOi*) are used to generate new molecular structures that are expected to accelerate the identification of new drugs, and other GenAI models help enhance medical images and assist in diagnosing diseases.

These are just a few highlights. While GenAI is still in its early stages, it is probably fair to say that this capability has the potential to drive innovation across multiple industries.

So what are the technical components of GenAI? Broadly speaking, we can include several components in GenAI: LLMs, embeddings (floating point representations of text or other types of content) that are stored in vector databases, and related technologies and libraries. Let's establish a few definitions.

Large Language Models

A *large language model* is a type of AI system designed to process and interpret written language. An LLM is considered "large" because of its huge number of parameters (GPT-3 (*https://oreil.ly/NrsAX*), an earlier model, contained 175 billion parameters), extensive and diverse training data, complex and deep architecture, significant computational resource requirements, and scalability and performance capabilities. Today's most powerful LLMs are literally trained on virtually all data in the public internet. We're talking about billions of sentences or text snippets that the model uses to learn and become proficient in understanding how humans communicate through words.

Training an LLM is a complex, time-consuming, and costly exercise. During training, an LLM examines massive amounts of text to learn the intricate patterns and structures of language. It becomes an expert at analyzing grammar, context, and the meanings behind words and sentences. This extensive training enables the model to mimic humanlike language abilities, letting it communicate in a quite realistic conversational manner.

Several examples of LLMs include those available from OpenAI (*https://oreil.ly/UZdp7*), Google (*https://oreil.ly/zIiH1*), Hugging Face (*https://oreil.ly/4zaL3*), and others.

Embeddings

An *embedding* is a compact, continuous representation of data used to capture the essence or latent features of the input data. The goal of embeddings is to transform high-dimensional data, such as documents, images, and other content, into a lower-dimensional space, where each point in the embedding space corresponds to a specific data sample or object.

Embeddings in GenAI are essential because they enable the models to learn meaningful representations of the data, capturing important patterns and relationships. By learning a compact representation, generative models can generate new data that closely resembles the training data, allowing them to create realistic and diverse samples in various domains, such as images, music, text, and more.

There are several examples of embedding models, which are typically much smaller than their LLM cousins, available from OpenAI (*https://oreil.ly/Suhir*), Google (*https://oreil.ly/Bs6MH*), Anthropic (*https://oreil.ly/-jtjI*), and others.

Vector Databases

A *vector database* is a collection of vector representations, or embeddings, that encode various attributes, features, or characteristics of data. The superpower of a vector database is its ability to efficiently perform "nearest neighbor search." Imagine you have a massive dataset with thousands or even millions of data points, and you want to find the most similar or closest ("nearest neighbors") data points to a specific query point. The vector database can quickly identify the data points that are most like the query point based on their vector representations.

Beyond nearest-neighbor search, a vector database offers the benefit of efficient retrieval and manipulation of data. By storing data in vector representations, we can work with lower-dimensional, continuous representations of the original data. This can speed up computation times and allow us to perform tasks like dimensionality reduction, data clustering, and classification more effectively.

Vector databases are used to identify relevant "context" that accompanies a prompt, which is submitted to an LLM for processing. Common (as of this writing) vector databases include Pinecone (*https://oreil.ly/bTfrj*) and Chroma (*https://oreil.ly/PIJK1*), although this field is rapidly changing and undoubtedly many more will emerge.

Prompts

A *prompt* is the starting point for interacting with a GenAI model. It can be a question, a partial sentence, a phrase, or any other text that is submitted to the GenAI model. The prompt provides the necessary cues for the model to understand the desired output and generate content that is aligned with the user's expectations.

You have probably provided prompts if you have used common tools such as Open-AI's ChatGPT, which has a cloud-based LLM with a frontend that lets a user ask a question. The prompt is the text you enter that gets submitted to ChatGPT's LLM.

Challenges

Despite GenAI's seemingly great power, there are still gaps and limitations. An LLM can sometimes be unable to answer queries in a realistic manner, which is referred to as *hallucinations*. According to Google (*https://oreil.ly/YMWGB*), these hallucinations "can be caused by a variety of factors, including insufficient training data, incorrect assumptions made by the model, or biases in the data used to train the model. AI hallucinations can be a problem for AI systems that are used to make important decisions, such as medical diagnoses or financial trading."

There are also practical shortcomings for any but the largest of enterprises, as the costs and time involved in training LLMs are extensive, measured in the tens and hundreds of millions of dollars and many months of time. Today, only the large internet giants are able to make the investment necessary to create a competitive LLM.

In addition, there is a cutoff time when a LLM's training is completed and any information, data, or events after that cutoff period are omitted, which means the data that the LLM learns from might be outdated by the time the model is released. Language is dynamic, and current events constantly reshape the world we live in, so LLMs may struggle to keep up with trends, slang, or emerging concepts, leading to inaccuracies or outdated responses in real-world scenarios.

Another limitation is potential bias in the training data. Since LLMs learn from publicly available text data, they might unintentionally absorb biases present in the data sources. For instance, if a specific website or forum has a biased view on certain topics, the model could reflect that bias in its outputs, such as gender bias where models were trained on gender stereotypes like "traditional jobs," which may emphasize particular gender roles. As a result, LLMs might not always provide fully objective or balanced answers, which could be problematic, especially with sensitive or controversial topics.

Additionally, LLMs have been criticized for their inability to fully understand context or maintain coherent conversations over extended interactions, although this is changing as vendors optimize their LLMs. LLMs can generate text that seems impressive at first glance, but they may struggle to maintain context and relevance in more extended conversations, leading to responses that become nonsensical or irrelevant.

Finally, virtually all enterprise data—information about customers, products, employees, and so on—is considered private, sensitive, or confidential, meaning that LLMs today are not trained on enterprise data. So as with data, information, or events that emerge after the training cutoff period, LLMs are blind to enterprise data. Because LLMs don't have access to this proprietary information, their ability to provide precise answers or insights in certain enterprise-specific domains may be limited. There are solutions to this, such as fine-tuning (*https://oreil.ly/1OFBP*), where selected layers of a pretrained LLM are trained on new data, typically using content from verified sources to bind and constrain LLM responses.

Data Mesh and Generative AI

Data Mesh and GenAI together give organizations the foundational data platform to make it much easier for GenAI to find, consume, share, and trust enterprise data. Data Mesh, data products, and data contracts offer new capabilities for AI enablement:

- Improve data quality
- Elevate models as primary artifacts
- Consume models inside data products
- Generate data product code
- Complement data product capabilities

Let's dig a bit deeper into each of these.

Improve Data Quality with Generative AI

The adage "garbage in, garbage out" highlights the importance of quality data for achieving valuable outputs from AI models. Essentially, the better the data fed into an AI model is, the better the results it will produce. This principle underscores the necessity for meticulous data curation and management to ensure that AI systems operate effectively and generate meaningful insights.

Data Mesh advocates for a decentralized approach to data management, where individual teams take ownership of their data domains. This decentralized ownership encourages better maintenance and stewardship of data quality at its source. And data products are carefully curated datasets tailored to specific uses, ensuring that the data available is not only high quality but also relevant and fit for purpose.

In addition, data contracts provide clear agreements between data products (and data providers and consumers in general), outlining the standards and expectations for data quality, structure, and availability, thus fostering consistency and reliability. And our "certification" approach (described in Chapter 11), built on a data-contract foundation, provides the transparency required to convey trust that the data product's quality—its adherence to its data contract—can be attested to.

By adopting these frameworks, organizations can create a robust data ecosystem that enhances the performance of GenAI models. Quality data inputs lead to quality outputs, facilitating better decision making and innovation. This integrated approach not only elevates data quality but also simplifies the process of finding, consuming, sharing, and trusting data, thereby maximizing the potential of GenAI.

Elevate Models as Primary Artifacts

According to McKinsey & Company (*https://oreil.ly/RBY74*), "Most data scientists, nowadays, say that over half their time is taken up with data wrangling—just trying to solve some of these problems. But solving those problems is a prerequisite to capturing any value at all." The work required to find, clean, organize, and prepare data for analysis requires an inordinate amount of time and effort, which is taken away from the primary objective of delivering valuable insights.

To address this, we suggest offering models as primary artifacts in data products. When AI models are bundled with their associated documentation, notebooks, and programs, the models are no longer standalone entities but rather become integrated components of a comprehensive data product. This integration provides detailed documentation that explains the model's architecture, training processes, and the data it was trained on, along with notebooks that illustrate practical applications and provide examples of usage.

Such comprehensive packaging makes it easier for data scientists to understand the capabilities as well as the inputs and outputs of each model, the assumptions made during its development, and the model's potential limitations. This transparency builds trust and reduces the cognitive load on data scientists, allowing them to focus more on analysis and less on preparatory work.

This approach significantly streamlines the workflow for data scientists and saves time and money. They no longer need to search extensively to find relevant models or decipher how to use them effectively. With models being part of a well-defined data product, data scientists can quickly access all of the necessary information in one place.

This bundling fosters a deeper understanding and confidence in the AI models, as data scientists can see how the models are intended to be used and can easily replicate or adapt the provided examples for their specific needs. Consequently, this approach not only enhances efficiency and productivity but also promotes a more collaborative and transparent AI development environment, ultimately accelerating the capture of value from AI initiatives.

Consume Models Inside Data Products

AI models will likely soon become integral components within data products, functioning as primary data transformation tools rather than external adjuncts. This means that AI models are now embedded directly into data products, playing a crucial role in transforming raw, ingested data into valuable insights.

Today, though, most AI models are probably used externally as adjunct components and not as part of the data product. When the control of the AI model is independent of the data product, that can complicate the integration process and overall system governance. Separate control can lead to difficulties in ensuring that the AI model adheres to the same quality standards, security protocols, and compliance requirements as the data product. This fragmented control can also hinder the ability to implement cohesive updates, track changes, and maintain consistency across the entire data-processing pipeline. And integrating external AI models often requires additional interfaces and middleware, increasing complexity and potential points of failure.

Integration of AI models as core transformation components within data products addresses this issue: as data is ingested, AI models can apply advanced algorithms to cleanse, structure, and analyze the data. This makes ownership of the end-to-end transformation—from ingestion through to AI-enabled transformation—the responsibility of the data product team. Any issues with the AI processing, versioning of the model, or compatibility of data with the model are the clear responsibility of the data product, which leads to faster evolution of the AI model (new features) as well as more rapid resolution of issues.

Generate Data Product Code

One of the most popular capabilities of GenAI is code generation. Because it understands natural language prompts and programming contexts, GenAI—having been trained on vast datasets of code—can easily produce high-quality code snippets, functions, and even entire programs.

A common use case today is to use GenAI to create boilerplate code, which is often repetitive and time-consuming to write. For example, setting up a new web application involves writing standard code for configurations, database connections, and user authentication. GenAI can automate these routine tasks by generating the necessary boilerplate code, allowing developers to focus on the more complex and unique aspects of the project. This not only improves efficiency but also ensures that the generated code follows best practices and is consistent across different projects. Figure 13-1 illustrates a very simple yet extremely powerful example of generating a FastAPI server, with an excellent explanation of how to run the server and how to call the generated server's endpoint—all created from a simple English request (the prompt).

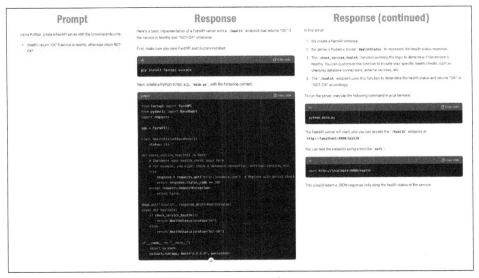

Figure 13-1. Prompt to generate an OpenAPI Specification

For Data Mesh, this code-generation capability can speed up the development of data product components, including consumption APIs, ingestion pipelines, and transformation logic. And GenAI can assist in integrating APIs and third-party services, which can be complicated because of varying documentation and implementation requirements. By analyzing API documentation and understanding the developer's needs, GenAI can generate the necessary code to establish connections, handle data exchange, and manage error responses in data product pipelines or transformation code.

Complement Data Product Capabilities

A tedious and time-consuming aspect of creating data products is generating accurate, comprehensive metadata. Metadata includes descriptions, definitions, and other contextual information essential for understanding and using the data effectively. AI models can be trained to scrape metadata from relevant documents, websites, and internal repositories. By parsing through vast amounts of text, LLMs can extract key pieces of information, such as data definitions, usage guidelines, and source details, ensuring accuracy and consistency.

In addition to streamlining metadata creation, AI can enhance data discovery through natural language interfaces. Navigating an enterprise Data Mesh and finding data products can be challenging, but with the integration of LLMs, users can interact with Data Mesh using everyday language, without needing to understand complex query languages or database structures. Vector databases and embeddings enable data product metadata to be indexed in a way that captures its semantic meaning rather than just its textual content. This allows for more nuanced and accurate search capabilities.

Climate Quantum and Generative AI

So how do these components interact in our Climate Quantum use case? Let's look at the following capabilities, as shown in Figure 13-2:

- Simplifying climate data search
- Analyzing and summarizing climate data
- Creating disclosure reports
- Generating code to simplify climate data consumption

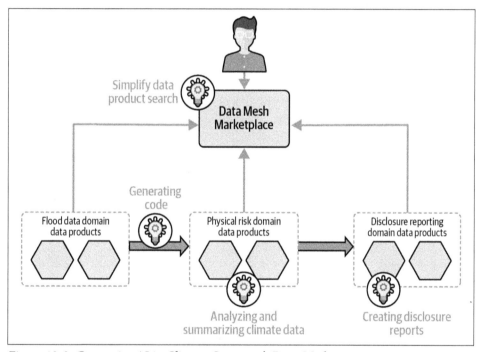

Figure 13-2. Generative AI in Climate Quantum's Data Mesh

Simplifying Climate Data Search

GenAI's natural language and semantic search capabilities offer a significant advantage in efficiently finding climate data. With the ability to understand the intent behind user queries and interpret complex climate-related terms, GenAI enables more accurate and relevant search results.

Users can pose questions in plain language, and the AI model can process those queries, analyze their meaning, and retrieve climate data that matches the context of the question. This simplified search process enhances data accessibility, fosters a deeper understanding of climate patterns, and facilitates informed decision making and advancements in climate science and policy.

GenAI can also be instructed to tag climate data automatically, making it easier to categorize and organize the information. By identifying key variables, regions, and temporal aspects within the data, the LLMs can create relevant tags or keywords. For instance, the model can tag weather data with attributes like temperature, precipitation, humidity, and location details. In a data landscape that contains thousands of data sources and formats, these tags help organize the vast climate data landscape.

Analyzing and Summarizing Climate Data

Climate data often consists of large, complex datasets, including weather observations, satellite imagery, and climate models. These datasets are rich in information but can be challenging to analyze and interpret because of their sheer volume and complexity.

GenAI plays a crucial role in managing this complexity by processing and analyzing the data and extracting key patterns and trends. For instance, weather observations collected from numerous sensors worldwide produce an overwhelming amount of data that GenAI can analyze to identify trends, such as temperature changes, precipitation patterns, and shifts in wind speeds. This automated analysis reduces the time and effort required for human experts to sift through the data manually.

Creating Disclosure Reports

Physical risk models incorporate a wide range of data sources, including environmental data, geographic information, and socioeconomic factors, to assess potential risks such as natural disasters, climate impacts, and other physical hazards.

GenAI takes the output from physical risk models and excels at creating boilerplate material that forms the bulk of disclosure-reporting documents. Standardized templates with sections like executive summaries, risk assessments, and mitigation strategies are developed by GenAI, which provides consistent language and terminology. GenAI can automatically update boilerplate content based on the latest data and regulatory changes, maintaining the relevance and compliance of the reports. This automation of routine content creation allows for efficient, consistent report generation across multiple instances.

Beyond boilerplate content, GenAI customizes reports to meet specific governance and regulatory needs by generating relevant, stakeholder-specific content. This involves conducting a contextual analysis to understand the requirements of different audiences, such as investors, regulators, and governance bodies.

Generating Code to Simplify Climate Data Processing

With the vast amounts of climate data being collected from diverse sources, integrating this data into applications and analytical tools can be time-consuming and challenging. GenAI can generate code snippets that facilitate this integration, ensuring seamless data flow from source to analytical tools.

For instance, it can ingest data from various climate data sources, clean it, and even fix some data errors. Or it can create connectors and APIs that allow data to be ingested into downstream pipelines and applications. This not only speeds up the development process but also ensures that data is consistently and accurately integrated across different platforms, enabling more effective use of climate data for analysis and decision making.

Summary

GenAI is popular today because it delivers real value. For Data Mesh, GenAI offers several capabilities that drive speed and agility in summarizing and analyzing data, generating code, and processing vast amounts of data. Since GenAI is still in its infancy and improvements arrive almost daily, it is clear that we are seeing only the tip of the iceberg in terms of the opportunities it presents to Data Mesh.

CHAPTER 14

Establishing Data Mesh Teams

Just like a natural ecosystem, Data Mesh consists of interconnected components that work together to create a thriving environment for data-driven value creation. But Data Mesh is a *sociotechnical* capability, which means that it has technology elements as well as social elements—or more specifically, organizational and cultural considerations.

Today, many enterprises focus mostly on the technical aspects at the expense of understanding the social aspects. In fact, many practitioners would tell you that technology is a relatively small part of a successful Data Mesh implementation. In our experience, the 80/20 rule applies: 80% of the effort, time, and cost in a Data Mesh implementation (and data product implementation) is spent trying to win over and influence people to adopt a new approach to organizational and cultural issues—one that emphasizes decentralization, local autonomy, new roles, and new governance techniques.

So these "organizational and cultural issues" are a big topic, which we address in this and the next chapter. In this chapter, we focus on the teams that are involved in Data Mesh: the data product team as well as the teams they interact with. The next chapter looks at the broader operating model: how teams interact, how they are governed, and how they are incentivized.

Team Topologies in Data Mesh

To describe the teams in the Data Mesh ecosystem, we leverage the concept of *team topologies*, adapted from Matthew Skelton and Manuel Pais's book *Team Topologies: Organizing Business and Technology Teams for Fast Flow* (IT Revolution). As shown in Figure 14-1, the core team in our discussion is the data product team (Skelton and Pais's stream-aligned team), which owns, manages, and governs data products. We will also touch briefly on the data platform and data enabling teams, which support data product teams.

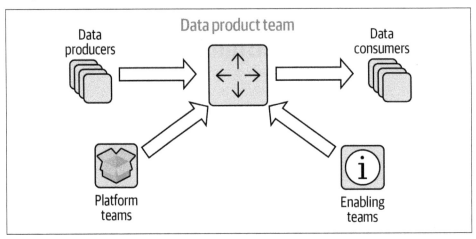

Figure 14-1. Data Mesh team topology

The Data Product Team

Data product teams are self-contained, autonomous units within an organization that are responsible for the end-to-end delivery of data products and services in Data Mesh. They are typically organized around specific business domains or product areas, which enhances their understanding of the domain and enables them to make informed decisions. With their dedicated focus on a particular data product or service, data product teams can develop deep expertise and a comprehensive understanding of the data and its implications within the specific domain.

A data product team has a clear scope and boundaries, typically centered on a specific domain, database, set of tables, or files. The team is accountable for all aspects of the data product's lifecycle, including data ingestion, consumption, discovery, and observability, as well as for ensuring the data product's overall success in delivering value to the organization.

Each data product team works independently and has the local autonomy to make decisions regarding its data products. This autonomy and independence allow for faster decision making and shorter feedback loops, which are essential for delivering data-driven solutions efficiently.

Key roles and responsibilities

The structure of a data product team, shown in Figure 14-2, can vary depending on the specific requirements of the data product that the team is working on. The team is led by a DPO who holds accountability for the success of the data product.

Other roles within the team may include metadata management, data management and security, consumption services, ingestion services, and release management. Each role contributes to different aspects of the data product's lifecycle and ensures its smooth operation and delivery of value to the organization.

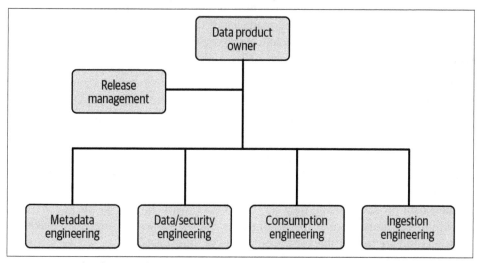

Figure 14-2. The data product team

It's important to note that while these roles are commonly found within data product teams, the team's specific structure and composition can vary depending on the organization and the nature of the data product being developed. In some cases, perhaps where scope is limited, data product teams may be quite small, but in other cases, they may be larger (the "two pizza team" (*https://oreil.ly/U_l2R*), about five to eight people, is probably a reasonable maximum).

Now let's look at how an individual data product team is organized and explore key team roles and responsibilities.

Data product owner

The data product team is led by a data product owner who has overall accountability for the success of the data product. This role plays a crucial part in defining and prioritizing the product backlog to ensure that the development team focuses on delivering the most valuable features first. The DPO is responsible for understanding customer needs, setting the vision for the data product, and communicating this vision to the team. They work closely with stakeholders to gather requirements and feedback, translating these into user stories and acceptance criteria.

While the DPO in agile practices may not necessarily have a traditional hierarchical leadership role, our experience is that successful data product managers often have a broader scope that encompasses strategic responsibilities such as needs analysis (as well as market analysis for external-facing data products), long-term product vision, roadmap planning, funding acquisition, and socialization (as well as go-to-market strategies for external-facing data products). They are also involved in the daily development activities and focus as much on the overall business success of the product. So just as the DPO is the manager of the data product, our experience is that a successful DPO is also the technical spokesperson—and even the leader—of the data product.

Now, we do expect this may get some pushback: where do you find a person with all these skills? Do all these skills need to be in one person's role? Can the DPO leverage other team members to fulfill these responsibilities? The simple answer to each of these questions is an emphatic yes!

Data product teams are agile and are designed to be locally autonomous. This does not mean that they operate in isolation but rather that they own all decisions related to their data product. As such, our experience is that successful DPOs act as the CEOs of their data products; while they serve customers with specific needs and need to fit within regulatory or other constraints, the buck stops with them. They make the decisions and are responsible for the outcomes of those decisions.

Let's take a look at the other capabilities in the data product team.

Release management

The purpose of release management is to coordinate the evolution of the data product. While this may not be a full-time position on the team (and is typically fulfilled by an engineer on the team), the release management role works closely with all members of the team to integrate changes into the release process and effectively communicate updates to stakeholders and users of the data product. Here are some of the most important responsibilities and skills of a data product release manager.

The release manager is responsible for planning and coordinating the release of data products. They work closely with the DPO, development team, and other stakeholders to define release schedules, establish release criteria, and coordinate the release process. They ensure that releases are well planned, align with business objectives, and meet quality standards.

The release manager works with team members to establish an effective release-management process (typically integrated with an organization's DevSecOps processes). To do this effectively, the release manager identifies potential risks and impacts associated with data product releases and develops strategies to mitigate them.

Effective communication is key to successful release management. Working with the DPO, the release manager is responsible for communicating release plans, progress, and impacts to stakeholders, including data product team members, business users, and technical teams.

Metadata engineering

Metadata management addresses considerations related to structures that capture the relevant information about data products and their artifacts. Metadata engineers define metadata attributes, relationships, and classifications that enable effective data discovery, understanding, and usage. For the purposes of this discussion, we use the term *metadata engineer* to refer to the role addressing this capability, although typically, it is a shared role performed by a data administrator or data engineer.

The metadata engineer is responsible for documenting and cataloging metadata in the Data Mesh Marketplace. They ensure that metadata is properly described, tagged, and indexed to facilitate easy search, retrieval, and understanding (and consistent semantics) of data products.

In keeping with this, the metadata engineer is responsible for establishing and enforcing metadata governance policies and processes. They define standards, guidelines, and best practices for metadata management, ensuring that metadata is captured, documented, and maintained consistently across data products. They play a key role in ensuring data quality and compliance with regulatory requirements.

Data contracts are another form of metadata that extend into service-level and quality expectations. The metadata engineer defines the data contracts that provide the necessary information to support data access, transformation, and data quality management. Using data contracts, they ensure the quality and integrity of data in the data product by performing assessments of data quality, implementing data validation rules, and resolving any issues or inconsistencies in metadata. They collaborate with data owners, data stewards, and other stakeholders to improve the quality and completeness of metadata, ensuring its reliability for data discovery and decision making.

One last area of responsibility is analysis of data lineage. The metadata engineer establishes processes and tools to capture and maintain data lineage information *within* the data product. They track the origins, transformations, and dependencies of data products to enable impact analysis and traceability. And they work with other data product teams to maintain a "chain of evidence" that tracks lineage *between* data products.

Data and security engineering

Data management is responsible for the overall architecture of the data product. For the purposes of this discussion, we use the term *data engineer* to refer to the role addressing this capability, although it may be a role shared with an enterprise's data platform team.

The data engineer translates business requirements into a logical and physical representation within the data product. They analyze business processes; identify relevant entities, attributes, and relationships; and capture them in a data model that is implemented in the data product. The data manager is responsible for the efficient storage, organization, and access mechanisms required to implement the data model while also ensuring (typically with the data platform team) that backup and recovery procedures are established and enacted.

This data security engineer is responsible for protecting data from unauthorized access, breaches, or misuse, although the role may be shared with an enterprise's data platform team and/or enterprise security team. In addition, the data security manager implements safeguards to ensure compliance with data protection regulations, such as GDPR or HIPAA, and works closely with enterprise IT and security teams to establish data security protocols.

Consumption engineering

The consumption engineering capability builds, supports, and evolves the services needed to consume the data in the data product. They design and develop interoperable interfaces—APIs, queries, and streaming, for example—and provide the necessary tools and services for users to access and utilize the data effectively. Recognizing the importance and technical depth of this capability, the consumption manager role is typically staffed by a full-time engineer.

The consumption engineer is responsible for designing and developing the services that allow consumers to access and consume data from data products. They work closely with DPOs, data engineers, and other stakeholders to understand consumer requirements and design service interfaces that meet their needs.

The consumption engineer ensures that the consumption services are interoperable with various systems, tools, and technologies used by consumers. They apply modern data integration techniques and standards, such as RESTful APIs, message queues, or event-driven architectures, to provide seamless integration between data products and consumer systems to support data-driven applications and workflows.

Once the consumption services are deployed, the consumption engineer provides ongoing support and maintenance to address any issues or performance concerns related to the consumption services, and they work closely with consumers to ensure smooth operation of the consumption services. To do this, the consumption engineer monitors and optimizes the performance and scalability of the consumption services. They analyze service-usage patterns, identify potential bottlenecks, and implement optimizations to enhance service performance and ensure scalability as data volumes and consumer demands increase.

The consumption engineer also works closely with other members of the data product team. Working with metadata engineering, they ensure that metadata is used appropriately and documentation is available for the consumption services. Together, they document service interfaces, data schemas, and usage guidelines to facilitate consumer understanding and adoption.

The consumption engineer works with security engineering to ensure the security and access control of the consumption services. Together, they implement authentication, authorization, and encryption mechanisms to protect data and restrict access based on consumer roles and permissions.

Ingestion engineering

Ingestion engineering designs, builds, and maintains the services responsible for ingesting data into data products within a Data Mesh. They design and develop data pipelines or workflows that enable the extraction, transformation, and loading of data into the data products. They employ various techniques and tools to facilitate seamless, automated data-ingestion processes. Because of the importance of this role, ingestion engineering is staffed by a full-time engineer.

Ingestion engineering establishes connectivity with various data sources, including databases, APIs, file systems, streaming platforms, or other external systems. They work closely with data source owners and administrators to define the integration requirements, establish secure connections, and ensure the efficient extraction of data from the sources.

They also focus on optimizing the performance and efficiency of data-ingestion processes. Ingestion engineering analyzes the ingestion workflows, identifies performance bottlenecks, and implements optimizations to enhance the speed, scalability, and reliability of data ingestion. They work with other members of the data product team to ensure that data-ingestion processes adhere to enterprise policies and regulatory compliance requirements, and they collaborate with data governance teams and stakeholders to establish data-quality standards, data-privacy measures, and data-classification rules.

Ingesting data from various sources can involve challenges, such as discrepancies, errors, or exceptions in the data. Ingestion engineering is responsible for implementing error-handling mechanisms and exception-management processes. They should have strong troubleshooting and problem-solving skills to identify and resolve issues with data promptly.

Platform Teams

Platform teams play a crucial role in supporting and enabling the work of other data product teams within the Data Mesh ecosystem. These teams focus on providing the necessary tools, utilities, and technical services that make it easier for data product teams to perform their tasks efficiently and effectively. Platform teams act as a central resource, offering shared services and capabilities that can be utilized by multiple teams across the organization.

Depending on your perspective, there could be a general platform team that handles all capabilities consumed by the data product, or there could be individual platform teams that offer services to the data product team. In most enterprises we have seen, there is no homogeneous single platform that the data product team consumes; rather, there are multiple platforms—separate data, API, and security platforms, for example—so we will use the plural form.

The primary goal of data platform teams is to remove any friction or barriers that other teams may encounter during their development and delivery processes. They build and maintain the underlying infrastructure, frameworks, and services that streamline the development, deployment, and operation of software products or services. By providing these "X-as-a-Service" wrapping full- or near-full-stack—ideally, self-serve—capabilities, platform teams allow other teams to focus on their specific areas of expertise without having to reinvent the wheel.

The scope of platform teams can vary depending on the organization's needs and priorities. They may include teams specializing in areas such as cloud infrastructure, APIs, security, networking, or any other technical domain that is critical for supporting the organization's software development efforts.

Enabling Teams

Last, but definitely not least, are enabling teams. Enabling teams are specialized groups within an organization that provide support and expertise to other teams to help them overcome obstacles and address specific needs. These teams act as consultants or advisers, offering guidance, resources, and solutions to help teams navigate challenges and achieve their goals.

Enabling teams collaborate closely with other Data Mesh teams, working in short bursts or on a project basis to provide targeted assistance. Enabling teams bring their expertise and knowledge to bear on specific problems or areas where additional support is needed and can take different forms depending on the organization and its specific needs.

They may include steering groups, enterprise governance and architecture teams, training groups, or any other specialized teams that can offer insights and assistance in specific domains. The common thread is that these teams typically have deep knowledge and experience or influence in specific areas and can provide valuable guidance, best practices, and resources to help teams succeed.

By leveraging the expertise of enabling teams, data product teams can benefit from specialized support and knowledge without having to build the same capabilities within every individual team. Enabling teams help foster collaboration, knowledge sharing, and innovation across the organization by providing targeted support to teams facing challenges or pursuing opportunities.

Climate Quantum Teams

Climate Quantum's team structure reflects the structure discussed in this chapter. But we will add a bit of detail, shown in Figure 14-3, about the mix of team skills.

	Skills	Data Product Owner	Release Mgmt	Metadata Engineering	Data and Security Engineering	Consumption Engineering	Ingestion Engineering
Technical Skills	Data Architecture	X		X	X		
	Database Management	X		X	X	X	X
	Data Quality / Governance		X	X		X	X
	Data Science / Programming					X	X
	Data Security / Privacy Mgmt	X		X	X	X	X
Infrastructure and Security	DevSecOps		X		X	X	X
	Ops / Performance Mgmt				X		
	Cloud Platforms / APIs				X	X	X
Business Skills	Domain Knowledge	X	X	X	X	X	X
	Executive Communications	X	X			X	X
	Business Acuman / Financials	X					

Figure 14-3. Climate Quantum team skills matrix

Climate Quantum's DPO is the spokesperson as well as the business and technical leader for their data product. This expanded role reflects the near-100% federated landscape of climate data (and data products), as there is only a minimal shared platform team and few enabling teams within a given domain. Simply put, the data product team is designed to be largely self-sufficient. The DPO in particular must be a "jack of all trades" and be equipped with relatively deep technical as well as business and financial skills.

Release management within a data product team takes on two responsibilities: they manage the evolution of the data product, but just as important, they play a key role in communicating its evolution and especially its changes to a potentially wide-ranging community of users. As such, it is not surprising to see a balance between technical and business skills for this role.

Metadata engineering establishes artifacts for many teams and hence requires some depth in technical skills but also has depth in security and deep domain knowledge. Data and security engineering requires similar skills but also specializes in infrastructure skills.

Consumer and ingestion engineering look quite similar in makeup. They have deep technical skills complemented by business skills. But they also have the basic infrastructure capabilities that enable them to build and implement core technical components and interfaces within the data product.

Summary

In this chapter, we explored the concept of establishing an effective data product team within a Data Mesh. We discussed the organizational structure and roles within a Data Mesh, including data product teams, platform teams, and enabling teams.

As they say, it takes a village to raise a child. Similarly, it takes a community of teams to create a flourishing data product. And while a data product team is responsible for the end-to-end delivery of services required by a data product, they interact with many other teams—producer teams, consumer teams, platform teams, and enabling teams—to deliver value.

CHAPTER 15

Defining a Data Mesh Operating Model

An operating model serves as a blueprint for how an organization functions, detailing the interactions and processes that enable it to achieve its goals. This model encompasses aspects such as organizational structure, technology, and workflows, providing a comprehensive framework for executing business strategies.

In this chapter, we will build on the previous chapter's focus on individual teams and explain how teams are bound together using a Data Mesh operating model. We will discuss how Data Mesh with its decentralized approach involves rethinking traditional centralized data management paradigms and embracing a more distributed, agile, and domain-centric approach.

Characteristics of an Operating Model

An *operating model* is a blueprint that defines how an organization conducts business, delivering value through its operations. It aligns people, processes, and technology to achieve strategic goals. In the context of data products or Data Mesh, the operating model guides how data—or more specifically, data products—are managed, shared, and utilized within an organization, ensuring that data initiatives align with business objectives and strategies.

One key objective of an operating model is to establish clear roles and responsibilities, ensuring that each team and individual knows their specific functions and how they contribute to the broader organizational goals. We will use the descriptions of Data Mesh teams from Chapter 14 to show how these teams interact more broadly.

Another important characteristic of an operating model is the establishment of efficient processes that describe how tasks and activities are carried out within the organization. For Data Mesh, this means establishing standardized processes for governance, quality, and lifecycle management of data products.

Integration of technology is also a crucial aspect of an operating model. This involves selecting and implementing the right technological tools and platforms to support the organization's operations. The operating model should facilitate a technology landscape that is easy to access, agile, scalable, and conducive to the decentralized nature of Data Mesh, enabling seamless interaction and data sharing across different domains.

Furthermore, an operating model emphasizes the importance of communication and collaboration among different units within an organization. Effective communication channels and collaboration practices ensure that teams can work together seamlessly, sharing insights and expertise.

The Operating Model Continuum

There are several destinations on the operating model continuum, as shown in Figure 15-1.

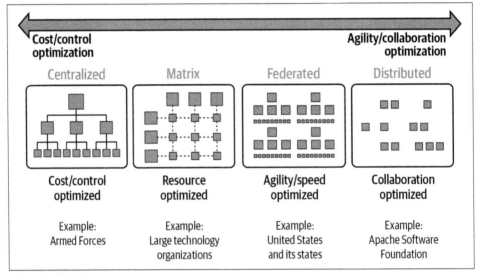

Figure 15-1. The operating model continuum

Centralized Organizations

Centralized organizations, exemplified by a nation's armed forces, are characterized by their emphasis on cost optimization and control. They often employ a strict hierarchy with top-down decision making, which establishes a clear chain of command where decisions and directives flow from the top level of the organization down to the lower levels. Such a hierarchy ensures that all parts of the organization are aligned with the central vision and policies, which is critical for maintaining uniformity in practices and standards. In industries where consistency and uniformity are essential, like manufacturing or finance, this centralized approach can be particularly effective. The predictability and control afforded by a centralized model are conducive to streamlined processes and clear accountability, ensuring that the entire organization moves cohesively toward its objectives.

However, the advantages of a centralized organizational model are accompanied by certain disadvantages, particularly related to its rigid structure. The top-down approach to decision making can lead to a bureaucratic, inflexible environment, and in situations where quick, responsive decision making is required, this rigidity can be a significant handicap. The lack of local autonomy means that decisions are made by those at the top, often detached from realities on the ground and frontline insights. This can result in decisions that are not well suited to local or departmental needs, leading to inefficiencies and frustration among employees. Moreover, the centralization of decision making can create bottlenecks, as all major decisions must go through a few high-level executives, slowing the organization's ability to respond to changes in the market or internal challenges.

Matrixed Organizations

Matrixed organizations, on the other hand, feature dual reporting relationships and cross-functional teams, which contribute to a dynamic, collaborative work environment. In this model, employees typically report to both a functional manager and a project manager, integrating expertise from various disciplines into one team. For instance, an employee in a technology company might report to an IT department manager (functional manager) as well as a project manager leading a specific initiative, such as developing a new software product. This dual-reporting structure is intended to optimize utilization of skills and expertise, ensuring that project teams have access to a diverse range of talents and perspectives. Cross-functional teams in a matrixed setup bring together specialists from different areas, such as engineering, marketing, and finance, fostering a holistic approach to project development and problem solving.

One significant advantage of matrixed organizations is efficiency in resource allocation. The flexibility of the matrix structure allows for the optimal deployment of human resources across various projects, as employees can be assigned tasks that best fit their skills and experience, irrespective of their departmental affiliation. This not only maximizes use of the workforce but also contributes to a more agile and adaptable organization. In large technology organizations, where project scopes and resource needs can fluctuate rapidly, this ability to swiftly reallocate resources is particularly beneficial. It ensures that projects are not delayed because of resource shortages and that employees are consistently engaged in meaningful, challenging work, contributing to higher levels of job satisfaction and productivity.

Matrixed organizations also face notable challenges, particularly in terms of management complexity and increased managerial overhead. The dual reporting lines can lead to confusion and conflict, as employees may receive competing directives or priorities from their functional and project managers. This complexity requires effective communication and clear role definitions to avoid ambiguities and conflicts. Additionally, the need to coordinate among multiple managers and teams can lead to increased management overhead, with more time spent on meetings and communication to align on objectives and strategies. In large technology companies, where projects are often complex and involve many stakeholders, this can result in slower decision-making processes and potential inefficiencies. Managers in a matrixed organization need to possess strong leadership and conflict-resolution skills to navigate these complexities effectively and maintain a productive work environment.

Federated Organizations

Federated organizations are typically structured in a way that combines multiple levels of governance, each with a degree of autonomy yet all bound together by a set of common policies and regulations. This structure is particularly evident in complex entities like the United States, where each individual state retains its sovereignty over specific local responsibilities while agreeing to adhere to certain overarching policies and regulations set by the federal government. The governance within a federated organization is tiered, with some decisions and policies being made at the highest level and others at more localized levels.

One of the primary advantages of federated organizations is the greater degree of local autonomy and decision-making power they offer. In the context of the European Union, member states have the freedom to make decisions on many internal matters, allowing them to address local needs and preferences effectively. This autonomy is crucial in ensuring that the diverse cultural, economic, and political contexts of each member are taken into account. Local autonomy fosters a sense of ownership and responsibility among the members, as they are not merely following directives from a central authority but are actively involved in the governance process. This can lead to more effective and tailored policy implementations, as decisions are made by those who are closely acquainted with the specific contexts and challenges.

However, the federated structure brings with it a certain complexity in decision making. The need to align and coordinate policies across different levels of governance can lead to lengthy negotiations and compromises. In the EU, reaching consensus among all member states can be a challenging and time-consuming process, especially on contentious issues where national interests may diverge. This complexity can sometimes slow the decision-making process, leading to delays in policy implementation. Furthermore, the need to accommodate diverse viewpoints can result in policies that are less effective or diluted in their impact. The challenge for federated organizations lies in finding the right balance between respecting local autonomy and ensuring efficient and effective decision making at the broader level.

Distributed Organizations

Finally, *distributed* organizations are characterized by their open, decentralized decision-making processes and a self-governing approach. This model is exemplified by entities like the Apache Software Foundation (*https://apache.org*) (ASF), where projects are managed independently by various teams dispersed across different locations. In a distributed organization, decision-making authority is not centralized in a single management hierarchy but is spread across multiple nodes or units within the organization. Each unit operates with a high degree of autonomy, making decisions that are best suited to their specific context and objectives. This structure is often enabled and supported by digital communication technologies that facilitate coordination and collaboration among geographically dispersed teams.

One of the key advantages of distributed organizations is the high degree of local autonomy and decision-making power they provide. This autonomy allows for decisions to be made closer to where they will have their impact, leading to more responsive and contextually appropriate outcomes. For example, in the ASF, various project teams are empowered to make decisions regarding their specific software projects, leading to more efficient and innovative development processes.

Additionally, distributed organizations tend to have minimal bureaucratic overhead. Without the need for a large central administrative structure, these organizations can operate more leanly, reducing costs and increasing operational efficiency. The decentralized nature also encourages a more entrepreneurial and innovative environment, as teams are not constrained by a rigid central policy.

The distributed model comes with its own set of challenges, particularly in terms of decision-making complexity. The lack of a centralized decision-making authority can sometimes lead to inconsistencies and difficulties in maintaining a unified strategic direction. In the case of the ASF, coordinating efforts and maintaining consistency across numerous independent projects can be a complex task. The challenge lies in ensuring that all the autonomous units or teams are aligned with the overall objectives and values of the organization while retaining their independence. Additionally, in the absence of a central authority, conflict resolution and the enforcement of standards and policies can become more complicated. The success of a distributed organization like the ASF depends heavily on the establishment of strong shared values and objectives, along with effective communication channels and collaborative tools that enable disparate teams to work toward common goals while respecting one another's autonomy.

Data Mesh Operating Model

In our Data Mesh operating model, we extend the scope beyond the realm of individual data product teams and interactions across the entire Data Mesh and all of its teams. This holistic approach helps harness the full potential of a decentralized data architecture, ensuring that the collective output of various data products synergizes into a unified, strategic asset for the organization. In general, the operating model of your organization has a significant influence on your technology choices, as shown in Figure 15-2, and hence has implications for how you evolve your Data Mesh (and data products).

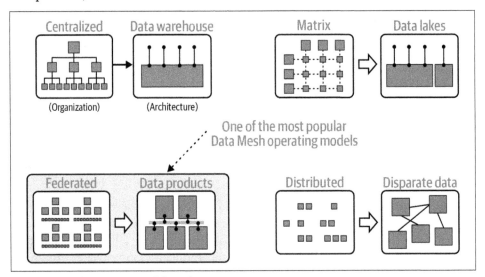

Figure 15-2. Operating model implications

Let's make a few comments here so that you don't read too much into this diagram. First, the illustration is a sweeping generalization; most organizations have a mix of operating models and architectures. Second, this does not imply that Data Mesh can operate only in one of these models (although federated organizations have a natural affinity to Data Mesh's federated principles and approach). In fact, Data Mesh can operate at a smaller scale in discrete parts of an organization, even within those organizations that have a centralized disposition.

While Data Mesh is clearly driving toward a federated model, in our experience, each organization is unique and has a mix of several operating models, each implemented in different parts of the enterprise. Now, that is not necessarily a problem—in many cases, there are already organizational boundaries (geographic or product units) that delineate the boundaries of one operating model from another. Within large groups, there may be multiple smaller groups, each structured in a way that aligns to that group's culture and business objectives. Nevertheless, it is important to understand the advantages and disadvantages of each operating model to be able to plan your approach for your Data Mesh and data products.

Some of these trade-offs are described quite well through Conway's law (although it is called a "law," it is more of a practical observation and simplification of a complex topic). The principles of Conway's law (*https://oreil.ly/Iu1aU*), to paraphrase, state that an organization's systems mirror its organization and communication structures. This applies to Data Mesh too, especially since most enterprises are federated (although their IT organizations may not be, particularly centralized IT groups, the problems of which were elaborated upon in Zhamak Dehghani's original *Data Mesh* book).

In a federated model, the autonomy granted to various units aligns with the Data Mesh principle of domain-oriented decentralized data ownership and architecture. Each unit in a federated organization can manage its data products, making decisions that best serve the local context yet consuming broader enterprise platforms or adhering to organizational standards and principles.

This regional focus fostered by Conway's law often results in data products that are finely tuned to local market needs and regulatory landscapes. While this approach enhances the effectiveness of data products in specific regions, it can inadvertently lead to fragmentation in a global data strategy, manifesting as data silos and challenges in cross-regional collaboration. Organizations striving for a unified global data perspective might struggle to integrate these diverse, regionally focused data products into a harmonious whole.

Nevertheless, it is important to note that there is no one-size-fits-all. You will just need to be cognizant that it may be harder to change your organization's structure and operating model to accommodate Data Mesh than it may be to have Data Mesh change to accommodate your organizational culture and operating model.

Understanding your operating model is one thing. Once your operating model is understood or established, what are the stages of its maturity? To answer this question, in the next section we propose a "Data Mesh Maturity Model."

Data Mesh Maturity Model

The Capability Maturity Model (*https://oreil.ly/DOofD*) (CMM) is a popular framework used in software engineering to improve and refine an organization's software-development process. Developed by the Software Engineering Institute at Carnegie Mellon University, CMM is structured around five maturity levels: initial, repeatable, defined, managed, and optimizing. Each level represents a different stage in process maturity, providing a clear path for continuous improvement. At the initial level, processes are often ad hoc and chaotic, while the highest level, optimizing, signifies a stage where processes are continuously refined and improved through proactive problem solving and innovation. Progression through these levels enables an organization to transition gradually from an unstructured, often unpredictable software-development process to a mature, disciplined, and efficient one.

The benefits of implementing CMM in an organization are multifaceted. First, it provides a clear and structured roadmap for process improvement, which is critical for managing complex software development projects. By adhering to the stages of CMM, organizations can achieve more predictable project outcomes, enhanced quality control, and increased efficiency. This systematic approach also helps identify performance bottlenecks and areas that require improvement. Furthermore, as organizations ascend the maturity levels, they become better equipped to handle large-scale, complex projects. The organization reduces the risk of project failures and enhances customer satisfaction by consistently delivering high-quality software. The CMM framework also encourages a culture of continuous learning and improvement, fostering innovation and keeping the organization adaptable in a rapidly evolving technological landscape.

Developing a Data Mesh Maturity Model based on the principles of software engineering's CMM and incorporating Data Mesh principles offers a structured path for organizations to enhance their data-management capabilities. This model provides a roadmap for evolving from rudimentary, unstructured data handling to a mature, sophisticated, and decentralized approach to data management. As shown in Figure 15-3, mapping the Data Mesh Maturity Model directly to the levels of CMM provides a structured approach to enhancing an organization's data capabilities.

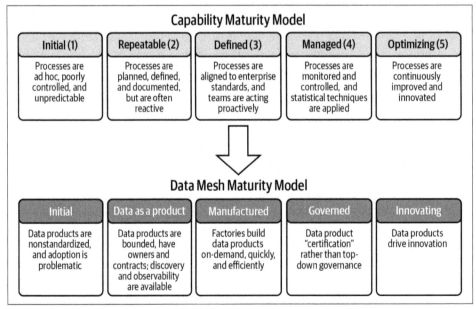

Figure 15-3. The Data Mesh Maturity Model

Let's explore this mapping:

Initial (level 1, equal to CMM level 1)

Data management is often chaotic and unstandardized, and data products exist as proofs of concept. Organizations at the initial level face significant challenges in adopting a consistent approach to handling data, as there are no clear structures or standards in place. Data products are often developed in an ad hoc manner, leading to issues in scalability, reliability, and integration. This stage is characterized by a recognition of the need for change and an understanding of the limitations of current data practices.

Data as a product (level 2)

At this level, the concept of treating data as a product is established. Data products are clearly defined and bounded, and they have dedicated owners who are responsible for their lifecycles. Contracts are in place to ensure quality and consistency, and interfaces for discovery and observability are available, making data more accessible and usable. This stage marks a significant shift toward a more structured and strategic approach to data management, aligning it more closely with business objectives.

Manufactured (level 3)

The manufactured stage sees the emergence of data product factories, which streamline the creation of data products. These factories are capable of producing data products on demand, quickly, and efficiently, thanks to standardized processes and automation. This level represents a maturity in operational efficiency, where the focus is on scaling up data production while maintaining quality and adherence to standards. The approach is systematic, and the production of data products becomes more predictable and reliable.

Governed (level 4)

Here, traditional top-down governance models are replaced with data product "certification" (discussed in previous chapters), indicating a more decentralized, autonomous approach to governance. This stage focuses on ensuring compliance, quality, and security through standardized certification processes. Data teams have a high degree of local autonomy for implementing data governance in their data products, fostering a sense of ownership and accountability. This level of maturity reflects a balance between flexibility and control, which is crucial for maintaining order in a diverse and dynamic data ecosystem.

Innovating (level 5)

At the innovating level, data products are not just well managed but also drive business innovation. Data products are leveraged as a key strategic asset, with organizations increasingly looking to data products to explore new opportunities, improve decision making, and gain competitive advantages. This stage is characterized by a culture that values data-driven insights and encourages experimentation and creative use of data. The organization's data capabilities are fully integrated with its strategic objectives, fostering an environment where data continually adds value and drives growth.

At each stage, Data Mesh benefits the organization by promoting domain-specific autonomy, ensuring that data is treated as a valuable product, and encouraging a decentralized yet governed approach. Once again, we can see that alignment with real-world practices such as CMM provides a clear path for organizations to evolve their Data Mesh practices systematically, enhancing their overall data maturity in line with evolving business needs and technological advancements.

Climate Quantum's Data Mesh Operating Model

Although Climate Quantum's use case has focused on data products in three domains (flood, physical risk, and disclosure reporting), the climate data domain (which includes the flood domain) is particularly suitable for the federated operating model that Data Mesh advocates, as shown in Figure 15-4.

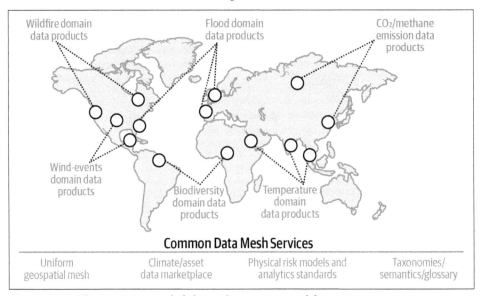

Figure 15-4. Climate Quantum's federated operating model

Climate Quantum's data and its producers are scattered across the globe. There are multiple data producers, each operating with its own set of objectives (providing commercial services versus a public good, for example), its own format (multiple satellite formats, for example), and its own frequency of publication (some are daily, some monthly, and some annually). And importantly, each data product has its own owner.

With multiple DPOs, Climate Quantum is organized in a federated operating model, where each data product team is independent and makes its own decisions. But it operates under a common Data Mesh platform that ensures that the ecosystem has a minimal set of common services:

Uniform geospatial mesh
Provides a consistent mechanism for managing location coordinates

Climate/asset data marketplace
The marketplace for all of Climate Quantum's data products

Standards, taxonomies, and glossaries
Provide a consistent set of semantics for all data products and their artifacts

Summary

In this chapter, we discussed operating-model options for your Data Mesh. The Data Mesh operating model serves as a blueprint for how the Data Mesh organization (data product teams, platform teams, enabling teams, and related groups) functions, detailing the interactions and processes that enable it to achieve its goals. But it's important to remember that there is no perfect fit: your operating model will need to work in your organization. Nevertheless, we hope we have given you enough insights to make Data Mesh fit much more easily into your organization.

CHAPTER 16

Establishing a Practical Data Mesh Roadmap

This chapter offers a pragmatic roadmap for Data Mesh implementation, building on the foundational understanding established in previous chapters. Recognizing the multifaceted nature of this undertaking, we explore how to navigate the complex interplay of technology, organizational culture and operating model, data-product creation, and governance that is required to put together a practical and feasible Data Mesh roadmap.

Here are a few quick notes to provide additional context for our roadmap:

- Our goal is to lay out the various streams of work required to get to that desirable end state. While this is somewhat comprehensive, that doesn't mean it's intended only for large organizations. Rather, this roadmap should be viewed as a set of capabilities that you should consider, but it's up to you to pick and choose what you need.

- The roadmap appears as streams with sequenced steps, which may lead some readers to assume that this is a "waterfall" approach. This is absolutely not the case. Rather, each stream can happen somewhat independently and in parallel, with touch points between them. And each stream can operate in an agile fashion, delivering needed components iteratively.

- The roadmap has timescales (in months). These are meant to be indicative, not prescriptive, as we recognize that each organization's capability and processes are different. The timescales are offered more as relative comparisons among the various streams of work.

Roadmap Structure

As you embark on the journey of implementing Data Mesh, it's crucial to have a structured roadmap to guide you through the various phases of this transformative process. The Enterprise Data Mesh Roadmap, shown in Figure 16-1, is not a one-size-fits-all solution but rather a flexible framework that can be adapted to the specific needs and context of each organization.

The journey toward an enterprise Data Mesh starts with a strategy and roadmap stream where you lay out the foundational vision for your Data Mesh initiative. The roadmap then follows four streams of work that operate largely in parallel and somewhat independently (with interlocks at various points, which we describe later) to establish your enterprise Data Mesh:

- Technology stream
- Factory stream
- Operating model stream
- Socialization stream

Finally, once the foundation for your Data Mesh has been established, these streams come together into a rollout stream where you create and deploy (and maintain and evolve) data products at scale and reap the value from your Data Mesh.

So let's dig a bit deeper into each stream.

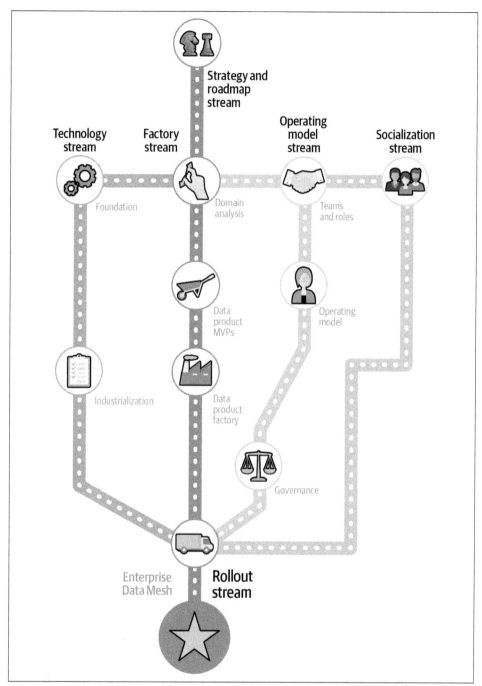

Figure 16-1. *The Enterprise Data Mesh Roadmap*

Strategy and Roadmap Stream

The strategy and roadmap stream, shown in Figure 16-2, establishes the business and technical vision and execution plan for your enterprise Data Mesh. This phase is characterized by a brief but comprehensive top-down approach that aligns the Data Mesh initiative with the broader strategic objectives of the organization. It is executed by a small team with strong business and technical skills.

The stream starts with an assessment of the current data landscape, including existing capabilities and gaps. This assessment is then used to define a clear vision and set of objectives for Data Mesh, ensuring alignment with the overall business strategy. The approach emphasizes stakeholder engagement, risk assessment, and the establishment of a governance framework to guide the implementation process. The key deliverables are as follows:

Data Mesh 101
: This Data Mesh introduction and communications pack contains presentations, FAQ documents, and educational videos that will help introduce Data Mesh to a broad audience across the enterprise. It will explain the fundamental concepts of Data Mesh, such as decentralized data ownership, domain-oriented data product design, and self-serve data infrastructure. The pack is intended to be used for onboarding, workshops, and ongoing education to ensure that all stakeholders have a baseline understanding of the initiative.

Conceptual architecture
: This deliverable includes architectural diagrams, component specifications, and infrastructure blueprints that highlight components of Data Mesh and data products. The documentation will give technical teams a clear understanding of the structure and interconnectivity of data products, data pipelines, and storage within Data Mesh, outlining how each contributes to the overall ecosystem.

Roadmap
: This granular, actionable plan describes how you will roll out Data Mesh across the enterprise. It delineates the stages of implementation, from initial proofs of concept to full-scale operationalization, with clear indicators for progress, accountability, and iterative review points.

Business outcomes
: This list of outcomes highlights potential efficiency gains, improvements in data quality, and other strategic advantages anticipated from the Data Mesh implementation. It connects each outcome to specific business objectives, providing a compelling case for investment and a benchmark for measuring success.

Risks
: This is a list of potential risks that will need to be mitigated.

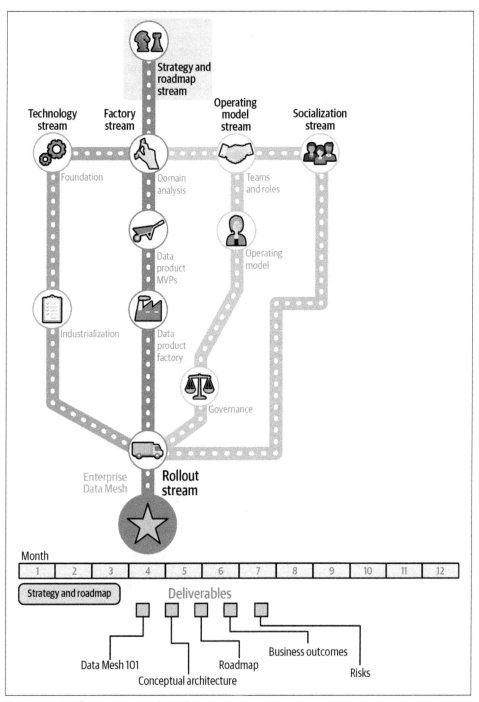

Figure 16-2. The strategy and roadmap stream

The strategy and roadmap stream describes the business outcomes for your Data Mesh and a practical plan—your roadmap—to achieving those outcomes. This stream creates a clear articulation of the goals, strategic importance, and expected benefits of Data Mesh. This phase results in a detailed implementation roadmap, comprehensive architectural documentation, and educational materials to ensure that all stakeholders are informed and aligned.

Technology Stream

The technology stream, shown in Figure 16-3, builds and industrializes the technical components in your enterprise Data Mesh. It plays a pivotal role in the implementation of a Data Mesh, setting the stage for a robust, scalable, and secure data infrastructure. This stream is dedicated to building a strong technological foundation that underpins the entire Data Mesh architecture. The stream's duration may appear to be brief, but it's important to recognize that many enterprises already possess elements of the required technology stack, such as databases and security infrastructure. These existing assets provide a head start, although the timeline may extend if foundational technologies are not yet in place.

The primary goal of the technology stream is to establish a suite of foundational technology capabilities that streamline the discovery, consumption, sharing, and governance of data across the enterprise. This involves the orchestration of various technology components, ensuring that they are seamlessly integrated and aligned with the overarching objectives of your Data Mesh. To achieve this, the technology stream is divided into two distinct yet interconnected phases: the foundational phase and the industrialization phase.

The foundational phase is focused on building the core technology components that form the backbone of your Data Mesh. It encompasses the deployment and configuration of essential technologies such as databases, security infrastructure, data quality management capabilities, and data contracts. The aim is to create a solid base upon which your Data Mesh can be built, ensuring that the infrastructure is robust, flexible, and capable of handling the diverse data needs of the enterprise.

The industrialization phase follows the foundational buildout. This phase is about scaling the capabilities established in the foundational phase, enhancing security, and preparing the infrastructure for widespread adoption and evolution. It involves integrating the Data Mesh components into the broader enterprise environment, emphasizing security, operability, and observability. The industrialization phase ensures that your Data Mesh is not just a static framework but rather a dynamic, evolving ecosystem capable of adapting to changing business needs and technological advancements.

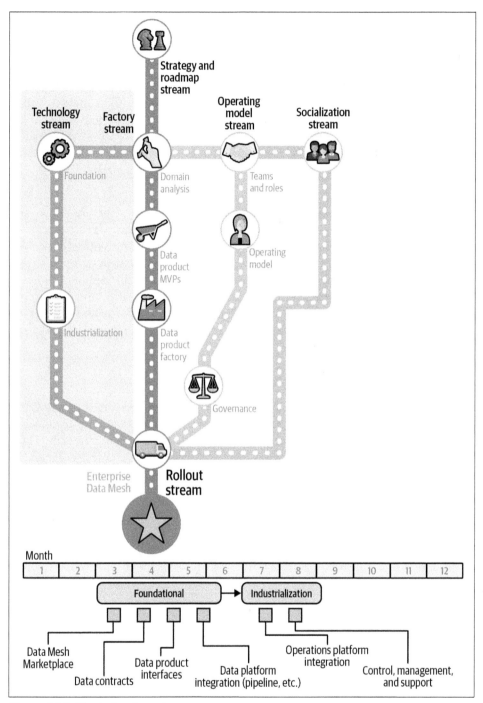

Figure 16-3. The technology stream

Foundational phase deliverables

The foundational phase deliverables are as follows:

Data Mesh Marketplace
> The foundational phase will prioritize the creation of a Data Mesh Marketplace that serves as the central directory for all data products. This marketplace is engineered to facilitate robust search capabilities, comprehensive discovery, and detailed observability of the data ecosystem. It incorporates advanced metadata management to ensure that data products can be easily located, understood, and managed, enhancing the operational efficiency of your Data Mesh.

Data contracts
> Data contracts serve as formal agreements that define the structure, usage, and governance of shared data within your Data Mesh. These contracts are crucial for establishing clear, consistent guidelines on data sharing, ownership, and accountability, ensuring a standardized approach to data management across different teams and departments. The data contracts will detail the responsibilities of data providers and consumers, requirements for data quality, and compliance standards. Common data contract templates and policy enforcement libraries are established at this point to make it easy to implement data contracts broadly in all data products.

Data product interfaces
> Data products have several interfaces (discovery, observability, operability, ingestion, and consumption), each of which will be designed and implemented. Common libraries, templates, and tools are developed to make it easy to integrate discovery, operability, and observability capabilities into all data products. These interfaces become the primary way that other data products and components interact with the data product.

Data platform integrations
> Data products are connected into the broader Data Mesh fabric and data platforms. Common ingestion and consumption services are implemented (for example, to implement pipelines or APIs) that make it easy to connect data products into enterprise platforms.

Industrialization phase deliverables

The industrialization phase deliverables are as follows:

Operations platform integration
> Ensuring resilience, security, and supportability involves the integration of Data Mesh components into the enterprise's operational environment. This includes setting up processes for systematic log collection, alert generation, and the forwarding of critical operational events to security and operations management

consoles. The aim is to create a cohesive operational landscape that enables smooth functioning and management of your Data Mesh across various environments. In addition, security components are integrated to safeguard all foundational components. This will include the deployment of encryption for data at rest and in transit, rigorous identity management, role-based access control, and OAuth 2.0 protocols for API security. For regulated industries, the security framework will integrate advanced zero-trust architectures, ensuring that security measures are robust, scalable, and compliant with industry standards.

Control, management, and support
We include here the establishment of a robust support structure, including automated processes and workflows to ensure that your Data Mesh is seamlessly integrated into the enterprise's technology support framework. This support system will be crafted to provide rapid assistance for issues, streamlined updates, and maintenance procedures, ensuring that your Data Mesh remains reliable and effective in supporting enterprise-wide data operations.

To summarize, the technology stream focuses on establishing foundational, scalable technology capabilities for enterprise-wide data management in two phases: the foundational phase, which builds the core technology components such as databases, security infrastructure, and data quality management; and the industrialization phase, which scales these capabilities for broader adoption and enhanced security.

Factory Stream

The factory stream, shown in Figure 16-4, uses a "test and learn" approach to deliver an initial set of proofs of concept and MVPs, culminating in the creation of repeatable processes to scale delivery of data products. It is an agile and dynamic phase within the Data Mesh implementation journey, operating in tandem with the technological advancements established in the technology stream. The essence of the factory stream lies in its ability to translate theoretical models into tangible, operational results through a series of iterative and progressive steps. By orchestrating proofs of concept and MVPs, this stream focuses on validating the practicality of the Data Mesh framework and refining the operational model before scaling up to a full-fledged production environment.

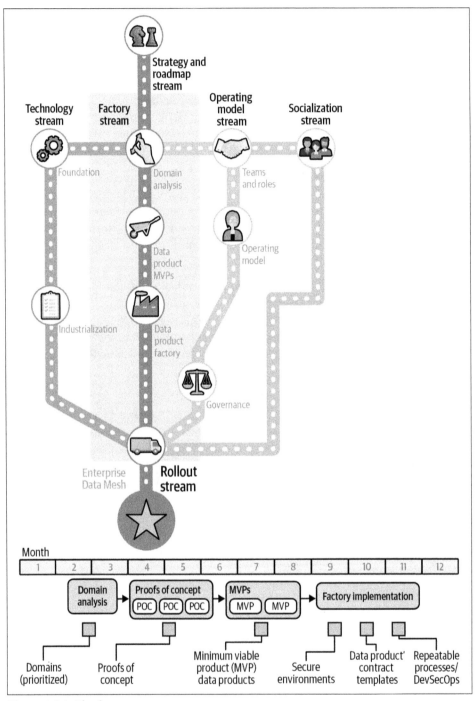

Figure 16-4. The factory stream

The key deliverables are as follows:

Domains list
    This is a prioritized list of candidate domains for future data products.

Proofs of concept
    This collection of proofs of concept is designed to validate various components and roles within your Data Mesh that address and mitigate risks identified during the strategy stream. The proofs of concept serve as a testing ground for new tools, technologies, and operational roles, such as the data product owner.

Minimum viable products
    Several MVP data products are implemented and deployed to production to "test and learn" the operational capabilities required for data products. The goal of these MVPs is to exercise the end-to-end delivery process, from initial development through to production deployment. Each MVP is crafted to deliver business value while providing insights into your Data Mesh's functionality and operability.

Secure environments
    This is a set of environments where data can be maintained securely. Ideally, these environments, supported by DevSecOps, can be established very quickly.

Data product templates
    A guide outlines the templates necessary for the at-scale creation and deployment of data products. This blueprint will serve as the manual for establishing the data product factory.

Repeatable processes and DevSecOps
    Here, you codify and document your learnings from your proofs of concept and MVPs and implement the repeatable processes required to build, secure, and deploy data products at scale.

To summarize, the factory stream emphasizes an agile, iterative approach to developing and scaling data products. Initially, you focus on delivering proofs of concept and MVPs to validate the Data Mesh framework and address potential risks identified during the strategy stream. Deliverables created in this stream include a portfolio of proofs of concept, blueprints for MVPs, and a comprehensive data product factory blueprint, all aimed at establishing repeatable processes for scaling delivery of data products.

Operating Model Stream

The operating model stream shown in Figure 16-5 defines the DPO role, the structure of the data product team, and the processes required to support your enterprise Data Mesh. (Operating models are described in detail in Chapter 15.) This stream is a critical component of the Data Mesh implementation process that focuses on the organizational aspect of delivering data products. It is within this stream that the practical orchestration of people, processes, and technology takes place to form a cohesive unit capable of realizing the Data Mesh vision. The journey begins with a deep dive into the organization's existing structure, scrutinizing and realigning it to foster a data-centric culture that emphasizes efficiency, effectiveness, and agility.

This stream is tasked with addressing some of the most significant challenges in adopting Data Mesh, such as dismantling silos, fostering cross-functional collaboration, and cultivating a shared sense of ownership over data assets. By establishing clear roles, responsibilities, and communication pathways, the operating model stream sets the stage for a transformative approach to data governance and utilization.

The key deliverables are as follows:

Data product team definition
> This document describes the roles and responsibilities of a data product team. This is a crucial document that usually fosters a fair amount of debate as it is the first public declaration of the degree of local autonomy required by data product teams as well as the skills needed to become somewhat self-sufficient.

Operating model definition
> This is a framework that outlines the roles and responsibilities within your Data Mesh and the broader enterprise community. It includes the definition of an ecosystem of teams and their interactions.

Data product team mobilization (first team)
> While this may be more of a milestone than a deliverable, the implementation of a running, productive data product is nevertheless an important event. This event, more than any others, is the first opportunity to "test drive" many of the core principles of Data Mesh (ownership, data as a product, clear boundaries, etc.).

Certification and governance policy
> We have stated in previous chapters that the dynamic nature of data products provides the opportunity to move from a top-down data governance posture to one of certification. This policy defines how you will implement this certification process and describes the governance roles and responsibilities of the data product team and its governance partners.

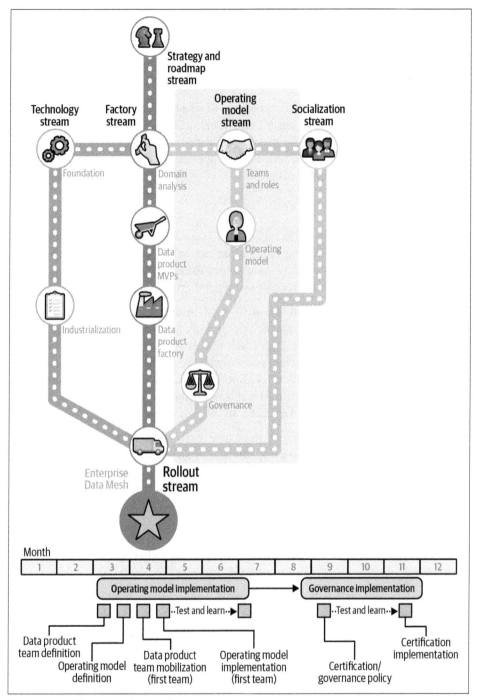

Figure 16-5. The operating model stream

Certification implementation
 With the certification policy in hand, you can now implement and operationalize your policy. At this point, you establish the automation to support certification, certification reporting, and regular stakeholder engagement to govern your data products.

By addressing each task and incorporating the key inputs, the operating model stream builds a robust foundation for the operational success of your Data Mesh. It ensures that the transition to a more agile, data-centric organization is not only strategic but also supported by a well-defined operational framework that can adapt to future challenges and opportunities.

Socialization Stream

The socialization stream, shown in Figure 16-6, is used to communicate data-product success stories while building the momentum needed to scale your enterprise Data Mesh. This stream is pivotal yet often underestimated because it is the conduit for cultural transformation within an organization embarking on a Data Mesh journey.

This stream goes beyond the dissemination of information; it is about fostering a data-driven culture, nurturing stakeholder buy-in, and cultivating a shared understanding and enthusiasm for the Data Mesh initiative. It's not merely about informing—it's about engaging, convincing, and rallying the entire organization around the new data paradigm. And it is about continuous learning. The challenge here is not only to communicate the technicalities and benefits but also to articulate the vision in a manner that resonates with and educates all levels of the enterprise.

In this stream, socialization is not a passive process; it is active and strategic, requiring deliberate planning and execution. It is an ongoing dialogue, a narrative that evolves and grows with your Data Mesh, designed to align the organization's heartbeat with the rhythm of data-centric operations and decision making.

The key deliverables are as follows:

Education sessions and awareness building
 These events are primarily targeted at an internal audience, where you educate and build awareness of your Data Mesh initiative.

Executive presentations, lunch and learn, MVP celebrations
 These events also primarily have an internal focus, but at this point in your Data Mesh journey, you will talk about not only progress but also actual successes. It almost goes without saying, but a strategic approach to engaging with stakeholders ensures, and builds momentum for, their continuous involvement, contribution, and support for the Data Mesh project.

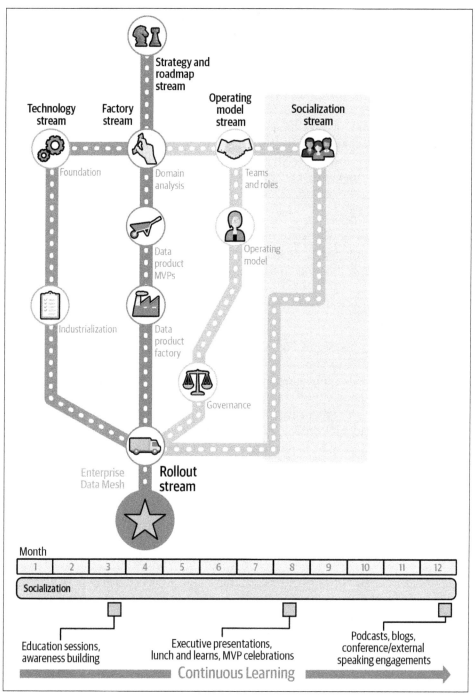

Figure 16-6. The socialization stream

Podcasts, blogs, conference and speaking engagements
> This is both internal as well as external outreach, and if done well, it becomes a fantastic way to engage with the broader technical community and attract talent.

Continuous learning
> The goal is to provide regular training sessions, workshops, and resources to keep employees updated on the latest trends, technologies, and best practices in Data Mesh. Promoting continuous learning ensures that all stakeholders remain informed and capable of effectively implementing and utilizing the Data Mesh framework. This fosters a culture of adaptability and innovation, enabling the organization to maximize the benefits of the Data Mesh initiative and stay competitive in a data-driven landscape.

By addressing these deliverables, the socialization stream ensures that the transition to Data Mesh is not only a technical implementation but also a cultural shift that the entire organization embraces and champions. It is through this stream that Data Mesh becomes part of the organizational language, its narrative, and ultimately, its identity.

Rollout Stream

The rollout stream, shown in Figure 16-7, is dedicated to building and operating data products at scale in your enterprise Data Mesh. It is the final yet continuous phase of the Data Mesh implementation, where the focus shifts to maximizing the delivery of data products to drive business outcomes and value. This stage marks the transition from the foundational setup of technology and factory capabilities to the active scaling and deployment of data products across the organization. Here, the emphasis is not just on launching data products but also on ensuring that they deliver maximum value rapidly and efficiently. The rollout stream is an ongoing process, constantly evolving as new data products are ideated, developed, and integrated into the business ecosystem.

The key deliverables are as follows:

Data products (1–n)
> Your objective is to use the capabilities built in previous streams to deliver data products at scale. To support this, you typically have a detailed plan that outlines the strategy for deploying new data products, including timelines, resource allocation, and integration with existing systems. To keep track of the benefits (and costs), you typically also create a framework for measuring and tracking the business value delivered by each data product, ensuring alignment with organizational goals and objectives.

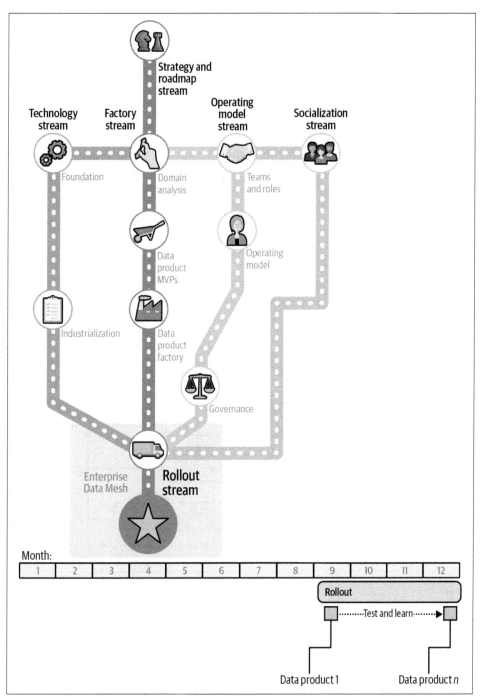

Figure 16-7. The rollout stream

The ultimate goal of the rollout stream is to realize the full potential of Data Mesh by delivering a steady stream of data products that contribute to the organization's strategic objectives. It's a dynamic process that aligns closely with the evolving needs of the business, ensuring that Data Mesh remains a relevant and valuable asset.

Climate Quantum's Data Mesh Roadmap

Climate Quantum's Data Mesh journey, shown in Figure 16-8, starts with a strategy and roadmap stream where we lay the foundational vision and execution plan for our Data Mesh. This involves defining the business and technical goals or "making climate risk analytics easy to find, consume, share, and trust." Climate Quantum also identifies several priority business domains (including the flood, physical risk, and disclosure reporting domains mentioned in previous chapters) that will guide its roadmap.

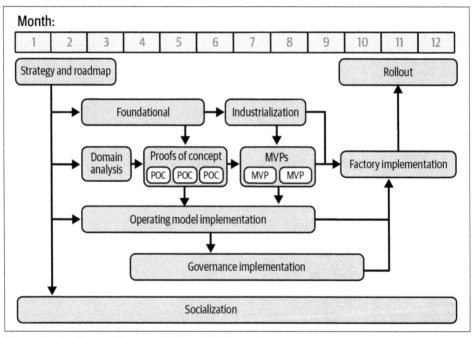

Figure 16-8. Climate Quantum's Data Mesh roadmap

Next (reading from top to bottom) is the technology stream. In this stream, Climate Quantum establishes the platforms and infrastructure necessary for its Data Mesh, including geospatial services, query platforms, API platforms, and governance tools. Climate Quantum starts this stream by selecting and implementing key platforms (and related tools and libraries) and then makes them production worthy.

The factory stream is initiated concurrently with the technology stream. Here, Climate Quantum focuses on building data products at scale. Initial activities aim to build skills and "test and learn" Data Mesh capabilities by experimenting with proofs of concept and eventually deploying data products for the flood, physical risk, and disclosure domains as MVPs.

Also concurrently, Climate Quantum's operating model stream addresses the organizational changes required to support Data Mesh. This involves defining roles and responsibilities needed to build successful data product teams. Because of the near fully federated set of owners and regional distribution of climate data, Climate Quantum designs its operating model to provide a lightweight set of common standards and certification needs and then delegate implementation to data product teams, thereby providing the local autonomy as well as the agility, scalability, and effective governance required to deliver at scale.

Climate Quantum's socialization stream operates continuously as a communication vehicle to keep stakeholders aware of progress as well as to communicate and "sell" Data Mesh's capabilities and benefits broadly throughout the organization. The socialization stream focuses on engaging and educating stakeholders (banks, insurers, asset managers, technology partners, etc.) to build a shared understanding and commitment to Climate Quantum's vision.

Last, Climate Quantum's rollout stream is about expanding the implementation, scaling its Data Mesh across different climate domains.

Summary

At this point, we hope that you have seen a somewhat comprehensive yet practical roadmap to establish your enterprise Data Mesh. We start with a strategy and roadmap stream that lays out the business and technical game plan for Data Mesh. Our roadmap offers four parallel streams that specify the foundational technology components, create a factory to build the tools and templates for developing data products at scale, define an operating model to adapt Data Mesh to your organization and culture, and implement a socialization stream that lets you tell your story and set the stage for growth. Finally, a rollout stream is where we apply the investments made in previous streams.

It is safe to say that any journey worth taking will be rewarding but will also have its potholes and speed bumps. This is normal. But we hope that the roadmap we offer will let you see the potholes before you fall into them and effectively navigate the speedbumps so that they don't slow you down.

Index

E

El (end of life), 84
embeddings (GenAI), 183
empowered DPO, 32-33
enabling teams, 200-201
encryption, infrastructure experience plane, 111
endpoints, links to, 52, 53
enterprise-grade data products, 21
   deployability, 22
   documentation, comprehensive, 22
   observability, 22
   operability, 22
   reliability, 21
   security, 21
Er (error rate), 84
Es (end of support), 84
event capture, 135
experience planes
   capability model, 110
      data product experience plane, 112-113
      infrastructure experience plane, 111-112
      mesh experience plane, 113-114
   data product experience plane, 105, 107-108
   infrastructure experience plane, 105, 106-107
   mesh experience plane, 105, 108-109
expertise, 68

F

FAIR data products
   accessibility, 20
   findability, 20
   interoperability, 20
   reuse, 20
federated computational governance, 18
federated governance model data product certification, 166-167
federated organizations, operating models and, 206-207
feedback loops, 115-116
   mesh experience plane, 114
files, 50
findability (FAIR principles), 20
Fy (frequency of update), 84

G

Ga (general availability), 84

gateways, 56-57
GenAI, 181
   code generation, 187-188
   data quality and, 185
   embeddings, 183
   LLMs (large language models), 182
      bias in training, 184
      context, 184
      hallucinations, 184
      training, 184
   metadata generation, 188
   prompts, 183
   report generation, 190-191
   searches and, 189-190
   uses, 181
   vector databases, 183
governance (see data governance)
governance interfaces, 61
   (see also data governance)
GPT-3, 182

H

Health Insurance Portability and Accountability Act (HIPAA), 7
HIPAA (Health Insurance Portability and Accountability Act), 7
human lineage, tribal knowledge, 74-76

I

IaC (infrastructure as code), infrastructure experience plane, 111
identity management, 132, 138-141
images, 25
infrastructure experience plane, 105, 106-107
   capability model, 111-112
infrastructure services, 64
ingestion engineering, data product teams, 199
ingestion interfaces, 57-58
ingestion, bulk methods, 58
interaction services, 63
interoperability (FAIR principles), 20
interpolated data, 43

L

large language models (LLMs) (see LLMs)
licenses, artifacts, 53
lifecycle, 27-29
links to endpoints

About the Authors

Jean-Georges "JGP" Perrin is the chief innovation officer at AbeaData, focusing on building innovative and modern data tooling. He is also chair of the Open Data Contract Standard (ODCS) at the Linux Foundation project Bitol, cofounder of AIDA User Group, and author of multiple books, including *Implementing Data Mesh* (O'Reilly) and *Spark in Action*, 2nd edition (Manning). He is passionate about software engineering and all things data. His latest endeavors bring him to more and more data engineering, data governance, industrialization of data science, and his favorite theme, Data Mesh. He is proud to have been recognized as a Lifetime IBM Champion, a PayPal Champion, and a Data Mesh MVP. Jean-Georges shares over 25 years of experience in the IT industry as a presenter and participant at conferences and publishing articles in print and online media. His blog is visible at *http://jgp.ai*. He enjoys exploring upstate New York and New England with his wife and kids when not immersed in tech, which he loves.

Eric Broda has been working in financial services for over three decades and has been a technology executive at, and consultant to, large banks, insurers, and payments firms. Today, Eric runs a boutique consulting company that designs, architects, and implements Data Mesh, data ecosystem, and generative AI solutions. Eric is also playing an active role in addressing the global climate change challenge where he is leading a team at an international nonprofit that is using Data Mesh and generative AI to build a climate data catalog and components in support of an open source global climate-related physical risk analytics system.

Colophon

The animal on the cover of *Implementing Data Mesh* is an American grass spider, also known as a funnel-web spider. There are many species of grass spider (*Agelenopsis*), all of which are harmless and common in gardens and yards. They are brown with lighter markings on their bodies.

Grass spiders build slippery, funnel-shaped webs in low-lying vegetation. The spiders sit at the center of the funnel and spring into action when prey touches the web. Once prey is captured, the grass spiders carry it back to the funnel's center with them.

Grass spiders are common and active from late spring through early fall. Many of the animals on O'Reilly covers are endangered; all of them are important to the world.

The cover illustration is by Karen Montgomery, based on an antique line engraving from a loose plate, source unknown. The series design is by Edie Freedman, Ellie Volckhausen, and Karen Montgomery. The cover fonts are Gilroy Semibold and Guardian Sans. The text font is Adobe Minion Pro; the heading font is Adobe Myriad Condensed; and the code font is Dalton Maag's Ubuntu Mono.

O'REILLY®

Learn from experts.
Become one yourself.

Books | Live online courses
Instant answers | Virtual events
Videos | Interactive learning

Get started at oreilly.com.

Printed in the USA
CPSIA information can be obtained
at www.ICGtesting.com
JSHW050559201024
72016JS00010B/198

9 781098 156220